Arsenal: Prayers Declarations and Decrees That Will Move Heaven and Shake Hell

Apostle Paula Ferguson

Published by FOSA Publishing LLC, 2025.

While every precaution has been taken in the preparation of this book, the publisher assumes no responsibility for errors or omissions, or for damages resulting from the use of the information contained herein.

ARSENAL: PRAYERS DECLARATIONS AND DECREES THAT WILL MOVE HEAVEN AND SHAKE HELL

First edition. May 16, 2025.

Copyright © 2025 Apostle Paula Ferguson.

ISBN: 979-8992303988

Written by Apostle Paula Ferguson.

Table of Contents

Dedication 1
How to Use This Book: Arsenal: Prayers, Declarations, and Decrees That Will Move Heaven and Shake Hell 5
Glossary 11
Introduction: Arsenal: Prayers, Declarations, and Decrees That Will Move Heaven and Shake Hell 13
  Chapter 1: Family Restoration 17
  Family Restoration Prayer 23
  Family Restoration Declarations and Decrees 25
  Chapter 2: Business and Wealth 29
  Business and Wealth Prayer 35
  Business and Wealth Declarations and Decrees 37
  Chapter 3: Health and Healing 39
  Health and Healing Prayer 45
  Health and Healing Declarations and Decrees 47
  Chapter 4: Delay Breaking 49
  Delay Breaking Prayer 55
  Delay Breaking Declarations and Decrees 57
  Chapter 5: Victory Over Enemies 59
  Victory Over Enemies Prayer 65
  Victory Over Enemies Declarations and Decrees 67
  Chapter 6: Purpose and Identity 69
  Purpose and Identity Prayer 75
  Purpose and Identity Declarations and Decrees 77
  Chapter 7: Spiritual Warfare and Protection 79
  Spiritual Warfare and Protection Prayer 85
  Spiritual Warfare and Protection Declarations and Decrees 87
  Chapter 8: Fruitfulness and Productivity 89
  Fruitfulness and Productivity Prayer 95
  Fruitfulness and Productivity Declarations and Decrees 97
  Chapter 9: Restoration and Deliverance 99
  Restoration and Deliverance Prayer 105
  Restoration and Deliverance Declarations and Decrees 107

Chapter 10: Favor, Scholarships, and Opportunities 109
Favor, Scholarships, and Opportunities Prayer 115
Favor, Scholarships, and Opportunities Declarations and Decrees 117
Chapter 11: Technological Warfare and Protection 119
Technological Warfare and Protection Prayer 127
Technological Warfare and Protection Declarations and Decrees 129
Chapter 12: Christ Consciousness and Awakening 131
Christ Consciousness and Awakening Prayer 139
Christ Consciousness and Awakening Declarations and Decrees 141
Chapter 13: Emotional and Relational Healing 145
Emotional and Relational Healing Prayer 153
Emotional and Relational Healing Declarations and Decrees 155
Chapter 14: Spiritual Discernment and Wisdom 157
Spiritual Discernment and Wisdom Prayer 165
Spiritual Discernment and Wisdom Declarations and Decrees 167
Chapter 15: Community and National Transformation 169
Community and National Transformation Prayer 177
Community and National Transformation Declarations and Decrees 179
Chapter 16: Freedom from Fear and Anxiety 181
Freedom from Fear and Anxiety 187
Freedom from Fear and Anxiety 189
Chapter 17: Intercession for Others 191
Intercession for Others 199
Intercession for Others 201
Chapter 18: Cross-Category Decrees 203
Cross-Category Decrees 209
Cross-Category Decrees 211
Complete List of Declarations and Decrees: Arsenal: Prayers, Declarations, and Decrees That Will Move Heaven and Shake Hell 213
Appendix: Morning Warfare Prayer Points 239
Appendix: Scripture Index 247
Dear Warrior of the Kingdom, ... 257

Dedication

This book, *Arsenal: Prayers, Declarations, and Decrees That Will Move Heaven and Shake Hell*, is dedicated to the extraordinary individuals who have profoundly shaped my spiritual journey, empowering me to walk boldly in the authority of God's Word. Their love, guidance, and teachings have been the cornerstone of this work, and I honor them with deep gratitude.

To my beloved husband, **Apostle Craig Ferguson**, my best friend, provider, and the embodiment of God's love. You have been and remain such a firm foundation; watching your walk with Christ has made me desire to do better. You are humble, yet you've taught me the difference between real and false humility. From the moment you entered my life, no matter what I've done, you have been my first cheerleader, encouraging me to succeed and catching me when I falter, never letting me call it failure but saying, *"Honey, this is how we learn."* You consistently guide me back to truth with your steadfast words: *"Let's see what the Word of God says."* Your authenticity and love overflow, giving more than what meets the eye. You will forever be the toughest act to follow—in fact, the show stops with you, and I am forever grateful for you.

To my dearest and blessed friend, **Denise Michelle Ray**, my spiritual partner and intercessor for nearly 20 years. Before I understood my own identity, you stood by my side, declaring God's promises over my life and refusing to let me dwell in complaint or despair. Your words have been my lifeline: *"Talk to God more than you talk to me,"* you'd say, redirecting my focus to the Father. When I grew weary of being the first to apologize, even when wronged, you'd lovingly challenge me: *"I know it's hard. It's hard being the first one to die on the cross, the first one to be hated, the first one to be crucified for something you didn't do... Oh wait, that was Christ, not you. I'm sorry, what were you saying?"* In that moment, you became my friend for life, always pointing me back to the Word and the heart of God.

To **all the pastors, preachers, teachers, and mentors** who have poured into my life—thank you for speaking over me, guiding me, and teaching me how to sow the Word. Your leadership has been the catalyst that positioned me for the miraculous.

And I am **Apostle Paula Ferguson.** During my walk with God, I have always declared over myself since I was a young girl that I am a human computer—whatever I need to know, God downloads into me. Time and again, I've seen this truth manifest; when I lack knowledge, God provides it in moments, with no explanation other than His faithfulness to my declarations. Through the anointing of the Holy Spirit, I've watched God shift circumstances, change rules, regulations, policies, and procedures, all because of the words I speak in alignment with His Word. The spiritual realm recognizes God's authority, His power, and my authority as His child in the earth. When I open my mouth and declare His promises, things change—whether I see it immediately or not.

This book is a testament to the power of prayers, declarations, and decrees, forged through the influence of these remarkable individuals and my own journey of faith. "I Did Us", and now I pass this weapon to you. These are your cheat codes, your weapons of spiritual warfare. Use them to speak God's Word, shift atmospheres, move heaven and shake hell.

Welcome to *Arsenal: Prayers, Declarations, and Decrees That Will Move Heaven and Shake Hell*. This book is more than words on a page; it is a spiritual arsenal, equipping you to wield the authority God has given you as His child. Through my journey, I've learned that the words we speak, when rooted in God's Word, carry the power to shift circumstances, transform outcomes, and bring heaven's promises into the earth while disrupting the plans of hell.

The individuals to whom this book is dedicated—my husband, Apostle Craig Ferguson; my Blessed friend, Denise Michelle Ray; and all the pastors, preachers, teachers, and mentors have each played a pivotal role in teaching me the power of prayer, declarations, and decrees. Their influence, alongside my own walk with God, has shown me that when we speak God's Word with faith and authority, the spiritual realm responds, and the impossible becomes possible.

In these pages, you will find prayers, declarations, and decrees grounded in Scripture, designed to empower you to approach God boldly, negotiate in the courts of heaven, and expect miracles in the physical realm. I've seen legs grow, bodies healed, and circumstances shift because of the principles shared here. You, too, can see God move in your life as you declare His promises with confidence.

"I Did Us"—I saw God's Word come to life through my declarations. Now, it's your turn. These are your cheat codes, your spiritual weapons. Take them, speak them, and watch heaven move and hell shake on your behalf.

With faith and expectation,
Apostle Paula Ferguson

How to Use This Book: Arsenal: Prayers, Declarations, and Decrees That Will Move Heaven and Shake Hell

When you step into a doctor's office, you expect precision. A throbbing headache doesn't call for an antacid, and a stomachache doesn't send you to a dentist. Every ailment demands a specific diagnosis, a targeted remedy, and a treatment tailored to the root cause. So it is in the spiritual realm, where the battles you face—whether in your family, finances, health, or destiny—require exact, faith-filled responses. **Arsenal: Prayers, Declarations, and Decrees That Will Move Heaven and Shake Hell** is your divine prescription, a sacred armory equipped with 323 Spirit-inspired proclamations to confront every challenge, dismantle every stronghold, and unleash the promises of God in your life.

This book is not a passive read; it is a living weapon, a battle cry, a catalyst for supernatural breakthrough. Crafted under the apostolic anointing of Apostle Paula Ferguson, these decrees are forged in the fire of God's Word, designed to shift atmospheres, break chains, and manifest the Kingdom in every sphere of your existence. Just as a physician discerns your symptoms before prescribing medicine, you are called to identify your spiritual battles and select the decrees that align with your need. A proclamation for financial overflow will not heal a fractured relationship; a decree for technological protection will not awaken your spiritual consciousness. Like a skilled surgeon wielding a scalpel, you must apply the right tool with precision and authority.

The Power of Your Words

God spoke, and the universe was formed (Genesis 1:3). As His image-bearer, you carry that same creative authority in your tongue: "Death and life are in the power of the tongue" (Proverbs 18:21). The declarations and decrees in this book are not mere words; they are divine instructions, backed by Heaven's authority, that command circumstances to align, principalities to bow, and blessings to flow. When you speak these decrees, you partner with the Holy Spirit, activating the covenant promises that are your inheritance as a joint-heir with Christ (Romans 8:17).

This power comes with responsibility. Just as a doctor prescribes medication with specific instructions—dosage, timing, consistency—you must wield these decrees with faith, intentionality, and perseverance. A single dose of medicine won't cure a chronic condition; a single decree, spoken without conviction, won't move a mountain. You are called to be a relentless warrior, declaring God's truth until the enemy flees and the promise manifests.

How to Use This Book

To unleash the full power of **Arsenal**, approach it as a sacred encounter with the Spirit of God. Here's how to engage with these decrees to see Heaven move and hell tremble:

1. Diagnose Your Battle

Before you speak a decree, seek the Holy Spirit's guidance to pinpoint your spiritual need. Are you fighting for family unity? Financial breakthrough? Protection from digital attacks? A deeper alignment with Christ's consciousness? Each chapter is a specialized ward in God's spiritual hospital, addressing distinct areas of your life:

- **Family Restoration**: For healing relationships, protecting your children, and breaking generational curses.
- **Business and Wealth**: For financial overflow, debt cancellation, and marketplace influence.
- **Health and Healing**: For physical, mental, and emotional wholeness.
- **Delay Breaking**: For accelerating promises and shattering stagnation.
- **Victory Over Enemies**: For dismantling demonic assignments and witchcraft.
- **Purpose and Identity**: For walking in divine calling and authority.
- **Spiritual Warfare and Protection**: For shielding your life from spiritual attacks.
- **Fruitfulness and Productivity**: For expanding influence and bearing fruit.
- **Restoration and Deliverance**: For redeeming lost time and breaking bondages.
- **Favor, Scholarships, and Opportunities**: For open doors and supernatural advancement.

- **Technological Warfare and Protection**: For safeguarding against digital and algorithmic attacks.
- **Christ Consciousness and Awakening**: For aligning with divine truth and transcending illusions.
- **Emotional and Relational Healing**: For mending emotional wounds and restoring relationships.
- **Spiritual Discernment and Wisdom**: For navigating life with divine clarity.
- **Community and National Transformation**: For igniting revival and restoring godly order.
- **Freedom from Fear and Anxiety**: For anchoring your heart in God's peace.
- **Intercession for Others**: For lifting others in prayer and securing their breakthroughs.
- **Cross-Category Decrees**: For versatile proclamations that apply across multiple battles.

In prayer, ask, "Lord, what am I facing? Where do I need Your victory?" The Spirit will guide you to the chapter that matches your battle, just as a physician selects the right treatment for your symptoms.

2. Select Your Weapon

Turn to the chapter that corresponds to your need. Each decree is a precision-crafted arrow, anointed to strike the heart of your challenge. Read through the decrees, allowing the Holy Spirit to highlight those that resonate. For example:

- For a struggling marriage, proclaim, "I decree that my marriage is strengthened by love, patience, wisdom, and mutual respect" (Chapter 1, #7).
- For digital attacks, declare, "I decree that no technology will be used as a portal to invade my dreams, thoughts, or personal space" (Chapter 11, #11).
- For spiritual awakening, decree, "I declare that I am not separate from God — we are one, and nothing can separate me from divine

Source" (Chapter 12, #27).

Select one decree, several, or an entire chapter as led. Trust the Spirit's prompting, for He knows the exact words to shift your reality.

3. Speak with Authority

Your voice is a divine instrument, ordained to command creation and subdue the enemy (Genesis 1:28). Speak these decrees with boldness, faith, and conviction, as a royal priest declaring God's will (1 Peter 2:9). Follow these steps:

- **Create a Sacred Space**: Find a quiet place, free from distractions, to focus on God's presence.
- **Invite the Spirit**: Pray, "Father, anoint my words with Your power and align them with Your will."
- **Declare Aloud**: Speak each decree audibly, with confidence, as if addressing Heaven and the enemy. For example, proclaim, "I decree that the power of the tithe unlocks divine peace, wealth, and the flow of supernatural provision" (Chapter 12, #40) with unwavering faith.
- **Personalize as Needed**: Insert names or details (e.g., "I decree that [child's name] is called into the kingdom of light" from Chapter 1, #14).
- **Anchor in Scripture**: Meditate on the accompanying scripture (e.g., Malachi 3:10 for tithing) to fuel your faith.

4. Persist in Faith

Spiritual warfare is a lifestyle, not a one-time event. Just as a doctor prescribes a course of treatment, you must persist in declaring these decrees until breakthrough manifests. The enemy may resist, but "the one who endures to the end will be saved" (Matthew 24:13). Commit to:

- **Daily Declaration**: Speak your decrees morning and night, or as led, building spiritual momentum.
- **Expectant Faith**: Believe your words are shifting the unseen realm (Mark 11:24). Doubt is the enemy's weapon; faith is yours.

- **Worship and Praise**: Pair decrees with worship to amplify their power (Psalm 149:6-9). Sing, pray, or lift your hands to magnify God.
- **Track Breakthroughs**: Journal answered prayers and victories to strengthen your faith, noting God's movement.

5. Live the Decrees

These decrees are a way of life. Align your actions with your proclamations. If you decree financial prosperity (Chapter 2), give cheerfully (2 Corinthians 9:7). If you declare Christ Consciousness (Chapter 12), pursue daily prayer and meditation (Colossians 4:2). Your life must reflect the truth you proclaim, for "faith without works is dead" (James 2:26).

6. Share the Arsenal

This book is not for you alone. As God moves, share these decrees with your family, church, or community. Teach others to diagnose their battles, select their weapons, and speak with authority. Become a beacon of faith, showing how to move Heaven and shake hell. "Let the redeemed of the Lord say so" (Psalm 107:2).

A Call to Arms

You are not a victim; you are a warrior, clothed in God's armor (Ephesians 6:11), armed with the sword of the Spirit (Ephesians 6:17). These decrees are your battle cries, your divine prescriptions, your keys to God's promises. Whether facing a family crisis, financial lack, health attack, or spiritual awakening, there is a decree tailored for your victory.

Approach this book with reverence, for it carries Heaven's authority. Approach it with urgency, for the enemy prowls (1 Peter 5:8). Approach it with joy, for you have "authority to trample on snakes and scorpions and to overcome all the power of the enemy" (Luke 10:19). Declare, decree, and watch God's glory manifest in every area of your life.

Glossary

Apostolic Authority: The God-given spiritual authority delegated to believers, particularly those called as apostles, to teach, govern, and advance God's Kingdom through prayer, decrees, and leadership. In this book, it refers to the believer's ability to command spiritual outcomes in alignment with God's Word (Revelation 1:6).

Blood of Jesus: A reference to the sacrificial death of Jesus Christ, which provides atonement, protection, and victory over sin and demonic forces. Used in decrees to invoke divine covering and authority (Revelation 12:11).

Christ Consciousness: The state of aligning one's mind, thoughts, and actions with the truth and nature of Jesus Christ, reflecting His wisdom and divine perspective. In this book, it denotes a deep spiritual awakening to God's truth and oneness with Him, not a New Age concept (1 Corinthians 2:16; Romans 12:2).

Co-create with God: The act of partnering with God through faith-filled words and actions to bring His divine purposes into reality on earth. This reflects the believer's role in aligning earthly circumstances with Heaven's will (Ephesians 3:20).

Covenant Promises: The assurances and blessings God has pledged to His people through His Word, such as provision, protection, and favor. These are activated through faith and proclamation (Deuteronomy 7:9; Galatians 3:29).

Decree: A faith-filled, authoritative proclamation spoken aloud to command spiritual and physical realities to align with God's Word. Unlike a prayer, which petitions God, a decree declares what is already promised (Proverbs 18:21; Job 22:28).

Declaration: A bold statement of faith rooted in God's Word, spoken to affirm truth, shift atmospheres, or establish God's will. Similar to a decree but may focus on affirming identity or promises (Psalm 149:6-9).

Digital Bloodline Reset: A metaphorical term for cleansing one's digital footprint (e.g., online data, interactions) from spiritual or demonic influence through the authority of Jesus' blood. It addresses modern technological warfare (Colossians 1:20).

Generational Curse: A pattern of sin, bondage, or negative consequences passed down through family lines due to disobedience or spiritual strongholds. Decrees in this book break these curses through Christ's redemption (Galatians 3:13).

Joint-Heir with Christ: The believer's position as an inheritor of God's promises and Kingdom blessings alongside Jesus, granting authority and access to divine resources (Romans 8:17).

Morning Warfare Prayer Points: Concise, daily prayers designed to confront spiritual battles, establish God's authority, and set the tone for victory. These are practical tools for consistent spiritual warfare (Ephesians 6:12).

Spiritual Armory: A metaphorical collection of prayers, declarations, and decrees, likened to weapons for spiritual warfare. This book serves as an armory to equip believers against the enemy's schemes (Ephesians 6:17).

Spiritual Warfare: The battle against demonic forces, principalities, and strongholds that oppose God's purposes, fought through prayer, decrees, and faith. This book equips believers to engage in this warfare (Ephesians 6:12).

Stronghold: A demonic or mental barrier that hinders God's will, such as fear, addiction, or division. Decrees dismantle strongholds by aligning with God's truth (2 Corinthians 10:4).

Technological Warfare: Spiritual attacks facilitated through modern technology (e.g., algorithms, surveillance, digital manipulation). This book addresses these through targeted decrees for protection and authority (Luke 10:19).

Tithe: The biblical practice of giving one-tenth of one's income to God, which activates covenant blessings, provision, and protection. Referenced in decrees for financial overflow (Malachi 3:10).

Introduction: Arsenal: Prayers, Declarations, and Decrees That Will Move Heaven and Shake Hell

In the heart of every believer burns a divine spark, an unyielding authority bestowed by the Creator to shape destinies, shift atmospheres, and command the forces of darkness to flee. This is not a privilege; it is a mandate, a clarion call to rise as warriors of the Spirit, wielding the sword of God's Word to bring Heaven's reality to earth. I am Apostle Paula Ferguson, and under the anointing of the Holy Spirit, I present to you *Arsenal: Prayers, Declarations, and Decrees That Will Move Heaven and Shake Hell*—a sacred weapon forged for such a time as this.

The world is a battlefield. Families fracture under division, finances falter under lack, health succumbs to affliction, and nations groan under corruption. The enemy prowls, seeking to steal, kill, and destroy (John 10:10), but God has not left His people defenseless. This book is your spiritual armory, a collection of 323 meticulously crafted prayers, declarations, and decrees, each a divine arrow designed to pierce the heart of every challenge. From restoring your family to awakening your Christ consciousness, from breaking delays to shielding your digital life, these decrees span 18 distinct battlegrounds, ensuring no area of your life remains untouched by God's power.

As an apostle, I have walked the frontlines of spiritual warfare, witnessed the enemy's tactics, and seen the transformative power of God's promises dismantle strongholds. These decrees are not born of theory but of divine revelation, inspired by the Holy Spirit and anchored in the unyielding truth of Scripture. They are your tools to confront specific battles with precision, for just as a physician prescribes a targeted remedy, you must wield the right decree for the right challenge. A prayer for health will not break a financial curse; a decree for favor will not heal a wounded heart. This book equips you to diagnose your battle, select your weapon, and speak with the authority of one seated in heavenly places (Ephesians 2:6).

The spiritual realm is not passive; it responds to the voice of the redeemed. When you speak these decrees, you are not begging—you are commanding, as a joint-heir with Christ (Romans 8:17). You are aligning earth with Heaven, shattering the enemy's plans, and activating the covenant promises that are your birthright. Whether you're contending for your children's salvation, breaking generational curses, protecting your community from darkness, or transcending fear through God's peace, these pages hold the keys to your victory across 18 specialized chapters:

- Family Restoration: Heal relationships and break generational chains.
- Business and Wealth: Unlock financial overflow and marketplace influence.
- Health and Healing: Restore physical, mental, and emotional wholeness.
- Delay Breaking: Accelerate promises and shatter stagnation.
- Victory Over Enemies: Dismantle demonic assignments and witchcraft.
- Purpose and Identity: Walk boldly in your divine calling.
- Spiritual Warfare and Protection: Shield your life from spiritual attacks.
- Fruitfulness and Productivity: Expand your influence and bear abundant fruit.
- Restoration and Deliverance: Redeem lost time and break bondages.
- Favor, Scholarships, and Opportunities: Open doors of supernatural advancement.
- Technological Warfare and Protection: Safeguard against digital assaults.
- Christ Consciousness and Awakening: Align with divine truth and transcend illusions.
- Emotional and Relational Healing: Mend wounds and restore connections.
- Spiritual Discernment and Wisdom: Navigate life with divine clarity.
- Community and National Transformation: Ignite revival and restore godly order.
- Freedom from Fear and Anxiety: Anchor your heart in God's peace.
- Intercession for Others: Lift others to salvation and breakthrough.
- Cross-Category Decrees: Wield versatile proclamations for any

battle.

God's promises are universal, transcending borders, cultures, and traditions. Whether you come from a collectivist society where family includes extended kin, a region facing unique spiritual strongholds, or a denomination with distinct prayer practices, these decrees are yours to wield. Under the guidance of the Holy Spirit, adapt them to your cultural context—personalize names, traditions, or challenges as led, knowing that the authority of God's Word remains unchanging (Isaiah 55:11). As you engage the "Morning Warfare Prayer Points" in each chapter's Practical Application section, rise daily to command, "My Father, my God, I take authority!" These concise, anointed prayers empower believers across African, African American, Hispanic, Asian, Indigenous, and European contexts to dismantle evil, restore divine order, and unleash breakthroughs, uniting the global Body of Christ in victory, in Jesus' name. Amen.

Chapter 1: Family Restoration

The Sacred Blueprint of Family

In the heart of God's eternal design lies the family—a divine institution, a sacred fortress, and the first battleground of faith. Before churches were built or nations were formed, God established the family as the cornerstone of His Kingdom on earth, a living testament to His covenant love and unbreakable promises. **Chapter 1: Family Restoration** is not merely a collection of prayers; it is a spiritual armory, wielding 51 Spirit-inspired declarations and decrees to heal fractured homes, protect loved ones, and reset generational destinies. Rooted in the unyielding truth of Joshua 24:15—"As for me and my house, we will serve the Lord"—this chapter equips you to declare your family a stronghold of righteousness, a beacon of God's glory, and a unit of supernatural warfare against the enemy's schemes.

The family is under siege in these last days. The enemy, prowling like a roaring lion (1 Peter 5:8), targets marriages with division, children with rebellion, and bloodlines with curses, seeking to dismantle God's blueprint. Yet, God has not left you defenseless. These 51 decrees, forged in the fire of divine revelation and apostolic authority, are your weapons to break every chain, restore every breach, and co-create with God a legacy of faith (Ephesians 3:20). From mending broken marriages to shielding your children's destinies, from canceling generational curses to activating covenant blessings, this chapter empowers you to stand as a watchman over your household, declaring, "Not on my watch will the enemy prevail!"

Why Family Restoration Matters

The family is not just a social unit; it is the first altar of worship, the cradle of faith, and the foundation of spiritual warfare. When God created Adam and Eve, He called them to be fruitful, multiply, and have dominion (Genesis 1:28), establishing the family as the seedbed of His Kingdom purposes. A strong family is a threat to the enemy's agenda, for it produces warriors who carry God's glory across generations. Conversely, a fractured family is a foothold for the adversary, allowing division, strife, and curses to take root. **Family Restoration** is the cornerstone of this book because without a fortified home, no other battle—financial, health-related, or spiritual—can be fully won. As Psalm 127:1 declares, "Unless the Lord builds the house, those who build it labor in vain."

For those new to prayer, this chapter is a gentle yet powerful entry point. The decrees are like seeds planted in faith, requiring only your voice and trust to grow divine protection, love, and unity in your home. Speak them as a beginner, and God will honor your faith with miracles (Mark 11:24). For prayer generals, this chapter is an apostolic mandate, a call to wield your authority as a king and priest (Revelation 1:6) to dismantle demonic assignments, reset generational trajectories, and establish your family as a warfare unit (Ephesians 6:12). Every decree is a sword, cutting through the enemy's lies and planting promises that echo through your bloodline. Whether you're a novice or a seasoned intercessor, this chapter is vital, for the family is where faith is forged, love is nurtured, and Heaven's power transforms lives.

The Power of Targeted Decrees

Just as a physician prescribes a specific remedy for a specific ailment—no antacid for a headache, no dental visit for a stomachache—spiritual battles demand precise, targeted weapons. The 51 decrees in **Family Restoration** are tailored to address the unique challenges facing your household. Is your marriage strained by miscommunication? Declare, "I decree that communication is restored in my marriage" (#9). Are your children drifting from faith? Proclaim, "I decree that no matter how far my children have strayed, God brings them back to worship and praise Him" (#15). Is your bloodline plagued by curses? Decree, "I decree that every spirit of rebellion is broken off my bloodline" (#6). Each proclamation is a divine prescription, anointed to hit the root of your family's need, aligning your home with God's covenant promises.

These decrees are not mere words; they are creative forces, carrying the authority of Heaven to shift realities. Proverbs 18:21 reminds us, "Death and life are in the power of the tongue." When you speak these decrees, you partner with the Holy Spirit, activating the blood of Jesus to cover your family (Revelation 12:11) and angels to war on your behalf (Psalm 103:20). For new believers, this is a revelation: your voice, though untrained, is a weapon when aligned with God's Word. For generals, it's a reminder of your apostolic charge to co-create with God, resetting destinies with every proclamation (Ephesians 3:20). The decrees are your tools to build, protect, and restore, ensuring your family stands as a testimony of God's faithfulness.

A Fortress Under Siege

The enemy's assault on families is relentless. Marriages crumble under the weight of division, children fall prey to rebellion and worldly influences, and generational curses—addiction, poverty, strife—persist like inherited diseases. Yet, God's Word is clear: "No weapon formed against you shall prosper" (Isaiah 54:17). The decrees in this chapter confront these attacks head-on, addressing specific needs:

Marital Unity: Decrees like "I decree that my marriage is strengthened by love, patience, wisdom, and mutual respect" (#7) and "I decree that as my spouse and I align with God's will, the impossible becomes possible in our home" (#42) restore communication, love, and divine alignment.

Children's Destinies: Proclamations such as "I decree that my children excel in wisdom, favor, and understanding" (#1) and "I decree that my children are called into the kingdom of light, living healthy and happy lives dedicated to God" (#14) shield and guide your offspring.

Generational Breakthrough: Decrees like "I decree freedom in my bloodline, connected to newness through dedication to God" (#31) and "I decree that every generational curse operating in my bloodline is broken by the power of the blood of Jesus" (from **Restoration and Deliverance**, cross-referenced) break inherited strongholds.

Spiritual Warfare: Decrees like "I declare that my family is the first unit of spiritual warfare, standing as a fortified wall against the enemy" (#41) and "I declare that angels are assigned to my household, activated by God's Word spoken through our lips" (#37) position your family as a battle-ready force.

For those new to prayer, these decrees are simple to speak, requiring only faith to see God move. Imagine planting a seed in fertile soil—each word you utter is a seed of promise, watered by trust, that grows into a harvest of restoration. For generals, these decrees are strategic, apostolic weapons, enabling you to exercise dominion (Genesis 1:28) and reset your family's trajectory. You're not just praying; you're commanding, aligning earth with Heaven, and establishing a legacy of faith that echoes through generations.

The Apostolic Call to Family Restoration

As an apostle, I've seen the enemy's tactics firsthand—division sowing discord, rebellion stealing destinies, and curses binding bloodlines. But I've also witnessed the power of God's Word to restore what was lost, heal what was broken, and redeem what was stolen (Joel 2:25). **Family Restoration** is not optional; it's foundational. Without a united, faith-filled home, your spiritual battles lack a firm footing. A divided house cannot stand (Mark 3:25), but a restored family is a fortress, unshakable against the enemy's assaults. This chapter is your apostolic mandate to take up your authority as a king and priest (Revelation 1:6), declaring God's promises over your household with unwavering faith.

For new believers, this chapter is an invitation to step into your God-given authority. You may feel inexperienced, but your voice, when aligned with these decrees, carries the weight of Heaven. Speak, "I declare that as for me and my house, we serve the Lord" (#17), and trust God to honor your faith. For generals, this chapter is a call to strategic warfare. You understand that the family is the first unit of war, a divine alliance to confront the enemy (Ephesians 6:12). Decrees like "I decree that my family co-creates with God, resetting every area of our lives according to His divine plan" (#32) and "I declare that my family attracts divine opportunities, resources, wisdom, and strategies as we walk in God's ways" (#43) empower you to lead your household with apostolic precision, breaking cycles and building legacies.

Practical Application for All

Family Restoration is a chapter for every believer, from the novice to the general, because every family faces battles, and every home needs God's covering. Here's how to engage with this chapter:

For Those New to Prayer

Start Simple: Choose one or two decrees that resonate with your family's needs, such as "I decree that my family walks in unity, peace, and divine love, serving the Lord wholeheartedly" (#16). Speak them daily, aloud, with faith.

Trust God's Word: You don't need experience; you need trust. Hebrews 11:6 says, "Without faith it is impossible to please Him." Your words, backed by Scripture, are powerful.

Expect Results: Like a patient taking medicine, trust that each decree is working, even if results aren't immediate. Journal answered prayers to build your faith.

Pray with Family: If possible, gather your spouse or children to speak these decrees together, creating a unified front (Matthew 18:19).

For Prayer Generals

Diagnose Strategically: Identify the enemy's tactics in your family—division, rebellion, curses—and select decrees to counter them, like "I decree that nothing can stop my family's destiny in Christ except our own unbelief, and we choose faith" (#36).

Activate Angels: Use decrees like "I declare that angels are assigned to my household, activated by God's Word spoken through our lips" (#37) to engage heavenly forces (Psalm 103:20).

Lead with Authority: As a general, you're not just praying; you're commanding. Speak, "I declare that my family is the first unit of spiritual warfare, standing as a fortified wall against the enemy" (#41), with apostolic boldness.

Intercede for Generations: Use decrees like "I declare that my descendants possess the gates of their enemies" (#23) to secure blessings for future generations.

Practical Steps

Create a Prayer Space: Find a quiet place to focus, inviting the Holy Spirit to anoint your words.

Speak Daily: Declare 5–10 decrees each morning or night, personalizing them (e.g., insert your child's name in "I decree that [name] excels in wisdom, favor, and understanding" [#1]).

Combine with Worship: Pair decrees with praise, amplifying their power (Psalm 149:6-9). Sing or lift your hands to magnify God.

Live the Decrees: Align your actions with your words. If you decree marital unity, practice patience and love (Ephesians 5:33). If you declare protection, trust God's covering (Psalm 91:1).

The Eternal Impact of Family Restoration

The stakes are eternal. A restored family is not just a personal victory; it's a generational triumph, a ripple effect that transforms communities, churches, and nations. When you declare, "I declare that my family fulfills every divine purpose and assignment" (#25), you're not only securing your household but planting seeds for a legacy of righteousness (Proverbs 13:22). When you proclaim, "I decree that my family co-creates with God, resetting every area of our lives according to His divine plan" (#32), you're aligning your bloodline with God's eternal purposes, breaking cycles of destruction and building altars of worship.

For new believers, this chapter is a gateway to experiencing God's power. You may start with a simple decree, like "I declare unity, peace, and divine love over my household" (#18), and see God mend a strained relationship. That small victory will ignite your faith, showing you the authority you carry in Christ (Luke 10:19). For generals, this chapter is a strategic blueprint. You recognize that the family is the first unit of war, a divine alliance to confront the enemy's schemes. Decrees like "I declare that as sons and daughters of God, my family brings remedies to the groans of creation" (#45) empower you to lead with prophetic insight, transforming your home into a hub of God's glory (Romans 8:19).

A Call to Rise

Family Restoration is where the battle begins and the victory is won. It's where you declare, "I decree that my family is covered by the blood of Jesus, becoming a testimony of God's power, love, and faithfulness" (#12), and watch Heaven respond. It's where you stand, as a new believer or a general, and proclaim, "I decree that God calls my family unstoppable, and we embrace His divine identity for us" (#44), knowing the enemy trembles at your voice. This chapter is not just a tool; it's a mandate, a divine commission to fortify your home, reset your legacy, and establish God's Kingdom in your family.

For those new to prayer, start here. Speak these decrees with faith, and God will honor your trust, building your home on the rock of His Word (Matthew 7:24). For generals, lead here. Wield these proclamations with apostolic authority, knowing your family is a warfare unit, co-creating with God to shift generations (Ephesians 3:20). The enemy may rage, but the blood of Jesus prevails (Revelation 12:11). Rise, declare, and watch your family become a fortress of faith, a testimony of restoration, and a legacy of God's unending love.

Family Restoration Prayer

Morning Warfare Prayer Points: Restoring Covenant Families

My Father, my God, I take authority over my family; let Your covenant unite us, in Jesus' name. Father, let every divisive spirit refuse to operate in my household today. Lord, I command every curse against my family to be null and void, in Jesus' name. Father, my God, I pull down every demonic plot sowing discord in my home. I dismantle every generational bondage; my bloodline is free, in Jesus' name. Lord, restore my marriage with love and respect; let unity prevail. My Father, my God, cover my children with Your blood; guide them to Your light. Let Your angels encamp around my home, guarding our legacy. Lord, thank You for healing our wounds; my family shines with Your glory. Anoint my household with joy; let our unity testify of Your love, in Jesus' name. Amen.

Scriptures: Genesis 17:7, Ephesians 5:33, Colossians 1:13, Galatians 3:13, Psalm 147:3, Psalm 103:20

Family Restoration Declarations and Decrees

1. I decree that my children excel in wisdom, favor, and understanding (Proverbs 4:7).
2. I decree that scholarships, favor, and supernatural opportunities manifest in my children's lives (Psalm 5:12).
3. I decree that my descendants are mighty in the land (Psalm 112:2).
4. I decree that my children and grandchildren walk in divine favor and success (Deuteronomy 28:11).
5. I decree that no weapon formed against my children prospers (Isaiah 54:17).
6. I decree that every spirit of rebellion is broken off my bloodline (Ephesians 6:12).
7. I decree that my marriage is strengthened by love, patience, wisdom, and mutual respect (Ephesians 5:33).
8. I decree that every attack against my marriage is overturned by God's power (Psalm 18:2).
9. I decree that communication is restored in my marriage (Colossians 4:6).
10. I decree that every wall of division in my marriage is torn down (Ephesians 2:14).
11. I decree that covenant blessings flow in my marriage and family line (Deuteronomy 7:9).
12. I decree that my family is covered by the blood of Jesus, becoming a testimony of God's power, love, and faithfulness (Revelation 12:11).
13. I decree that every breach in my family is repaired, and every broken heart is mended (Psalm 147:3).
14. I decree that my children are called into the kingdom of light, living healthy and happy lives dedicated to God (Colossians 1:13).
15. I decree that no matter how far my children have strayed, God brings them back to worship and praise Him (Luke 15:20).

16. I decree that my family walks in unity, peace, and divine love, serving the Lord wholeheartedly (Psalm 133:1).
17. I declare that as for me and my house, we serve the Lord (Joshua 24:15).
18. I declare unity, peace, and divine love over my household (John 17:21).
19. I declare that my family walks in covenant with the Most High God (Genesis 17:7).
20. I declare restoration over every broken relationship in my family (Joel 2:25).
21. I declare freedom and divine health over my descendants (3 John 1:2).
22. I declare that my family leaves a legacy of righteousness (Proverbs 13:22).
23. I declare that my descendants possess the gates of their enemies (Genesis 22:17).
24. I declare that generational wealth, wisdom, and favor flow through my family (Deuteronomy 28:8).
25. I declare that my family fulfills every divine purpose and assignment (Jeremiah 1:5).
26. I declare that, by the blood and promise of Jesus Christ, I am the seed of Abraham, progressing and going forth (Galatians 3:29).
27. I receive the blessing of Abraham in my life and my children's lives (Galatians 3:14).
28. I decree that no spirit of darkness takes my children; they live healthy and happy lives (Psalm 91:10).
29. I decree that my children live long, healthy lives, free from curses (Psalm 91:16).
30. I decree that everything my children touch prospers (Deuteronomy 28:2).
31. I decree freedom in my bloodline, connected to newness through dedication to God (Romans 6:4).
32. I decree that my family co-creates with God, resetting every area of our lives according to His divine plan (Ephesians 3:20).
33. I declare that God's power, exceeding all I can ask or imagine,

energizes my household to fulfill His purpose (Ephesians 3:20).
34. I decree that God never abandons my family, empowering us to press forward in unity and strength (Deuteronomy 31:6).
35. I declare that as a king and priest under God, I lead my family in righteousness through the blood of Jesus (Revelation 1:6).
36. I decree that nothing can stop my family's destiny in Christ except our own unbelief, and we choose faith (Philippians 4:13).
37. I declare that angels are assigned to my household, activated by God's Word spoken through our lips (Psalm 103:20).
38. I decree that my soul surrenders to the authority of my spirit, aligning my family with God's truth (Psalm 42:5).
39. I declare that my spirit is fully surrendered to the Holy Spirit, guiding my family into all truth (John 16:13).
40. I decree that my body submits to the authority of my soul, enabling my family to walk in divine health (3 John 1:2).
41. I declare that my family is the first unit of spiritual warfare, standing as a fortified wall against the enemy (Ephesians 6:12).
42. I decree that as my spouse and I align with God's will, the impossible becomes possible in our home (Matthew 19:26).
43. I declare that my family attracts divine opportunities, resources, wisdom, and strategies as we walk in God's ways (Proverbs 3:5-6).
44. I decree that God calls my family unstoppable, and we embrace His divine identity for us (Isaiah 54:17).
45. I declare that as sons and daughters of God, my family brings remedies to the groans of creation (Romans 8:19).
46. I decree that my family's words activate Heaven's power, resetting generational blessings in our bloodline (Proverbs 18:21).
47. I declare that our alignment with the Holy Spirit fortifies our home, making us a beacon of God's glory (John 17:22).
48. I decree that every member of my family walks in the authority of Christ, commanding breakthroughs in His name (Luke 10:19).
49. I declare that God's exceeding power flows through our family, surpassing every limitation and obstacle (Ephesians 3:20).
50. I decree that our family's unity in faith moves mountains, establishing God's Kingdom in our home (Mark 11:23).

51. I declare that as we co-create with God, our family is a living testimony of His unstoppable power and love (Psalm 115:14).

Chapter 2: Business and Wealth

The Divine Mandate for Prosperity

In God's eternal design, wealth and business are not merely means of survival but divine tools for advancing His Kingdom and fulfilling His purposes on earth. **Chapter 2: Business and Wealth** is a spiritual armory, equipped with 28 Spirit-inspired declarations and decrees to unlock financial overflow, cancel debts, and establish marketplace influence. Rooted in the unshakable promise of Deuteronomy 8:18—"It is He who gives you the ability to produce wealth"—this chapter empowers you to declare your finances and business endeavors as conduits of God's glory, breaking every chain of lack and aligning your resources with Heaven's economy.

The enemy seeks to bind believers in financial bondage, stifle business growth, and hinder Kingdom impact (John 10:10). Yet, God has not left you defenseless. These 28 decrees, forged in the fire of divine revelation and apostolic authority, are your weapons to dismantle strongholds of poverty, activate supernatural provision, and co-create with God a legacy of abundance (Philippians 4:19). From canceling debts to opening doors of opportunity, from anointing your hands for wealth to funding God's work, this chapter equips you to stand as a steward of Heaven's resources, declaring, "Not on my watch will lack prevail!"

Why Business and Wealth Matter

Wealth and business are not secular pursuits; they are sacred assignments, entrusted to believers to steward for God's glory. When God blessed Abraham, He promised to make him a blessing to all nations (Genesis 12:2-3), and as heirs of that promise (Galatians 3:29), you are called to wield wealth and influence to advance the Kingdom. A prosperous believer is a threat to the enemy's agenda, for they fund ministries, create opportunities, and demonstrate God's faithfulness. Conversely, financial lack is a foothold for the adversary, fostering fear, division, and limitation. **Business and Wealth** is foundational to this book because without financial freedom, your ability to impact other areas—family, community, or ministry—is constrained. As Malachi 3:10 declares, "Bring the whole tithe into the storehouse... and see if I will not throw open the floodgates of heaven."

For those new to prayer, this chapter is an accessible entry point. The decrees are seeds of faith, requiring only your voice and trust to cultivate provision and opportunity. Speak them as a beginner, and God will honor your faith with breakthroughs (Mark 11:24). For prayer generals, this chapter is an apostolic mandate, a call to wield your authority as a king and priest (Revelation 1:6) to break financial curses, reset economic destinies, and establish your business as a warfare unit (Ephesians 6:12). Every decree is a sword, cutting through the enemy's lies and planting promises that echo through your legacy. Whether you're a novice or a seasoned intercessor, this chapter is vital, for wealth is where stewardship is tested, influence is expanded, and God's provision transforms lives.

The Power of Targeted Decrees

Just as a physician prescribes a specific remedy for a specific ailment—no antacid for a headache, no dental visit for a stomachache—financial battles demand precise, targeted weapons. The 28 decrees in **Business and Wealth** are tailored to address the unique challenges facing your finances and business. Are you burdened by debt? Declare, "I decree an abundance of divine debt cancellation" (#1). Is your business stagnant? Proclaim, "I decree that supernatural doors of business and wealth open now" (#9). Are you seeking influence? Decree, "I decree that I am anointed to be a marketplace influencer, walking in wisdom and favor" (#18). Each proclamation is a divine prescription, anointed to hit the root of your financial need, aligning your resources with God's covenant promises.

These decrees are not mere words; they are creative forces, carrying the authority of Heaven to shift realities. Proverbs 18:21 reminds us, "Death and life are in the power of the tongue." When you speak these decrees, you partner with the Holy Spirit, activating the blood of Jesus to cover your finances (Revelation 12:11) and angels to war on your behalf (Hebrews 1:14). For new believers, this is a revelation: your voice, though untrained, is a weapon when aligned with God's Word. For generals, it's a reminder of your apostolic charge to co-create with God, resetting financial destinies with every proclamation (Ephesians 3:20). The decrees are your tools to build, protect, and multiply, ensuring your business and wealth stand as a testimony of God's faithfulness.

A Marketplace Under Siege

The enemy's assault on finances is relentless. Debts pile up, opportunities are blocked, and businesses falter under economic pressures and spiritual attacks. Yet, God's Word is clear: "The blessing of the Lord brings wealth, without painful toil for it" (Proverbs 10:22). The decrees in this chapter confront these attacks head-on, addressing specific needs:

- **Debt Cancellation**: Decrees like "I decree an abundance of divine debt cancellation" (#1) and "I decree that my debts are canceled, and supernatural provision is my portion" (#4) break the chains of financial bondage.
- **Business Growth**: Proclamations such as "I decree that supernatural doors of business and wealth open now" (#9) and "I decree that clients and contracts locate me supernaturally" (#10) unlock opportunities and expansion.
- **Marketplace Influence**: Decrees like "I decree that I am anointed to be a marketplace influencer, walking in wisdom and favor" (#18) and "I decree that every meeting, transaction, and negotiation is guided by divine wisdom" (#19) position you as a Kingdom leader.
- **Kingdom Funding**: Decrees like "I decree that I fund the Kingdom of God with joy and abundance" (#7) and "I decree that I create programs, institutions, and legacies that serve the Lord" (#8) align your wealth with God's purposes.

For those new to prayer, these decrees are simple to speak, requiring only faith to see God move. Imagine planting a seed in fertile soil—each word you utter is a seed of provision, watered by trust, that grows into a harvest of abundance. For generals, these decrees are strategic, apostolic weapons, enabling you to exercise dominion (Genesis 1:28) and reset your financial trajectory. You're not just praying; you're commanding, aligning earth with Heaven, and establishing a legacy of prosperity that echoes through generations.

The Apostolic Call to Business and Wealth

As an apostle, I've seen the enemy's tactics firsthand—poverty sowing fear, lack stealing opportunities, and financial curses binding destinies. But I've also witnessed the power of God's Word to restore what was lost, multiply what was sown, and redeem what was stolen (Joel 2:25). **Business and Wealth** is not optional; it's foundational. Without financial freedom, your ability to fulfill God's purposes is limited. A prosperous house stands firm (Psalm 112:3), but a bound one struggles to shine. This chapter is your apostolic mandate to take up your authority as a king and priest (Revelation 1:6), declaring God's promises over your finances with unwavering faith.

For new believers, this chapter is an invitation to step into your God-given authority. You may feel inexperienced, but your voice, when aligned with these decrees, carries the weight of Heaven. Speak, "I declare that the works of my hands are blessed" (#20), and trust God to honor your faith. For generals, this chapter is a call to strategic warfare. You understand that wealth is a weapon, a divine resource to confront the enemy's schemes (Ephesians 6:12). Decrees like "I decree that my hands are anointed to gain wealth" (#2) and "I declare that I live under Heaven's economy, unmoved by the world's economy" (#26) empower you to lead with apostolic precision, breaking cycles of lack and building legacies of abundance.

Practical Application for All

Business and Wealth is a chapter for every believer, from the novice to the general, because every life faces financial battles, and every calling needs God's provision. Here's how to engage with this chapter:

For Those New to Prayer

- **Start Simple**: Choose one or two decrees that resonate with your financial needs, such as "I declare that financial overflow is my portion" (#25). Speak them daily, aloud, with faith.
- **Trust God's Word**: You don't need experience; you need trust. Hebrews 11:6 says, "Without faith it is impossible to please Him." Your words, backed by Scripture, are powerful.
- **Expect Results**: Like a patient taking medicine, trust that each decree is working, even if results aren't immediate. Journal answered prayers to build your faith.
- **Give in Faith**: If possible, pair decrees with acts of giving, creating a unified front of faith (2 Corinthians 9:7).

For Prayer Generals

- **Diagnose Strategically**: Identify the enemy's tactics in your finances—debt, stagnation, curses—and select decrees to counter them, like "I decree that I am free from every spirit of financial bondage" (#13).
- **Activate Angels**: Use decrees like "I decree that God's warring angels bring everything stored up for me, including wealth" (#17) to engage heavenly forces (Hebrews 1:14).
- **Lead with Authority**: As a general, you're not just praying; you're commanding. Speak, "I decree that sudden promotions, business expansions, and new income streams flow to me" (#12), with apostolic boldness.
- **Intercede for Legacy**: Use decrees like "I declare that the wealth of the wicked is laid up for me" (#24) to secure blessings for future generations.

Practical Steps

- **Create a Prayer Space**: Find a quiet place to focus, inviting the Holy Spirit to anoint your words.
- **Speak Daily**: Declare 5–10 decrees each morning or night, personalizing them (e.g., insert your business's name in "I declare that [name] prospers" [#21]).
- **Combine with Worship**: Pair decrees with praise, amplifying their power (Psalm 149:6-9). Sing or lift your hands to magnify God.
- **Live the Decrees**: Align your actions with your words. If you decree provision, practice generosity (Proverbs 11:25). If you declare wisdom, seek God's guidance in decisions (James 1:5).

The Eternal Impact of Business and Wealth

The stakes are eternal. Prosperous finances are not just a personal victory; they're a generational triumph, a ripple effect that transforms families, communities, and nations. When you declare, "I decree that I fund the

Kingdom of God with joy and abundance" (#7), you're not only securing your wealth but planting seeds for a legacy of righteousness (Proverbs 13:22). When you proclaim, "I decree that I create programs, institutions, and legacies that serve the Lord" (#8), you're aligning your resources with God's eternal purposes, breaking cycles of lack and building altars of impact.

For new believers, this chapter is a gateway to experiencing God's power. You may start with a simple decree, like "I declare that every business endeavor prospers" (#21), and see God open a door of opportunity. That small victory will ignite your faith, showing you the authority you carry in Christ (Luke 10:19). For generals, this chapter is a strategic blueprint. You recognize that wealth is a warfare tool, a divine resource to confront the enemy's schemes. Decrees like "I declare that ideas, creativity, and witty inventions flow through me" (#23) empower you to lead with prophetic insight, transforming your business into a hub of God's glory (Isaiah 60:11).

A Call to Rise

Business and Wealth is where the battle for provision begins and the victory is won. It's where you declare, "I decree that my hands are anointed to gain wealth" (#2), and watch Heaven respond. It's where you stand, as a new believer or a general, and proclaim, "I declare that I live under Heaven's economy, unmoved by the world's economy" (#26), knowing the enemy trembles at your voice. This chapter is not just a tool; it's a mandate, a divine commission to fortify your finances, reset your legacy, and establish God's Kingdom through your wealth.

For those new to prayer, start here. Speak these decrees with faith, and God will honor your trust, building your finances on the rock of His Word (Matthew 7:24). For generals, lead here. Wield these proclamations with apostolic authority, knowing your wealth is a warfare unit, co-creating with God to shift generations (Ephesians 3:20). The enemy may rage, but the promises of God prevail (Deuteronomy 28:12). Rise, declare, and watch your business and wealth become a fortress of provision, a testimony of abundance, and a legacy of God's unending faithfulness.

Business and Wealth Prayer

Morning Warfare Prayer Points: Commanding Financial Dominion

My Father, my God, I take authority over my finances; let wealth flow to me, in Jesus' name. Father, let every spirit of lack refuse to operate in my business today. Lord, I command every debt to be canceled; provision overtakes me, in Jesus' name. My Father, my God, I pull down every demonic barrier blocking my financial breakthroughs. I dismantle every generational curse of poverty; my bloodline prospers, in Jesus' name. Lord, open doors no man can shut; let favor guide my transactions. Anoint my hands to produce wealth; my work glorifies You. Let Your angels deliver stored-up resources to my family. Lord, thank You for Your overflow; my business testifies of Your provision. Father, cause me to excel in the marketplace; let my cup run over, in Jesus' name. Amen.

Scriptures: Deuteronomy 8:18, Philippians 4:19, Psalm 90:17, Revelation 3:8, Galatians 3:13, Hebrews 1:14

Business and Wealth Declarations and Decrees

1. I decree an abundance of divine debt cancellation (Deuteronomy 15:1).
2. I decree that my hands are anointed to gain wealth (Deuteronomy 8:18).
3. I decree that I restore everything God has called me to restore (Joel 2:25).
4. I decree that my debts are canceled, and supernatural provision is my portion (Philippians 4:19).
5. I decree that I am the lender and not the borrower (Deuteronomy 28:12).
6. I decree that I own land and real estate (Psalm 37:29).
7. I decree that I fund the Kingdom of God with joy and abundance (Malachi 3:10).
8. I decree that I create programs, institutions, and legacies that serve the Lord (Isaiah 61:4).
9. I decree that supernatural doors of business and wealth open now (Revelation 3:8).
10. I decree that clients and contracts locate me supernaturally (Psalm 75:6-7).
11. I decree that favor establishes the work of my hands (Psalm 90:17).
12. I decree that sudden promotions, business expansions, and new income streams flow to me (Deuteronomy 28:2).
13. I decree that I am free from every spirit of financial bondage (Luke 4:18).
14. I decree that financial miracles chase and overtake me (Deuteronomy 28:2).
15. I decree that I owe no man anything but love (Romans 13:8).
16. I decree that everything stolen from my finances is restored sevenfold (Proverbs 6:31).
17. I decree that God's warring angels bring everything stored up for

me, including wealth (Hebrews 1:14).
18. I decree that I am anointed to be a marketplace influencer, walking in wisdom and favor (Daniel 1:20).
19. I decree that every meeting, transaction, and negotiation is guided by divine wisdom (James 1:5).
20. I declare that the works of my hands are blessed (Deuteronomy 28:12).
21. I declare that every business endeavor prospers (Psalm 1:3).
22. I declare that new contracts, divine clients, and financial increase locate me (Isaiah 60:11).
23. I declare that ideas, creativity, and witty inventions flow through me (Proverbs 8:12).
24. I declare that the wealth of the wicked is laid up for me (Proverbs 13:22).
25. I declare that financial overflow is my portion (Psalm 23:5).
26. I declare that I live under Heaven's economy, unmoved by the world's economy (Philippians 4:19).
27. I declare that doors of financial favor, business opportunities, and Kingdom partnerships open (Revelation 3:7).
28. I receive the wealth of the wicked stored up for the righteous (Proverbs 13:22).

Chapter 3: Health and Healing

The Divine Prescription for Wholeness

In God's eternal design, health is not merely the absence of sickness but a state of complete physical, mental, and emotional wholeness, reflecting His promise of abundant life (John 10:10). **Chapter 3: Health and Healing** is a spiritual armory, equipped with 23 Spirit-inspired declarations and decrees to restore your body, renew your mind, and heal your soul. Rooted in the unyielding truth of Isaiah 53:5—"By His wounds we are healed"—this chapter empowers you to declare your health as a testimony of God's power, breaking every chain of disease and aligning your well-being with Heaven's design.

The enemy assaults health with sickness, mental oppression, and emotional wounds, seeking to steal vitality and hinder your purpose (1 Peter 5:8). Yet, God has not left you defenseless. These 23 decrees, forged in the fire of divine revelation and apostolic authority, are your weapons to uproot infirmities, dismantle generational curses, and co-create with God a legacy of divine health (Exodus 15:26). From healing chronic conditions to protecting your mind from anxiety, from breaking cycles of disease to restoring restful sleep, this chapter equips you to stand as a guardian of your health, declaring, "Not on my watch will sickness prevail!"

Why Health and Healing Matter

Health is not a luxury; it is a divine mandate, the foundation of a vibrant life dedicated to God's purposes. When God formed humanity, He declared them "very good" (Genesis 1:31), endowing them with bodies as temples of the Holy Spirit (1 Corinthians 6:19). A healthy believer is a threat to the enemy's agenda, for they carry God's glory with strength, clarity, and resilience. Conversely, sickness and mental oppression are footholds for the adversary, fostering fear, distraction, and limitation. **Health and Healing** is foundational to this book because without wholeness, your ability to fulfill God's calling—whether in family, business, or ministry—is compromised. As 3 John 1:2 declares, "I pray that you may enjoy good health and that all may go well with you, even as your soul is getting along well."

For those new to prayer, this chapter is a gentle yet powerful entry point. The decrees are seeds of faith, requiring only your voice and trust to cultivate healing and restoration. Speak them as a beginner, and God will honor your faith with miracles (Mark 11:24). For prayer generals, this chapter is an apostolic mandate, a call to wield your authority as a king and priest (Revelation 1:6) to break curses of sickness, reset health destinies, and establish your body as a warfare unit (Ephesians 6:12). Every decree is a sword, cutting through the enemy's lies and planting promises that echo through your bloodline. Whether you're a novice or a seasoned intercessor, this chapter is vital, for health is where faith is tested, resilience is forged, and God's healing transforms lives.

The Power of Targeted Decrees

Just as a physician prescribes a specific remedy for a specific ailment—no antacid for a headache, no dental visit for a stomachache—health battles demand precise, targeted weapons. The 23 decrees in **Health and Healing** are tailored to address the unique challenges facing your body, mind, and emotions. Are you battling chronic illness? Declare, "I decree that complete healing flows through my bloodstream, organs, bones, and mind" (#1). Is your mental health under attack? Proclaim, "I decree that every assignment against my mental health—depression, anxiety, fear—is broken" (#4). Are generational diseases plaguing your family? Decree, "I decree that generational curses of sickness—epilepsy, tumors, diabetes, cancer—are broken" (#5). Each proclamation is a divine prescription, anointed to hit the root of your health need, aligning your well-being with God's covenant promises.

These decrees are not mere words; they are creative forces, carrying the authority of Heaven to shift realities. Proverbs 18:21 reminds us, "Death and life are in the power of the tongue." When you speak these decrees, you partner with the Holy Spirit, activating the blood of Jesus to cover your health (Revelation 12:11) and angels to war on your behalf (Psalm 103:20). For new believers, this is a revelation: your voice, though untrained, is a weapon when aligned with God's Word. For generals, it's a reminder of your apostolic charge to co-create with God, resetting health destinies with every proclamation (Ephesians 3:20). The decrees are your tools to heal, protect, and restore, ensuring your body and mind stand as a testimony of God's faithfulness.

A Body Under Siege

The enemy's assault on health is relentless. Diseases ravage bodies, mental oppression clouds minds, and emotional wounds fester, all designed to derail your purpose. Yet, God's Word is clear: "No weapon formed against you shall prosper" (Isaiah 54:17). The decrees in this chapter confront these attacks head-on, addressing specific needs:

- **Physical Healing**: Decrees like "I decree that complete healing flows through my bloodstream, organs, bones, and mind" (#1) and "I decree that tumors, chronic pain, diabetes, insomnia, and every disease are uprooted" (#2) restore your body to wholeness.
- **Mental and Emotional Health**: Proclamations such as "I decree that every assignment against my mental health—depression, anxiety, fear—is broken" (#4) and "I decree that my immune system, mind, and emotions are healed" (#13) shield your mind and emotions.
- **Generational Breakthrough**: Decrees like "I decree that generational curses of sickness—epilepsy, tumors, diabetes, cancer—are broken" (#5) and "I decree that every infirmity in my family bloodline is cursed and broken" (#11) break inherited strongholds.
- **Rest and Protection**: Decrees like "I decree that every enemy attacking me in my sleep through dreams is overthrown" (#6) and "I decree that I rest in perfect peace, for the Lord is with me" (#8) ensure restful sleep and spiritual protection.

For those new to prayer, these decrees are simple to speak, requiring only faith to see God move. Imagine planting a seed in fertile soil—each word you utter is a seed of healing, watered by trust, that grows into a harvest of wholeness. For generals, these decrees are strategic, apostolic weapons, enabling you to exercise dominion (Genesis 1:28) and reset your health trajectory. You're not just praying; you're commanding, aligning earth with Heaven, and establishing a legacy of divine health that echoes through generations.

The Apostolic Call to Health and Healing

As an apostle, I've seen the enemy's tactics firsthand—sickness sowing despair, mental oppression stealing clarity, and generational curses binding bloodlines. But I've also witnessed the power of God's Word to heal what was broken, restore what was lost, and redeem what was stolen (Jeremiah 30:17).

Health and Healing is not optional; it's foundational. Without wholeness, your ability to fulfill God's purposes is limited. A healthy body and mind stand firm (Psalm 30:2), but a sick one struggles to shine. This chapter is your apostolic mandate to take up your authority as a king and priest (Revelation 1:6), declaring God's promises over your health with unwavering faith.

For new believers, this chapter is an invitation to step into your God-given authority. You may feel inexperienced, but your voice, when aligned with these decrees, carries the weight of Heaven. Speak, "I declare that my body is the temple of the Holy Spirit—sickness cannot dwell here" (#19), and trust God to honor your faith. For generals, this chapter is a call to strategic warfare. You understand that health is a battlefield, a divine domain to confront the enemy's schemes (Ephesians 6:12). Decrees like "I decree that my body is restored from head to toe, free from sickness" (#14) and "I declare that divine health, strength, and peace are my inheritance" (#21) empower you to lead with apostolic precision, breaking cycles of disease and building legacies of vitality.

Practical Application for All

Health and Healing is a chapter for every believer, from the novice to the general, because every life faces health battles, and every body needs God's touch. Here's how to engage with this chapter:

For Those New to Prayer

- **Start Simple**: Choose one or two decrees that resonate with your health needs, such as "I declare that no sickness comes near my dwelling" (#15). Speak them daily, aloud, with faith.
- **Trust God's Word**: You don't need experience; you need trust. Hebrews 11:6 says, "Without faith it is impossible to please Him." Your words, backed by Scripture, are powerful.
- **Expect Results**: Like a patient taking medicine, trust that each decree is working, even if results aren't immediate. Journal answered prayers to build your faith.
- **Rest in Faith**: Pair decrees with rest and trust, creating a unified front of faith (Psalm 4:8).

For Prayer Generals

- **Diagnose Strategically**: Identify the enemy's tactics in your health—disease, mental oppression, curses—and select decrees to counter them, like "I decree that every infirmity in my family bloodline is cursed and broken" (#11).
- **Activate Angels**: Use decrees like "I declare that angels war on my behalf, fighting unseen battles" (from Chapter 7, cross-referenced) to engage heavenly forces (Psalm 103:20).
- **Lead with Authority**: As a general, you're not just praying; you're commanding. Speak, "I decree that long life is my portion" (#9), with apostolic boldness.
- **Intercede for Generations**: Use decrees like "I declare freedom and divine health over my descendants" (#22) to secure blessings for future generations.

Practical Steps

- **Create a Prayer Space**: Find a quiet place to focus, inviting the Holy Spirit to anoint your words.
- **Speak Daily**: Declare 5–10 decrees each morning or night, personalizing them (e.g., insert your name in "I decree that [name]'s body is restored from head to toe" [#14]).
- **Combine with Worship**: Pair decrees with praise, amplifying their power (Psalm 149:6-9). Sing or lift your hands to magnify God.
- **Live the Decrees**: Align your actions with your words. If you decree healing, practice healthy habits (1 Corinthians 6:19). If you declare peace, trust God's presence (Isaiah 26:3).

The Eternal Impact of Health and Healing

The stakes are eternal. A healed body and mind are not just a personal victory; they're a generational triumph, a ripple effect that transforms families, communities, and nations. When you declare, "I declare that I live and declare the works of the Lord" (#16), you're not only securing your health but planting seeds for a legacy of vitality (Psalm 91:16). When you proclaim, "I decree that divine healing flows through my family, breaking cycles of disease" (#12), you're aligning your bloodline with God's eternal purposes, breaking cycles of infirmity and building altars of wholeness.

For new believers, this chapter is a gateway to experiencing God's power. You may start with a simple decree, like "I declare that my strength is renewed like the eagle's" (#18), and see God restore your energy. That small victory will ignite your faith, showing you the authority you carry in Christ (Luke 10:19). For generals, this chapter is a strategic blueprint. You recognize that health is a warfare domain, a divine stronghold to confront the enemy's schemes. Decrees like "I declare freedom and divine health over my descendants" (#22) empower you to lead with prophetic insight, transforming your life into a hub of God's healing (Psalm 30:2).

A Call to Rise

Health and Healing is where the battle for wholeness begins and the victory is won. It's where you declare, "I decree that complete healing flows through my bloodstream, organs, bones, and mind" (#1), and watch Heaven respond. It's where you stand, as a new believer or a general, and proclaim, "I declare that divine health, strength, and peace are my inheritance" (#21), knowing the enemy trembles at your voice. This chapter is not just a tool; it's a mandate, a divine commission to fortify your body, reset your legacy, and establish God's Kingdom through your health.

For those new to prayer, start here. Speak these decrees with faith, and God will honor your trust, building your health on the rock of His Word (Matthew 7:24). For generals, lead here. Wield these proclamations with apostolic authority, knowing your body is a warfare unit, co-creating with God to shift generations (Ephesians 3:20). The enemy may rage, but the healing of Jesus prevails (Isaiah 53:5). Rise, declare, and watch your health become a fortress of wholeness, a testimony of restoration, and a legacy of God's unending power.

Health and Healing Prayer

Morning Warfare Prayer Points: Restoring Divine Health

My Father, my God, I take authority over my body; let Your healing flow through me, in Jesus' name. Father, let every spirit of sickness refuse to operate in my life today. Lord, I command every disease to be uprooted from my body, in Jesus' name. Father, my God, I pull down every demonic assignment attacking my health. I dismantle every generational curse of infirmity; my bloodline is whole, in Jesus' name. Lord, restore my strength like the eagle's; let vitality overtake me. My Father, my God, cover my sleep with Your peace; no oppression disturbs me. Father, let Your angels war for my wellness, guarding my body. Lord, thank You for Your stripes; my body testifies of Your healing. Father, anoint me with health; let my life shine with Your glory, in Jesus' name. Amen.

Scriptures: Isaiah 53:5, Psalm 30:2, Isaiah 40:31, Psalm 4:8, Galatians 3:13, Psalm 103:20

Health and Healing Declarations and Decrees

1. I decree that complete healing flows through my bloodstream, organs, bones, and mind (Isaiah 53:5).
2. I decree that tumors, chronic pain, diabetes, insomnia, and every disease are uprooted (Luke 4:39).
3. I decree that supernatural strength rises within me (Isaiah 40:31).
4. I decree that every assignment against my mental health—depression, anxiety, fear—is broken (Philippians 4:7).
5. I decree that generational curses of sickness—epilepsy, tumors, diabetes, cancer—are broken (Galatians 3:13).
6. I decree that every enemy attacking me in my sleep through dreams is overthrown (Psalm 4:8).
7. I decree that no demonic oppression touches me at night (Psalm 91:5).
8. I decree that I rest in perfect peace, for the Lord is with me (Isaiah 26:3).
9. I decree that long life is my portion (Psalm 91:16).
10. I decree that I enjoy the fruit of my labor in good health (Psalm 128:2).
11. I decree that every infirmity in my family bloodline is cursed and broken (Matthew 8:17).
12. I decree that divine healing flows through my family, breaking cycles of disease (Exodus 15:26).
13. I decree that my immune system, mind, and emotions are healed (Psalm 30:2).
14. I decree that my body is restored from head to toe, free from sickness (Jeremiah 30:17).
15. I declare that no sickness comes near my dwelling (Psalm 91:10).
16. I declare that I live and declare the works of the Lord (Psalm 118:17).
17. I declare that divine life flows through every cell, tissue, and organ (John 6:63).
18. I declare that my strength is renewed like the eagle's (Isaiah

40:31).
19. I declare that my body is the temple of the Holy Spirit—sickness cannot dwell here (1 Corinthians 6:19).
20. I declare that energy, vitality, and clarity of mind are my portion (Nehemiah 8:10).
21. I declare that divine health, strength, and peace are my inheritance (3 John 1:2).
22. I declare freedom and divine health over my descendants (Exodus 23:25).
23. I decree that there is no sickness, early death, suicide, accidents, or burglary for me or my children (Psalm 91:10).

Chapter 4: Delay Breaking

The Divine Acceleration of Promises

In God's eternal plan, every promise, assignment, and destiny moment is appointed for its season, yet the enemy seeks to delay, hinder, and stagnate what God has ordained (Habakkuk 2:3). **Chapter 4: Delay Breaking** is a spiritual armory, equipped with 22 Spirit-inspired declarations and decrees to shatter procrastination, accelerate divine timing, and unleash the suddenlies of God. Rooted in the unyielding truth of Isaiah 60:22—"When the time is right, I, the Lord, will make it happen"—this chapter empowers you to declare your life free from delays, aligning your path with Heaven's swift fulfillment.

The enemy's tactic is to bind believers in cycles of waiting, frustration, and missed opportunities, sowing doubt and despair (Ecclesiastes 3:11). Yet, God has not left you defenseless. These 22 decrees, forged in the fire of divine revelation and apostolic authority, are your weapons to break chains of stagnation, restore lost time, and co-create with God a legacy of accelerated breakthroughs (Joel 2:25). From advancing your business to fulfilling your ministry, from reclaiming opportunities to moving forward without bondage, this chapter equips you to stand as a catalyst of divine speed, declaring, "Not on my watch will delay prevail!"

Why Delay Breaking Matters

Delay is not merely a temporal inconvenience; it is a spiritual battlefield, where the enemy seeks to thwart God's purposes for your life. When God called you, He set a course for your destiny (Jeremiah 1:5), but delays can erode faith, dim vision, and weaken resolve. A believer free from delay is a threat to the enemy's agenda, for they seize divine moments, fulfill assignments, and demonstrate God's faithfulness. Conversely, stagnation is a foothold for the adversary, fostering unbelief and distraction. **Delay Breaking** is foundational to this book because without forward momentum, your ability to impact other areas—family, finances, or health—is hindered. As Psalm 37:23 declares, "The Lord makes firm the steps of the one who delights in Him."

For those new to prayer, this chapter is an accessible entry point. The decrees are seeds of faith, requiring only your voice and trust to cultivate acceleration and breakthrough. Speak them as a beginner, and God will honor your faith with miracles (Mark 11:24). For prayer generals, this chapter is an apostolic mandate, a call to wield your authority as a king and priest (Revelation 1:6) to dismantle demonic hindrances, reset destiny timelines, and establish your life as a warfare unit (Ephesians 6:12). Every decree is a sword, cutting through the enemy's lies and planting promises that propel you forward. Whether you're a novice or a seasoned intercessor, this chapter is vital, for momentum is where faith is ignited, purpose is fulfilled, and God's timing transforms lives.

The Power of Targeted Decrees

Just as a physician prescribes a specific remedy for a specific ailment—no antacid for a headache, no dental visit for a stomachache—battles against delay demand precise, targeted weapons. The 22 decrees in **Delay Breaking** are tailored to address the unique obstacles blocking your progress. Is your business stalled? Declare, "I decree that my business moves forward with supernatural momentum" (#5). Are promises unfulfilled? Proclaim, "I decree acceleration over every promise, assignment, and destiny moment" (#1). Is procrastination binding you? Decree, "I decree that chains of stagnation, procrastination, and delay are broken" (#9). Each proclamation is a divine prescription, anointed to hit the root of your delay, aligning your life with God's appointed time.

These decrees are not mere words; they are creative forces, carrying the authority of Heaven to shift realities. Proverbs 18:21 reminds us, "Death and life are in the power of the tongue." When you speak these decrees, you partner with the Holy Spirit, activating the blood of Jesus to cover your destiny (Revelation 12:11) and angels to war on your behalf (Hebrews 1:14). For new believers, this is a revelation: your voice, though untrained, is a weapon when aligned with God's Word. For generals, it's a reminder of your apostolic charge to co-create with God, resetting timelines with every proclamation (Ephesians 3:20). The decrees are your tools to advance, restore, and accelerate, ensuring your life stands as a testimony of God's faithfulness.

A Destiny Under Siege

The enemy's assault on your destiny is relentless. Opportunities slip away, finances lag, and ministries falter under the weight of delay, all designed to derail God's plan. Yet, God's Word is clear: "No weapon formed against you shall prosper" (Isaiah 54:17). The decrees in this chapter confront these attacks head-on, addressing specific needs:

- **Promise Fulfillment**: Decrees like "I decree acceleration over every promise, assignment, and destiny moment" (#1) and "I declare that every promise of God comes to pass without delay" (#16) align your life with divine timing.
- **Business and Finances**: Proclamations such as "I decree that my business moves forward with supernatural momentum" (#5) and "I decree that my finances catch up to the prophetic word over my life" (#6) unlock progress and provision.
- **Opportunity Restoration**: Decrees like "I decree that every lost opportunity is restored sevenfold" (#8) and "I decree that new doors no man can shut are opened" (#10) reclaim what was stolen.
- **Mental and Spiritual Freedom**: Decrees like "I decree that I cancel stinking thinking and strongholds delaying me" (#21) and "I decree that I move forward without bondage" (#22) break mental and spiritual barriers.

For those new to prayer, these decrees are simple to speak, requiring only faith to see God move. Imagine planting a seed in fertile soil—each word you utter is a seed of acceleration, watered by trust, that grows into a harvest of breakthroughs. For generals, these decrees are strategic, apostolic weapons, enabling you to exercise dominion (Genesis 1:28) and reset your destiny's trajectory. You're not just praying; you're commanding, aligning earth with Heaven, and establishing a legacy of divine timing that echoes through generations.

The Apostolic Call to Delay Breaking

As an apostle, I've seen the enemy's tactics firsthand—delays sowing doubt, stagnation stealing momentum, and hindrances binding destinies. But I've also witnessed the power of God's Word to restore what was lost, accelerate what was delayed, and redeem what was stolen (Amos 9:13). **Delay Breaking** is not optional; it's foundational. Without momentum, your ability to fulfill God's purposes is limited. A life in motion stands firm (Philippians 1:6), but a stalled one struggles to shine. This chapter is your apostolic mandate to take up your authority as a king and priest (Revelation 1:6), declaring God's promises over your timeline with unwavering faith.

For new believers, this chapter is an invitation to step into your God-given authority. You may feel inexperienced, but your voice, when aligned with these decrees, carries the weight of Heaven. Speak, "I declare that the season of waiting has ended, and suddenlies have begun" (#15), and trust God to honor your faith. For generals, this chapter is a call to strategic warfare. You understand that delay is a battlefield, a divine domain to confront the enemy's schemes (Ephesians 6:12). Decrees like "I decree that divine speed overtakes me" (#3) and "I declare immediate breakthroughs manifest in my life" (#17) empower you to lead with apostolic precision, breaking cycles of stagnation and building legacies of acceleration.

Practical Application for All

Delay Breaking is a chapter for every believer, from the novice to the general, because every life faces delays, and every destiny needs God's timing. Here's how to engage with this chapter:

For Those New to Prayer

- **Start Simple**: Choose one or two decrees that resonate with your needs, such as "I declare sudden miracles and divine turnarounds" (#18). Speak them daily, aloud, with faith.
- **Trust God's Word**: You don't need experience; you need trust. Hebrews 11:6 says, "Without faith it is impossible to please Him." Your words, backed by Scripture, are powerful.
- **Expect Results**: Like a patient taking medicine, trust that each decree is working, even if results aren't immediate. Journal answered prayers to build your faith.
- **Act in Faith**: Pair decrees with action, creating a unified front of faith (James 2:26).

For Prayer Generals

- **Diagnose Strategically**: Identify the enemy's tactics in your delays—stagnation, doubt, hindrances—and select decrees to counter them, like "I decree that chains of stagnation, procrastination, and delay are broken" (#9).

- **Activate Angels**: Use decrees like "I decree that destiny helpers locate me now" (#12) to engage heavenly forces (Hebrews 1:14).
- **Lead with Authority**: As a general, you're not just praying; you're commanding. Speak, "I decree that nothing stops or delays me" (#20), with apostolic boldness.
- **Intercede for Legacy**: Use decrees like "I declare that supernatural opportunities and divine timing align for my success" (#13) to secure blessings for future seasons.

Practical Steps

- **Create a Prayer Space**: Find a quiet place to focus, inviting the Holy Spirit to anoint your words.
- **Speak Daily**: Declare 5–10 decrees each morning or night, personalizing them (e.g., insert your goal in "I decree that [goal] moves forward with supernatural momentum" [#5]).
- **Combine with Worship**: Pair decrees with praise, amplifying their power (Psalm 149:6-9). Sing or lift your hands to magnify God.
- **Live the Decrees**: Align your actions with your words. If you decree acceleration, take steps forward (Psalm 37:23). If you declare freedom, reject doubt (Mark 11:23).

The Eternal Impact of Delay Breaking

The stakes are eternal. A life free from delay is not just a personal victory; it's a generational triumph, a ripple effect that transforms families, communities, and nations. When you declare, "I decree that every lost opportunity is restored sevenfold" (#8), you're not only securing your destiny but planting seeds for a legacy of fulfillment (Ecclesiastes 9:11). When you proclaim, "I decree that the next six months produce more fruit than the last six years" (#2), you're aligning your timeline with God's eternal purposes, breaking cycles of stagnation and building altars of progress.

For new believers, this chapter is a gateway to experiencing God's power. You may start with a simple decree, like "I declare that delay is broken permanently" (#14), and see God open a door. That small victory will ignite your faith, showing you the authority you carry in Christ (Luke 10:19). For generals, this chapter is a strategic blueprint. You recognize that delay is a warfare domain, a divine stronghold to confront the enemy's schemes. Decrees like "I declare that the power of delay is shattered" (#19) empower you to lead with prophetic insight, transforming your life into a hub of God's timing (Acts 2:2).

A Call to Rise

Delay Breaking is where the battle for momentum begins and the victory is won. It's where you declare, "I decree acceleration over every promise, assignment, and destiny moment" (#1), and watch Heaven respond. It's where you stand, as a new believer or a general, and proclaim, "I decree that nothing stops or delays me" (#20), knowing the enemy trembles at your voice. This chapter is not just a tool; it's a mandate, a divine commission to fortify your destiny, reset your timeline, and establish God's Kingdom through your progress.

For those new to prayer, start here. Speak these decrees with faith, and God will honor your trust, building your destiny on the rock of His Word (Matthew 7:24). For generals, lead here. Wield these proclamations with apostolic authority, knowing your life is a warfare unit, co-creating with God to shift generations (Ephesians 3:20). The enemy may rage, but the timing of God prevails (Ecclesiastes 3:1). Rise, declare, and watch your destiny become a fortress of momentum, a testimony of acceleration, and a legacy of God's unending faithfulness.

Delay Breaking Prayer

Morning Warfare Prayer Points: Accelerating Divine Timing

My Father, my God, I take authority over my destiny; let Your timing accelerate my promises, in Jesus' name. Father, let every spirit of stagnation refuse to hinder me today. Lord, I command every delay to be null and void, in Jesus' name. My Father, my God, I pull down every demonic barrier blocking my breakthroughs. Father, I dismantle every generational curse of postponement; my bloodline advances, in Jesus' name. Lord, restore my lost opportunities sevenfold; let speed overtake me. My Father, my God, align my steps with Your divine schedule; my purpose unfolds. Father, let Your angels clear my path, guarding my progress. Lord, thank You for Your suddenlies; my life testifies of Your acceleration. Father, anoint me with divine momentum; let my destiny shine with Your glory, in Jesus' name. Amen.

Scriptures: Habakkuk 2:3, Isaiah 60:22, Revelation 3:8, Galatians 3:13, Joel 2:25

Delay Breaking Declarations and Decrees

1. I decree acceleration over every promise, assignment, and destiny moment (Habakkuk 2:3).
2. I decree that the next six months produce more fruit than the last six years (Isaiah 60:22).
3. I decree that divine speed overtakes me (2 Samuel 22:30).
4. I decree that what took others years takes me months (Ecclesiastes 3:11).
5. I decree that my business moves forward with supernatural momentum (Psalm 75:6).
6. I decree that my finances catch up to the prophetic word over my life (Deuteronomy 28:2).
7. I decree that my ministry and purpose are not delayed (Acts 13:2).
8. I decree that every lost opportunity is restored sevenfold (Joel 2:25).
9. I decree that chains of stagnation, procrastination, and delay are broken (Isaiah 10:27).
10. I decree that new doors no man can shut are opened (Revelation 3:8).
11. I decree that my pathway is made straight, and my steps are ordered (Psalm 37:23).
12. I decree that destiny helpers locate me now (Hebrews 1:14).
13. I declare that supernatural opportunities and divine timing align for my success (Ecclesiastes 9:11).
14. I declare that delay is broken permanently (Isaiah 40:31).
15. I declare that the season of waiting has ended, and suddenlies have begun (Acts 2:2).
16. I declare that every promise of God comes to pass without delay (2 Peter 3:9).
17. I declare immediate breakthroughs manifest in my life (Psalm 18:29).
18. I declare sudden miracles and divine turnarounds (Psalm 126:2).

19. I declare that the power of delay is shattered (Isaiah 43:19).
20. I decree that nothing stops or delays me (Philippians 1:6).
21. I decree that I cancel stinking thinking and strongholds delaying me (2 Corinthians 10:5).
22. I decree that I move forward without bondage (John 8:36).

Chapter 5: Victory Over Enemies

The Divine Triumph Over Darkness

In God's eternal design, believers are called to walk in victory, clothed in His armor and armed with His authority to overcome every enemy (Ephesians 6:11). **Chapter 5: Victory Over Enemies** is a spiritual armory, equipped with 22 Spirit-inspired declarations and decrees to dismantle demonic assignments, break witchcraft, and establish your dominion over the forces of darkness. Rooted in the unyielding truth of Isaiah 54:17—"No weapon formed against you shall prosper"—this chapter empowers you to declare your life a stronghold of triumph, aligning your battles with Heaven's victory.

The enemy prowls like a roaring lion, deploying curses, sabotage, and spiritual attacks to steal, kill, and destroy (1 Peter 5:8). Yet, God has not left you defenseless. These 22 decrees, forged in the fire of divine revelation and apostolic authority, are your weapons to scatter demonic plans, silence word curses, and co-create with God a legacy of conquest (Romans 8:37). From overturning plots to commanding angelic protection, from breaking strongholds to walking in perpetual victory, this chapter equips you to stand as a warrior of the Kingdom, declaring, "Not on my watch will the enemy prevail!"

Why Victory Over Enemies Matters

Spiritual warfare is not optional; it is the reality of every believer's life. When God called you, He equipped you with authority to trample on snakes and scorpions and to overcome all the power of the enemy (Luke 10:19). A victorious believer is a threat to the enemy's agenda, for they expose his schemes, advance God's Kingdom, and demonstrate His power. Conversely, unchecked spiritual attacks are a foothold for the adversary, fostering fear, division, and destruction. **Victory Over Enemies** is foundational to this book because without triumph over darkness, your ability to thrive in other areas—family, finances, or health—is compromised. As Exodus 14:14 declares, "The Lord will fight for you; you need only to be still."

For those new to prayer, this chapter is an accessible entry point. The decrees are seeds of faith, requiring only your voice and trust to cultivate victory and protection. Speak them as a beginner, and God will honor your faith with breakthroughs (Mark 11:24). For prayer generals, this chapter is an apostolic mandate, a call to wield your authority as a king and priest (Revelation 1:6) to dismantle demonic networks, reset spiritual battlegrounds, and establish your life as a warfare unit (Ephesians 6:12). Every decree is a sword, cutting through the enemy's lies and planting promises that secure your triumph. Whether you're a novice or a seasoned intercessor, this chapter is vital, for victory is where faith is fortified, authority is exercised, and God's power transforms lives.

The Power of Targeted Decrees

Just as a physician prescribes a specific remedy for a specific ailment—no antacid for a headache, no dental visit for a stomachache—spiritual battles demand precise, targeted weapons. The 22 decrees in **Victory Over Enemies** are tailored to address the unique attacks facing your life. Are you facing demonic plots? Declare, "I decree that every demonic plot against me is overturned" (#2). Is witchcraft targeting your progress? Proclaim, "I decree that every satanic attack and witchcraft against my progress catches fire" (#11). Are word curses binding you? Decree, "I decree that every word curse over my life, destiny, or family is canceled" (#5). Each proclamation is a divine prescription, anointed to hit the root of your spiritual battle, aligning your life with God's victory.

These decrees are not mere words; they are creative forces, carrying the authority of Heaven to shift realities. Proverbs 18:21 reminds us, "Death and life are in the power of the tongue." When you speak these decrees, you partner with the Holy Spirit, activating the blood of Jesus to cover your battles (Revelation 12:11) and angels to war on your behalf (Psalm 91:11). For new believers, this is a revelation: your voice, though untrained, is a weapon when aligned with God's Word. For generals, it's a reminder of your apostolic charge to co-create with God, resetting spiritual battlegrounds with every proclamation (Ephesians 3:20). The decrees are your tools to conquer, protect, and triumph, ensuring your life stands as a testimony of God's power.

A Life Under Siege

The enemy's assault on your life is relentless. Demonic plots, witchcraft, and word curses seek to sabotage your destiny, while spirits of poverty and betrayal aim to bind your progress. Yet, God's Word is clear: "The Lord is my shield" (Psalm 3:3). The decrees in this chapter confront these attacks head-on, addressing specific needs:

- **Demonic Plots**: Decrees like "I decree that every demonic plot against me is overturned" (#2) and "I decree that the plans of the enemy are exposed and dismantled" (#3) scatter the enemy's schemes.
- **Witchcraft and Curses**: Proclamations such as "I decree that every word curse over my life, destiny, or family is canceled" (#5) and "I decree that every satanic attack and witchcraft against my progress catches fire" (#11) break spiritual bondage.
- **Angelic Protection**: Decrees like "I decree that angels of God war on my behalf" (#4) and "I decree that the angels of the Lord encamp around me and deliver me" (#7) activate heavenly forces.
- **Perpetual Victory**: Decrees like "I declare that I walk in perpetual victory and dominion" (#21) and "I decree that no weapon formed against me prospers; fear, worry, panic, and doubt leave now" (#22) establish lasting triumph.

For those new to prayer, these decrees are simple to speak, requiring only faith to see God move. Imagine planting a seed in fertile soil—each word you utter is a seed of victory, watered by trust, that grows into a harvest of triumph. For generals, these decrees are strategic, apostolic weapons, enabling you to exercise dominion (Genesis 1:28) and reset your spiritual battlefield. You're not just praying; you're commanding, aligning earth with Heaven, and establishing a legacy of conquest that echoes through generations.

The Apostolic Call to Victory Over Enemies

As an apostle, I've seen the enemy's tactics firsthand—plots sowing chaos, curses stealing destinies, and witchcraft binding progress. But I've also witnessed the power of God's Word to dismantle what was built against you, restore what was lost, and redeem what was stolen (Psalm 33:10). **Victory Over Enemies** is not optional; it's foundational. Without triumph over darkness, your ability to fulfill God's purposes is limited. A victorious life stands firm (Romans 8:37), but a besieged one struggles to shine. This chapter is your apostolic mandate to take up your authority as a king and priest (Revelation 1:6), declaring God's promises over your battles with unwavering faith.

For new believers, this chapter is an invitation to step into your God-given authority. You may feel inexperienced, but your voice, when aligned with these decrees, carries the weight of Heaven. Speak, "I declare that every witchcraft assignment is canceled by the blood of Jesus" (#15), and trust God to honor your faith. For generals, this chapter is a call to strategic warfare. You understand that spiritual warfare is a battlefield, a divine domain to confront the enemy's schemes (Ephesians 6:12). Decrees like "I decree that confusion falls into the camp of the enemy" (#9) and "I declare that principalities, powers, and rulers of darkness are defeated" (#18) empower you to lead with apostolic precision, breaking cycles of oppression and building legacies of victory.

Practical Application for All

Victory Over Enemies is a chapter for every believer, from the novice to the general, because every life faces spiritual battles, and every destiny needs God's protection. Here's how to engage with this chapter:

For Those New to Prayer

- **Start Simple**: Choose one or two decrees that resonate with your battles, such as "I declare that every delay, hindrance, sabotage, and attack is broken" (#19). Speak them daily, aloud, with faith.
- **Trust God's Word**: You don't need experience; you need trust. Hebrews 11:6 says, "Without faith it is impossible to please Him." Your words, backed by Scripture, are powerful.
- **Expect Results**: Like a patient taking medicine, trust that each decree is working, even if results aren't immediate. Journal answered prayers to build your faith.
- **Stand in Faith**: Pair decrees with trust, creating a unified front of faith (Ephesians 6:16).

For Prayer Generals

- **Diagnose Strategically**: Identify the enemy's tactics in your life—curses, witchcraft, sabotage—and select decrees to counter them, like "I decree that every hex, spell, enchantment, or incantation is broken" (#6).
- **Activate Angels**: Use decrees like "I decree that angels of God war on my behalf" (#4) to engage heavenly forces (Psalm 91:11).

- **Lead with Authority**: As a general, you're not just praying; you're commanding. Speak, "I decree that God fights my battles, ensuring victory over all enemies" (#14), with apostolic boldness.
- **Intercede for Legacy**: Use decrees like "I declare that the fire of God burns up every demonic assignment" (#20) to secure blessings for future generations.

Practical Steps

- **Create a Prayer Space**: Find a quiet place to focus, inviting the Holy Spirit to anoint your words.
- **Speak Daily**: Declare 5–10 decrees each morning or night, personalizing them (e.g., insert your name in "I decree that every demonic plot against [name] is overturned" [#2]).
- **Combine with Worship**: Pair decrees with praise, amplifying their power (Psalm 149:6-9). Sing or lift your hands to magnify God.
- **Live the Decrees**: Align your actions with your words. If you decree victory, walk in confidence (Romans 8:37). If you declare protection, trust God's shield (Psalm 3:3).

The Eternal Impact of Victory Over Enemies

The stakes are eternal. A life of victory is not just a personal triumph; it's a generational conquest, a ripple effect that transforms families, communities, and nations. When you declare, "I decree that I see my enemies no more" (#1), you're not only securing your life but planting seeds for a legacy of dominion (Genesis 22:17). When you proclaim, "I declare that I walk in perpetual victory and dominion" (#21), you're aligning your battles with God's eternal purposes, breaking cycles of oppression and building altars of triumph.

For new believers, this chapter is a gateway to experiencing God's power. You may start with a simple decree, like "I declare that every spirit of sabotage, betrayal, jealousy, and backbiting is silenced" (#16), and see God expose a plot. That small victory will ignite your faith, showing you the authority you carry in Christ (Luke 10:19). For generals, this chapter is a strategic blueprint. You recognize that spiritual warfare is a divine stronghold, a battlefield to confront the enemy's schemes. Decrees like "I decree that no weapon formed against me prospers; fear, worry, panic, and doubt leave now" (#22) empower you to lead with prophetic insight, transforming your life into a hub of God's victory (2 Corinthians 2:14).

A Call to Rise

Victory Over Enemies is where the battle against darkness begins and the victory is won. It's where you declare, "I decree that every demonic plot against me is overturned" (#2), and watch Heaven respond. It's where you stand, as a new believer or a general, and proclaim, "I declare that I walk in perpetual victory and dominion" (#21), knowing the enemy trembles at your voice. This chapter is not just a tool; it's a mandate, a divine commission to fortify your life, reset your battlefield, and establish God's Kingdom through your triumph.

For those new to prayer, start here. Speak these decrees with faith, and God will honor your trust, building your victory on the rock of His Word (Matthew 7:24). For generals, lead here. Wield these proclamations with apostolic authority, knowing your life is a warfare unit, co-creating with God to shift generations (Ephesians 3:20). The enemy may rage, but the authority of Christ prevails (Revelation 12:11). Rise, declare, and watch your life become a fortress of triumph, a testimony of conquest, and a legacy of God's unending power.

Victory Over Enemies Prayer

Morning Warfare Prayer Points: Overthrowing Demonic Schemes

My Father, my God, I take authority over my battles; let Your power scatter my enemies, in Jesus' name. Father, let every spirit of destruction refuse to operate against me today. Lord, I command every curse and hex to be null and void, in Jesus' name. My Father, my God, I pull down every demonic plot targeting my life. I dismantle every generational bondage of oppression; my bloodline triumphs, in Jesus' name. Lord, shield me with Your presence; let victory prevail. My Father, my God, grant me authority to tread on serpents; my enemies fall. Let Your angels war for my deliverance, guarding my peace. Lord, thank You for Your triumph; my life testifies of Your victory. Father, anoint me with boldness; let my battles shine with Your glory, in Jesus' name. Amen.

Scriptures: Psalm 33:10, Isaiah 54:17, Ephesians 6:12, Galatians 3:13, Psalm 91:11

Victory Over Enemies Declarations and Decrees

1. I decree that I see my enemies no more (Exodus 14:13).
2. I decree that every demonic plot against me is overturned (Psalm 33:10).
3. I decree that the plans of the enemy are exposed and dismantled (Job 5:12).
4. I decree that angels of God war on my behalf (Psalm 91:11).
5. I decree that every word curse over my life, destiny, or family is canceled (Numbers 23:23).
6. I decree that every hex, spell, enchantment, or incantation is broken (Isaiah 47:12-13).
7. I decree that the angels of the Lord encamp around me and deliver me (Psalm 34:7).
8. I decree that every demonic stronghold over my family is dismantled (2 Corinthians 10:4).
9. I decree that confusion falls into the camp of the enemy (Exodus 23:27).
10. I decree that divine justice is executed on my behalf (Psalm 89:14).
11. I decree that every satanic attack and witchcraft against my progress catches fire (Psalm 97:3).
12. I decree that every spirit of poverty is cast out (Luke 4:18).
13. I decree that God is my shield, causing every enemy to fall (Psalm 3:3).
14. I decree that God fights my battles, ensuring victory over all enemies (Exodus 14:14).
15. I declare that every witchcraft assignment is canceled by the blood of Jesus (Revelation 12:11).
16. I declare that every spirit of sabotage, betrayal, jealousy, and backbiting is silenced (Psalm 31:20).
17. I declare that every chain the enemy used to bind me is shattered (Acts 12:7).

18. I declare that principalities, powers, and rulers of darkness are defeated (Ephesians 6:12).
19. I declare that every delay, hindrance, sabotage, and attack is broken (Isaiah 54:17).
20. I declare that the fire of God burns up every demonic assignment (Hebrews 12:29).
21. I declare that I walk in perpetual victory and dominion (Romans 8:37).
22. I decree that no weapon formed against me prospers; fear, worry, panic, and doubt leave now (Isaiah 54:17).

Chapter 6: Purpose and Identity

The Divine Blueprint of Your Calling

In God's eternal design, you were created with a unique purpose, a divine calling that reflects His image and advances His Kingdom (Jeremiah 1:5). **Chapter 6: Purpose and Identity** is a spiritual armory, equipped with 28 Spirit-inspired declarations and decrees to awaken your gifts, align your heart with God's will, and establish your authority as a child of God. Rooted in the unyielding truth of Ephesians 2:10—"We are God's handiwork, created in Christ Jesus to do good works"—this chapter empowers you to declare your identity as a chosen vessel, breaking every lie of the enemy and stepping boldly into your destiny.

The enemy seeks to obscure your purpose with doubt, distraction, and false identities, aiming to derail God's plan for your life (John 10:10). Yet, God has not left you defenseless. These 28 decrees, forged in the fire of divine revelation and apostolic authority, are your weapons to dismantle confusion, stir your gifts, and co-create with God a legacy of impact (Romans 11:29). From walking in your divine assignment to expanding your influence, from rejecting worldly labels to embracing your heavenly authority, this chapter equips you to stand as a beacon of God's purpose, declaring, "Not on my watch will my calling be silenced!"

Why Purpose and Identity Matter

Your purpose and identity are not mere personal attributes; they are divine mandates, the foundation of a life that glorifies God. When God formed you, He knit you together with intention (Psalm 139:13-14), calling you to bear fruit and shine as a light (Matthew 5:16). A believer rooted in their God-given identity is a threat to the enemy's agenda, for they fulfill assignments, influence generations, and reflect God's glory. Conversely, confusion about purpose is a foothold for the adversary, fostering insecurity and ineffectiveness. **Purpose and Identity** is foundational to this book because without clarity of calling, your ability to thrive in other areas—family, finances, or health—is limited. As John 15:16 declares, "You did not choose me, but I chose you and appointed you so that you might go and bear fruit."

For those new to prayer, this chapter is an accessible entry point. The decrees are seeds of faith, requiring only your voice and trust to cultivate clarity and confidence. Speak them as a beginner, and God will honor your faith with revelation (Mark 11:24). For prayer generals, this chapter is an apostolic mandate, a call to wield your authority as a king and priest (Revelation 1:6) to break lies of the enemy, reset your calling, and establish your life as a warfare unit (Ephesians 6:12). Every decree is a sword, cutting through the enemy's deception and planting promises that anchor your identity. Whether you're a novice or a seasoned intercessor, this chapter is vital, for purpose is where faith is ignited, authority is claimed, and God's calling transforms lives.

The Power of Targeted Decrees

Just as a physician prescribes a specific remedy for a specific ailment—no antacid for a headache, no dental visit for a stomachache—battles over purpose demand precise, targeted weapons. The 28 decrees in **Purpose and Identity** are tailored to address the unique challenges blocking your calling. Are you unsure of your assignment? Declare, "I decree that I walk in my divine assignment" (#1). Are distractions dimming your focus? Proclaim, "I decree that my mind, heart, and will align with God's purpose" (#11). Are you held back by insecurity? Decree, "I decree that I am above average, created in God's image, fruitful, and good" (#24). Each proclamation is a divine prescription, anointed to hit the root of your identity crisis, aligning your life with God's eternal plan.

These decrees are not mere words; they are creative forces, carrying the authority of Heaven to shift realities. Proverbs 18:21 reminds us, "Death and life are in the power of the tongue." When you speak these decrees, you partner with the Holy Spirit, activating the blood of Jesus to cover your calling (Revelation 12:11) and angels to war on your behalf (Psalm 103:20). For new believers, this is a revelation: your voice, though untrained, is a weapon when aligned with God's Word. For generals, it's a reminder of your apostolic charge to co-create with God, resetting your purpose with every proclamation (Ephesians 3:20). The decrees are your tools to awaken, align, and advance, ensuring your life stands as a testimony of God's faithfulness.

A Calling Under Siege

The enemy's assault on your purpose is relentless. Lies of inadequacy, worldly distractions, and false identities seek to derail your destiny, while fear and doubt aim to silence your voice. Yet, God's Word is clear: "I have chosen you and appointed you" (John 15:16). The decrees in this chapter confront these attacks head-on, addressing specific needs:

- **Divine Assignment**: Decrees like "I decree that I walk in my divine assignment" (#1) and "I decree that I do not miss my moment of destiny" (#2) anchor you in God's purpose.
- **Gift Activation**: Proclamations such as "I decree that my gifts are stirred and sharpened by the Spirit" (#4) and "I decree that every gift inside me is awakened" (#10) unleash your potential.
- **Identity in Christ**: Decrees like "I declare that I am a new creation in Christ" (#14) and "I declare that I have the mind of Christ" (#15) reject false labels.
- **Influence and Impact**: Decrees like "I decree that my influence expands for God's glory" (#7) and "I decree that I carry solutions for my generation" (#9) position you as a Kingdom leader.

For those new to prayer, these decrees are simple to speak, requiring only faith to see God move. Imagine planting a seed in fertile soil—each word you utter is a seed of purpose, watered by trust, that grows into a harvest of impact. For generals, these decrees are strategic, apostolic weapons, enabling you to exercise dominion (Genesis 1:28) and reset your calling's trajectory. You're not just praying; you're commanding, aligning earth with Heaven, and establishing a legacy of purpose that echoes through generations.

The Apostolic Call to Purpose and Identity

As an apostle, I've seen the enemy's tactics firsthand—lies sowing doubt, distractions stealing focus, and false identities binding destinies. But I've also witnessed the power of God's Word to awaken what was dormant, restore what was lost, and redeem what was stolen (Joel 2:25). **Purpose and Identity** is not optional; it's foundational. Without clarity of calling, your ability to fulfill God's purposes is limited. A life rooted in divine identity stands firm (Ephesians 2:6), but a confused one struggles to shine. This chapter is your apostolic mandate to take up your authority as a king and priest (Revelation 1:6), declaring God's promises over your calling with unwavering faith.

For new believers, this chapter is an invitation to step into your God-given authority. You may feel inexperienced, but your voice, when aligned with these decrees, carries the weight of Heaven. Speak, "I declare that I am chosen, appointed, and equipped to bear fruit" (#16), and trust God to honor your faith. For generals, this chapter is a call to strategic warfare. You understand that purpose is a battlefield, a divine domain to confront the enemy's schemes (Ephesians 6:12). Decrees like "I decree that divine ideas, strategies, and inventions birth through me" (#8) and "I declare that I fulfill my assignment and leave nothing undone" (#21) empower you to lead with apostolic precision, breaking cycles of confusion and building legacies of impact.

Practical Application for All

Purpose and Identity is a chapter for every believer, from the novice to the general, because every life faces battles over calling, and every destiny needs God's clarity. Here's how to engage with this chapter:

For Those New to Prayer

- **Start Simple**: Choose one or two decrees that resonate with your calling, such as "I declare that I am a new creation in Christ" (#14). Speak them daily, aloud, with faith.
- **Trust God's Word**: You don't need experience; you need trust. Hebrews 11:6 says, "Without faith it is impossible to please Him." Your words, backed by Scripture, are powerful.
- **Expect Results**: Like a patient taking medicine, trust that each decree is working, even if results aren't immediate. Journal answered prayers to build your faith.
- **Seek God's Will**: Pair decrees with prayer, creating a unified front of faith (Colossians 4:2).

For Prayer Generals

- **Diagnose Strategically**: Identify the enemy's tactics in your calling—doubt, distraction, insecurity—and select decrees to counter them, like "I decree that I am bold, courageous, and effective in my calling" (#5).

- **Activate Angels:** Use decrees like "I receive all that God promised, releasing it in my life" (#22) to engage heavenly forces (Hebrews 1:14).
- **Lead with Authority:** As a general, you're not just praying; you're commanding. Speak, "I decree that I operate as God designed, fruitful and in the right place" (#28), with apostolic boldness.
- **Intercede for Legacy:** Use decrees like "I decree that my star shines brighter" (#26) to secure blessings for future generations.

Practical Steps

- **Create a Prayer Space:** Find a quiet place to focus, inviting the Holy Spirit to anoint your words.
- **Speak Daily:** Declare 5–10 decrees each morning or night, personalizing them (e.g., insert your name in "I decree that [name] walks in my divine assignment" [#1]).
- **Combine with Worship:** Pair decrees with praise, amplifying their power (Psalm 149:6-9). Sing or lift your hands to magnify God.
- **Live the Decrees:** Align your actions with your words. If you decree purpose, pursue God's calling (Philippians 2:13). If you declare authority, walk in confidence (Luke 10:19).

The Eternal Impact of Purpose and Identity

The stakes are eternal. A life rooted in purpose is not just a personal victory; it's a generational triumph, a ripple effect that transforms families, communities, and nations. When you declare, "I declare that I fulfill my assignment and leave nothing undone" (#21), you're not only securing your calling but planting seeds for a legacy of impact (Proverbs 13:22). When you proclaim, "I decree that I carry solutions for my generation" (#9), you're aligning your destiny with God's eternal purposes, breaking cycles of confusion and building altars of influence.

For new believers, this chapter is a gateway to experiencing God's power. You may start with a simple decree, like "I declare that I have the mind of Christ" (#15), and see God clarify your path. That small victory will ignite your faith, showing you the authority you carry in Christ (Luke 10:19). For generals, this chapter is a strategic blueprint. You recognize that purpose is a warfare domain, a divine stronghold to confront the enemy's schemes. Decrees like "I decree that my influence expands for God's glory" (#7) empower you to lead with prophetic insight, transforming your life into a hub of God's calling (Esther 4:14).

A Call to Rise

Purpose and Identity is where the battle for your calling begins and the victory is won. It's where you declare, "I decree that I walk in my divine assignment" (#1), and watch Heaven respond. It's where you stand, as a new believer or a general, and proclaim, "I declare that I am seated in heavenly places in Christ Jesus" (#17), knowing the enemy trembles at your voice. This chapter is not just a tool; it's a mandate, a divine commission to fortify your calling, reset your identity, and establish God's Kingdom through your purpose.

For those new to prayer, start here. Speak these decrees with faith, and God will honor your trust, building your purpose on the rock of His Word (Matthew 7:24). For generals, lead here. Wield these proclamations with apostolic authority, knowing your life is a warfare unit, co-creating with God to shift generations (Ephesians 3:20). The enemy may rage, but the calling of God prevails (Romans 11:29). Rise, declare, and watch your life become a fortress of purpose, a testimony of identity, and a legacy of God's unending faithfulness.

Purpose and Identity Prayer

Morning Warfare Prayer Points: Awakening Divine Calling

My Father, my God, I take authority over my purpose; let Your calling awaken in me, in Jesus' name. Father, let every spirit of doubt refuse to cloud my identity today. Lord, I command every lie of inadequacy to be null and void, in Jesus' name. My Father, my God, I pull down every demonic plot obscuring my destiny. I dismantle every generational curse of aimlessness; my bloodline shines, in Jesus' name. Lord, stir my gifts with Your fire; let clarity prevail. My Father, my God, align my steps with Your divine assignment; my purpose unfolds. Father, let Your angels guide my path, guarding my calling. Thank You for Your revelation; my life testifies of Your purpose. Father, anoint me with boldness; let my identity radiate Your glory, in Jesus' name. Amen.

Scriptures: Jeremiah 1:5, Ephesians 2:6, Galatians 3:13, Ephesians 1:17, John 15:16

Purpose and Identity Declarations and Decrees

1. I decree that I walk in my divine assignment (Jeremiah 1:5).
2. I decree that I do not miss my moment of destiny (Ecclesiastes 3:1).
3. I decree that doors aligning with God's purpose open (Revelation 3:8).
4. I decree that my gifts are stirred and sharpened by the Spirit (1 Timothy 4:14).
5. I decree that I am bold, courageous, and effective in my calling (Joshua 1:9).
6. I decree that I am fruitful in every good work (Colossians 1:10).
7. I decree that my influence expands for God's glory (Matthew 5:16).
8. I decree that divine ideas, strategies, and inventions birth through me (Proverbs 8:12).
9. I decree that I carry solutions for my generation (Esther 4:14).
10. I decree that every gift inside me is awakened (Romans 11:29).
11. I decree that my mind, heart, and will align with God's purpose (Philippians 2:13).
12. I decree that my heart is flooded with light, receiving wisdom and revelation (Ephesians 1:17).
13. I decree that I walk in integrity and humility as God elevates me (Psalm 75:6-7).
14. I declare that I am a new creation in Christ (2 Corinthians 5:17).
15. I declare that I have the mind of Christ (1 Corinthians 2:16).
16. I declare that I am chosen, appointed, and equipped to bear fruit (John 15:16).
17. I declare that I am seated in heavenly places in Christ Jesus (Ephesians 2:6).
18. I declare boldness to speak the truth in love (Ephesians 4:15).
19. I declare that divine authority flows through my words and actions (Luke 10:19).

20. I declare that I am a voice for the voiceless and a light in the darkness (Isaiah 58:10).
21. I declare that I fulfill my assignment and leave nothing undone (John 17:4).
22. I receive all that God promised, releasing it in my life (Hebrews 11:6).
23. I receive all that God has for me, productive and growing (2 Peter 1:8).
24. I decree that I am above average, created in God's image, fruitful, and good (Genesis 1:26-27).
25. I decree that I have dominion, rule, and reign, reflecting God's hand (Genesis 1:28).
26. I decree that my star shines brighter (Daniel 12:3).
27. I receive my inheritance in Jesus' name (Ephesians 1:11).
28. I decree that I operate as God designed, fruitful and in the right place (Psalm 139:14).

Chapter 7: Spiritual Warfare and Protection

The Divine Shield Against Darkness

In God's eternal design, believers are called to stand firm, shielded by His protection and armed with His authority to wage war against the forces of darkness (Ephesians 6:13). **Chapter 7: Spiritual Warfare and Protection** is a spiritual armory, equipped with 17 Spirit-inspired declarations and decrees to dismantle witchcraft, shield your life from attacks, and establish your safety under God's wings. Rooted in the unyielding truth of Psalm 91:1—"Whoever dwells in the shelter of the Most High will rest in the shadow of the Almighty"—this chapter empowers you to declare your life a fortress of divine protection, breaking every assault of the enemy and aligning your battles with Heaven's defense.

The enemy unleashes relentless attacks—witchcraft, oppression, and spiritual traps—seeking to infiltrate your mind, body, and home (1 Peter 5:8). Yet, God has not left you defenseless. These 17 decrees, forged in the fire of divine revelation and apostolic authority, are your weapons to scatter demonic networks, activate angelic protection, and co-create with God a legacy of safety (Psalm 91:11). From blinding monitoring spirits to covering your family with the blood of Jesus, from destroying dream attacks to dwelling in God's secret place, this chapter equips you to stand as a sentinel of the Kingdom, declaring, "Not on my watch will the enemy breach my defenses!"

Why Spiritual Warfare and Protection Matter

Spiritual warfare is not a peripheral concern; it is the heartbeat of a believer's life. When God redeemed you, He clothed you in His armor and gave you authority to bind and loose (Matthew 16:19), ensuring no evil can prevail against you. A protected believer is a threat to the enemy's agenda, for they stand unshaken, advance God's Kingdom, and reflect His power. Conversely, vulnerability to spiritual attacks is a foothold for the adversary, fostering fear, sickness, and chaos. **Spiritual Warfare and Protection** is foundational to this book because without a shield against darkness, your ability to thrive in other areas—family, finances, or purpose—is compromised. As Psalm 121:7 declares, "The Lord will keep you from all harm—He will watch over your life."

For those new to prayer, this chapter is an accessible entry point. The decrees are seeds of faith, requiring only your voice and trust to cultivate protection and victory. Speak them as a beginner, and God will honor your faith with deliverance (Mark 11:24). For prayer generals, this chapter is an apostolic mandate, a call to wield your authority as a king and priest (Revelation 1:6) to dismantle demonic assignments, reset spiritual defenses, and establish your life as a warfare unit (Ephesians 6:12). Every decree is a sword, cutting through the enemy's schemes and planting promises that secure your safety. Whether you're a novice or a seasoned intercessor, this chapter is vital, for protection is where faith is fortified, battles are won, and God's shield transforms lives.

The Power of Targeted Decrees

Just as a physician prescribes a specific remedy for a specific ailment—no antacid for a headache, no dental visit for a stomachache—spiritual battles demand precise, targeted weapons. The 17 decrees in **Spiritual Warfare and Protection** are tailored to address the unique attacks threatening your life. Are witchcraft assignments targeting you? Declare, "I decree that every witchcraft assignment is dismantled by fire" (#1). Are you plagued by night terrors? Proclaim, "I decree that dream attacks, night terrors, and oppression are destroyed" (#4). Do you need divine covering? Decree, "I declare that the blood of Jesus covers my mind, body, spirit, and home" (#12). Each proclamation is a divine prescription, anointed to hit the root of your spiritual threat, aligning your life with God's protection.

These decrees are not mere words; they are creative forces, carrying the authority of Heaven to shift realities. Proverbs 18:21 reminds us, "Death and life are in the power of the tongue." When you speak these decrees, you partner with the Holy Spirit, activating the blood of Jesus to cover your life (Revelation 12:11) and angels to war on your behalf (Psalm 91:11). For new believers, this is a revelation: your voice, though untrained, is a weapon when aligned with God's Word. For generals, it's a reminder of your apostolic charge to co-create with God, resetting spiritual defenses with every proclamation (Ephesians 3:20). The decrees are your tools to shield, conquer, and deliver, ensuring your life stands as a testimony of God's power.

A Life Under Siege

The enemy's assault on your life is relentless. Witchcraft, monitoring spirits, and dream attacks seek to infiltrate your peace, while sickness and oppression aim to weaken your resolve. Yet, God's Word is clear: "No evil will befall you, nor will any plague come near your dwelling" (Psalm 91:10). The decrees in this chapter confront these attacks head-on, addressing specific needs:

- **Witchcraft Dismantling**: Decrees like "I decree that every witchcraft assignment is dismantled by fire" (#1) and "I decree that every demonic network against my progress is scattered" (#3) break spiritual bondage.
- **Spiritual Protection**: Proclamations such as "I decree that the shield of the Lord surrounds my family and home" (#5) and "I decree that I am covered under God's wings, with no evil or plague near me" (#9) ensure divine covering.
- **Angelic Defense**: Decrees like "I decree that God's angelic armies surround me day and night" (#8) and "I declare that angels war on my behalf, fighting unseen battles" (#15) activate heavenly forces.
- **Deliverance from Oppression**: Decrees like "I decree that I am free of oppression" (#17) and "I declare that divine reinforcements overthrow the enemy's plans" (#16) secure lasting freedom.

For those new to prayer, these decrees are simple to speak, requiring only faith to see God move. Imagine planting a seed in fertile soil—each word you utter is a seed of protection, watered by trust, that grows into a harvest of safety. For generals, these decrees are strategic, apostolic weapons, enabling you to exercise dominion (Genesis 1:28) and reset your spiritual battlefield. You're not just praying; you're commanding, aligning earth with Heaven, and establishing a legacy of protection that echoes through generations.

The Apostolic Call to Spiritual Warfare and Protection

As an apostle, I've seen the enemy's tactics firsthand—witchcraft sowing chaos, oppression stealing peace, and spiritual traps binding destinies. But I've also witnessed the power of God's Word to dismantle what was sent against you, restore what was lost, and redeem what was stolen (Isaiah 61:1). **Spiritual Warfare and Protection** is not optional; it's foundational. Without a shield against darkness, your ability to fulfill God's purposes is limited. A protected life stands firm (Psalm 91:4), but a vulnerable one struggles to shine. This chapter is your apostolic mandate to take up your authority as a king and priest (Revelation 1:6), declaring God's promises over your safety with unwavering faith.

For new believers, this chapter is an invitation to step into your God-given authority. You may feel inexperienced, but your voice, when aligned with these decrees, carries the weight of Heaven. Speak, "I declare that I dwell in the secret place of the Most High" (#13), and trust God to honor your faith. For generals, this chapter is a call to strategic warfare. You understand that spiritual protection is a battlefield, a divine domain to confront the enemy's schemes (Ephesians 6:12). Decrees like "I decree that every monitoring and familiar spirit is blinded and cast out" (#2) and "I declare that divine protection is my portion every day" (#14) empower you to lead with apostolic precision, breaking cycles of attack and building legacies of safety.

Practical Application for All

Spiritual Warfare and Protection is a chapter for every believer, from the novice to the general, because every life faces spiritual attacks, and every destiny needs God's shield. Here's how to engage with this chapter:

For Those New to Prayer

- **Start Simple**: Choose one or two decrees that resonate with your battles, such as "I declare that divine protection is my portion every day" (#14). Speak them daily, aloud, with faith.
- **Trust God's Word**: You don't need experience; you need trust. Hebrews 11:6 says, "Without faith it is impossible to please Him." Your words, backed by Scripture, are powerful.
- **Expect Results**: Like a patient taking medicine, trust that each decree is working, even if results aren't immediate. Journal answered prayers to build your faith.
- **Rest in Faith**: Pair decrees with trust, creating a unified front of faith (Psalm 91:1).

For Prayer Generals

- **Diagnose Strategically**: Identify the enemy's tactics in your life—witchcraft, oppression, monitoring spirits—and select decrees to counter them, like "I decree that every demonic network against my progress is scattered" (#3).
- **Activate Angels**: Use decrees like "I decree that God's angelic armies surround me day and night" (#8) to engage heavenly forces (Psalm 91:11).
- **Lead with Authority**: As a general, you're not just praying; you're commanding. Speak, "I decree that every battle to destroy me is won by God" (#10), with apostolic boldness.
- **Intercede for Legacy**: Use decrees like "I decree that my bloodline is protected by the covenant of Jesus' blood" (#7) to secure blessings for future generations.

Practical Steps

- **Create a Prayer Space**: Find a quiet place to focus, inviting the Holy Spirit to anoint your words.
- **Speak Daily**: Declare 5–10 decrees each morning or night, personalizing them (e.g., insert your name in "I declare that the blood of Jesus covers [name]'s mind, body, spirit, and home" [#12]).
- **Combine with Worship**: Pair decrees with praise, amplifying their power (Psalm 149:6-9). Sing or lift your hands to magnify God.
- **Live the Decrees**: Align your actions with your words. If you decree protection, walk in peace (Philippians 4:7). If you declare deliverance, reject fear (2 Timothy 1:7).

The Eternal Impact of Spiritual Warfare and Protection

The stakes are eternal. A life shielded from darkness is not just a personal victory; it's a generational triumph, a ripple effect that transforms families, communities, and nations. When you declare, "I decree that sickness, accidents, premature death, and violence cannot touch us" (#6), you're not only securing your life but planting seeds for a legacy of safety (Psalm 91:10). When you proclaim, "I declare that I dwell in the secret place of the Most High" (#13), you're aligning your defenses with God's eternal purposes, breaking cycles of attack and building altars of protection.

For new believers, this chapter is a gateway to experiencing God's power. You may start with a simple decree, like "I declare that divine protection is my portion every day" (#14), and see God thwart an attack. That small victory will ignite your faith, showing you the authority you carry in Christ (Luke 10:19). For generals, this chapter is a strategic blueprint. You recognize that spiritual warfare is a divine stronghold, a battlefield to confront the enemy's schemes. Decrees like "I decree that I am free of oppression" (#17) empower you to lead with prophetic insight, transforming your life into a hub of God's protection (2 Kings 6:16-17).

A Call to Rise

Spiritual Warfare and Protection is where the battle against darkness begins and the victory is won. It's where you declare, "I decree that every witchcraft assignment is dismantled by fire" (#1), and watch Heaven respond. It's where you stand, as a new believer or a general, and proclaim, "I declare that the blood of Jesus covers my mind, body, spirit, and home" (#12), knowing the enemy trembles at your voice. This chapter is not just a tool; it's a mandate, a divine commission to fortify your defenses, reset your battlefield, and establish God's Kingdom through your protection.

For those new to prayer, start here. Speak these decrees with faith, and God will honor your trust, building your safety on the rock of His Word (Matthew 7:24). For generals, lead here. Wield these proclamations with apostolic authority, knowing your life is a warfare unit, co-creating with God to shift generations (Ephesians 3:20). The enemy may rage, but the shield of God prevails (Psalm 3:3). Rise, declare, and watch your life become a fortress of safety, a testimony of deliverance, and a legacy of God's unending power.

Spiritual Warfare and Protection Prayer

Morning Warfare Prayer Points: Securing Divine Protection

My Father, my God, I take authority over my spirit; let Your shield guard me, in Jesus' name. Father, let every demonic attack refuse to breach my peace today. Lord, I command every witchcraft scheme to be null and void, in Jesus' name. My Father, my God, I pull down every satanic plot invading my dreams. I dismantle every generational oppression; my bloodline is secure, in Jesus' name. Cover me with Your wings; let safety overtake me. Fortify my mind with Your truth; guide my stand. Father, let Your angels encamp around me, guarding my soul. Thank You for Your fortress; my life testifies of Your protection. Father, anoint me with resilience; let my faith shine with Your glory, in Jesus' name. Amen.

Scriptures: Psalm 91:1, Psalm 121:7, Psalm 91:11, Galatians 3:13, Psalm 4:8

Spiritual Warfare and Protection Declarations and Decrees

1. I decree that every witchcraft assignment is dismantled by fire (Psalm 97:3).
2. I decree that every monitoring and familiar spirit is blinded and cast out (2 Corinthians 4:4).
3. I decree that every demonic network against my progress is scattered (Psalm 68:1).
4. I decree that dream attacks, night terrors, and oppression are destroyed (Psalm 4:8).
5. I decree that the shield of the Lord surrounds my family and home (Psalm 3:3).
6. I decree that sickness, accidents, premature death, and violence cannot touch us (Psalm 91:10).
7. I decree that my bloodline is protected by the covenant of Jesus' blood (Hebrews 13:20).
8. I decree that God's angelic armies surround me day and night (Psalm 91:11).
9. I decree that I am covered under God's wings, with no evil or plague near me (Psalm 91:4).
10. I decree that every battle to destroy me is won by God (Exodus 14:14).
11. I decree that God goes before me, making crooked places straight (Isaiah 45:2).
12. I declare that the blood of Jesus covers my mind, body, spirit, and home (Revelation 12:11).
13. I declare that I dwell in the secret place of the Most High (Psalm 91:1).
14. I declare that divine protection is my portion every day (Psalm 121:7).
15. I declare that angels war on my behalf, fighting unseen battles (Hebrews 1:14).
16. I declare that divine reinforcements overthrow the enemy's plans (2

Kings 6:16-17).
17. I decree that I am free of oppression (Isaiah 61:1).

Chapter 8: Fruitfulness and Productivity

The Divine Mandate to Multiply

In God's eternal design, fruitfulness and productivity are not optional; they are divine commands, reflecting His call to multiply and fill the earth with His glory (Genesis 1:28). **Chapter 8: Fruitfulness and Productivity** is a spiritual armory, equipped with 18 Spirit-inspired declarations and decrees to expand your influence, multiply your impact, and bear abundant fruit for the Kingdom. Rooted in the unyielding truth of Psalm 1:3—"They are like a tree planted by streams of water, which yields its fruit in season"—this chapter empowers you to declare your life a flourishing garden, breaking every barrier to productivity and aligning your efforts with Heaven's abundance.

The enemy seeks to stifle your fruitfulness with barrenness, weariness, and limitation, aiming to diminish your Kingdom impact (John 10:10). Yet, God has not left you defenseless. These 18 decrees, forged in the fire of divine revelation and apostolic authority, are your weapons to dismantle obstacles, cultivate growth, and co-create with God a legacy of multiplication (Colossians 1:10). From increasing your business to amplifying your ministry, from overcoming barren places to reaping in joy, this chapter equips you to stand as a steward of God's abundance, declaring, "Not on my watch will fruitlessness prevail!"

Why Fruitfulness and Productivity Matter

Fruitfulness is not merely personal success; it is a divine mandate, the evidence of a life rooted in God's purpose. When God created humanity, He blessed them to be fruitful and multiply (Genesis 1:28), entrusting them to steward His creation and extend His Kingdom. A fruitful believer is a threat to the enemy's agenda, for they produce lasting impact, influence generations, and reflect God's glory. Conversely, barrenness and unproductivity are footholds for the adversary, fostering stagnation and despair. **Fruitfulness and Productivity** is foundational to this book because without multiplication, your ability to impact other areas—family, finances, or purpose—is constrained. As John 15:8 declares, "This is to my Father's glory, that you bear much fruit, showing yourselves to be my disciples."

For those new to prayer, this chapter is an accessible entry point. The decrees are seeds of faith, requiring only your voice and trust to cultivate growth and abundance. Speak them as a beginner, and God will honor your faith with increase (Mark 11:24). For prayer generals, this chapter is an apostolic mandate, a call to wield your authority as a king and priest (Revelation 1:6) to break cycles of barrenness, reset your productivity, and establish your life as a warfare unit (Ephesians 6:12). Every decree is a sword, cutting through the enemy's limitations and planting promises that yield a harvest. Whether you're a novice or a seasoned intercessor, this chapter is vital, for fruitfulness is where faith is expressed, impact is multiplied, and God's abundance transforms lives.

The Power of Targeted Decrees

Just as a physician prescribes a specific remedy for a specific ailment—no antacid for a headache, no dental visit for a stomachache—battles over productivity demand precise, targeted weapons. The 18 decrees in **Fruitfulness and Productivity** are tailored to address the unique obstacles hindering your increase. Is your business or ministry stagnant? Declare, "I decree increase over my business, ministry, family, and finances" (#2). Are you facing barrenness? Proclaim, "I decree that every barren place becomes fruitful" (#8). Do you seek greater impact? Decree, "I decree that my influence grows as I remain faithful" (#7). Each proclamation is a divine prescription, anointed to hit the root of your limitation, aligning your life with God's promise of abundance.

These decrees are not mere words; they are creative forces, carrying the authority of Heaven to shift realities. Proverbs 18:21 reminds us, "Death and life are in the power of the tongue." When you speak these decrees, you partner with the Holy Spirit, activating the blood of Jesus to cover your efforts (Revelation 12:11) and angels to war on your behalf (Psalm 103:20). For new believers, this is a revelation: your voice, though untrained, is a weapon when aligned with God's Word. For generals, it's a reminder of your apostolic charge to co-create with God, resetting your productivity with every proclamation (Ephesians 3:20). The decrees are your tools to multiply, expand, and flourish, ensuring your life stands as a testimony of God's faithfulness.

A Harvest Under Siege

The enemy's assault on your fruitfulness is relentless. Barrenness, weariness, and smallness seek to limit your impact, while obstacles block new territories and opportunities. Yet, God's Word is clear: "The blessing of the Lord brings wealth, without painful toil for it" (Proverbs 10:22). The decrees in this chapter confront these attacks head-on, addressing specific needs:

- **Multiplication**: Decrees like "I decree that I am fruitful and multiply in every area of my life" (#1) and "I decree increase over my business, ministry, family, and finances" (#2) unlock abundance.
- **Expansion**: Proclamations such as "I decree that I expand beyond former limitations" (#3) and "I decree that doors of new territories open for me" (#5) break barriers to growth.
- **Fruitful Impact**: Decrees like "I decree that my influence grows as I remain faithful" (#7) and "I declare that my work bears fruit and impacts many" (#15) position you as a Kingdom influencer.
- **Perseverance**: Decrees like "I decree that seeds sown in tears reap in joy" (#10) and "I decree that I do not grow weary, reaping in due season" (#11) ensure enduring productivity.

For those new to prayer, these decrees are simple to speak, requiring only faith to see God move. Imagine planting a seed in fertile soil—each word you utter is a seed of increase, watered by trust, that grows into a harvest of abundance. For generals, these decrees are strategic, apostolic weapons, enabling you to exercise dominion (Genesis 1:28) and reset your productivity's trajectory. You're not just praying; you're commanding, aligning earth with Heaven, and establishing a legacy of fruitfulness that echoes through generations.

The Apostolic Call to Fruitfulness and Productivity

As an apostle, I've seen the enemy's tactics firsthand—barrenness sowing scarcity, weariness stealing momentum, and limitations binding impact. But I've also witnessed the power of God's Word to multiply what was sown, restore what was lost, and redeem what was stolen (Psalm 115:14). **Fruitfulness and Productivity** is not optional; it's foundational. Without multiplication, your ability to fulfill God's purposes is limited. A fruitful life stands firm (Psalm 1:3), but a barren one struggles to shine. This chapter is your apostolic mandate to take up your authority as a king and priest (Revelation 1:6), declaring God's promises over your productivity with unwavering faith.

For new believers, this chapter is an invitation to step into your God-given authority. You may feel inexperienced, but your voice, when aligned with these decrees, carries the weight of Heaven. Speak, "I declare that the blessing of the Lord makes me rich without sorrow" (#17), and trust God to honor your faith. For generals, this chapter is a call to strategic warfare. You understand that fruitfulness is a battlefield, a divine domain to confront the enemy's schemes (Ephesians 6:12). Decrees like "I decree that what was small becomes mighty under God's hand" (#4) and "I declare that excellence flows through my hands" (#13) empower you to lead with apostolic precision, breaking cycles of limitation and building legacies of abundance.

Practical Application for All

Fruitfulness and Productivity is a chapter for every believer, from the novice to the general, because every life faces barriers to increase, and every calling needs God's multiplication. Here's how to engage with this chapter:

For Those New to Prayer

- **Start Simple**: Choose one or two decrees that resonate with your goals, such as "I declare that overflow is my portion—spiritually, financially, relationally" (#16). Speak them daily, aloud, with faith.
- **Trust God's Word**: You don't need experience; you need trust. Hebrews 11:6 says, "Without faith it is impossible to please Him." Your words, backed by Scripture, are powerful.
- **Expect Results**: Like a patient taking medicine, trust that each decree is working, even if results aren't immediate. Journal answered prayers to build your faith.
- **Work in Faith**: Pair decrees with effort, creating a unified front of faith (Luke 16:10).

For Prayer Generals

- **Diagnose Strategically**: Identify the enemy's tactics in your productivity—barrenness, weariness, obstacles—and select decrees to

counter them, like "I decree that every barren place becomes fruitful" (#8).
- **Activate Angels**: Use decrees like "I decree that I produce in abundance, stewarding all God gave me" (#18) to engage heavenly forces (Hebrews 1:14).
- **Lead with Authority**: As a general, you're not just praying; you're commanding. Speak, "I decree that new regions, audiences, and platforms are given for Kingdom impact" (#6), with apostolic boldness.
- **Intercede for Legacy**: Use decrees like "I declare that my work bears fruit and impacts many" (#15) to secure blessings for future generations.

Practical Steps

- **Create a Prayer Space**: Find a quiet place to focus, inviting the Holy Spirit to anoint your words.
- **Speak Daily**: Declare 5–10 decrees each morning or night, personalizing them (e.g., insert your project in "I declare that [project] bears fruit and impacts many" [#15]).
- **Combine with Worship**: Pair decrees with praise, amplifying their power (Psalm 149:6-9). Sing or lift your hands to magnify God.
- **Live the Decrees**: Align your actions with your words. If you decree fruitfulness, work diligently (Proverbs 22:29). If you declare increase, steward resources wisely (Luke 16:10).

The Eternal Impact of Fruitfulness and Productivity

The stakes are eternal. A fruitful life is not just a personal victory; it's a generational triumph, a ripple effect that transforms families, communities, and nations. When you declare, "I decree that I am like a tree planted by rivers, fruitful in season" (#9), you're not only securing your productivity but planting seeds for a legacy of abundance (Psalm 115:14). When you proclaim, "I declare that my work bears fruit and impacts many" (#15), you're aligning your efforts with God's eternal purposes, breaking cycles of barrenness and building altars of multiplication.

For new believers, this chapter is a gateway to experiencing God's power. You may start with a simple decree, like "I declare that I am productive in my purpose" (#12), and see God multiply your efforts. That small victory will ignite your faith, showing you the authority you carry in Christ (Luke 10:19). For generals, this chapter is a strategic blueprint. You recognize that fruitfulness is a warfare domain, a divine stronghold to confront the enemy's schemes. Decrees like "I decree that I produce in abundance, stewarding all God gave me" (#18) empower you to lead with prophetic insight, transforming your life into a hub of God's abundance (Isaiah 60:11).

A Call to Rise

Fruitfulness and Productivity is where the battle for increase begins and the victory is won. It's where you declare, "I decree that I am fruitful and multiply in every area of my life" (#1), and watch Heaven respond. It's where you stand, as a new believer or a general, and proclaim, "I declare that the blessing of the Lord makes me rich without sorrow" (#17), knowing the enemy trembles at your voice. This chapter is not just a tool; it's a mandate, a divine commission to fortify your productivity, reset your legacy, and establish God's Kingdom through your fruitfulness.

For those new to prayer, start here. Speak these decrees with faith, and God will honor your trust, building your productivity on the rock of His Word (Matthew 7:24). For generals, lead here. Wield these proclamations with apostolic authority, knowing your life is a warfare unit, co-creating with God to shift generations (Ephesians 3:20). The enemy may rage, but the abundance of God prevails (Psalm 23:5). Rise, declare, and watch your life become a fortress of fruitfulness, a testimony of multiplication, and a legacy of God's unending glory.

Fruitfulness and Productivity Prayer

Morning Warfare Prayer Points: Multiplying Divine Harvests

My Father, my God, I take authority over my endeavors; let Your blessing multiply me, in Jesus' name. Father, let every spirit of barrenness refuse to hinder my work today. Lord, I command every obstacle to my productivity to be null and void, in Jesus' name. I pull down every demonic barrier stifling my growth. Father, I dismantle every generational failure; my bloodline prospers, in Jesus' name. Lord, expand my influence with Your favor; let abundance overtake me. My Father, my God, anoint my hands for excellence; guide my efforts. Father, let Your angels guard my harvests, ensuring my increase. Thank You for Your provision; my life testifies of Your fruitfulness. Father, cause my work to flourish; let my success shine with Your glory, in Jesus' name. Amen.

Scriptures: Genesis 1:28, Psalm 1:3, Colossians 1:10, Galatians 3:13, Psalm 126:5

Fruitfulness and Productivity Declarations and Decrees

1. I decree that I am fruitful and multiply in every area of my life (Genesis 1:28).
2. I decree increase over my business, ministry, family, and finances (Psalm 115:14).
3. I decree that I expand beyond former limitations (Isaiah 54:2).
4. I decree that what was small becomes mighty under God's hand (Zechariah 4:10).
5. I decree that doors of new territories open for me (Isaiah 60:11).
6. I decree that new regions, audiences, and platforms are given for Kingdom impact (Mark 16:15).
7. I decree that my influence grows as I remain faithful (Matthew 25:21).
8. I decree that every barren place becomes fruitful (Psalm 1:3).
9. I decree that I am like a tree planted by rivers, fruitful in season (Psalm 1:3).
10. I decree that seeds sown in tears reap in joy (Psalm 126:5).
11. I decree that I do not grow weary, reaping in due season (Galatians 6:9).
12. I declare that I am productive in my purpose (Colossians 1:10).
13. I declare that excellence flows through my hands (Proverbs 22:29).
14. I declare that divine ideas and strategies flow daily (Proverbs 8:12).
15. I declare that my work bears fruit and impacts many (John 15:8).
16. I declare that overflow is my portion—spiritually, financially, relationally (Psalm 23:5).
17. I declare that the blessing of the Lord makes me rich without sorrow (Proverbs 10:22).
18. I decree that I produce in abundance, stewarding all God gave me (Luke 16:10).

Chapter 9: Restoration and Deliverance

The Divine Redemption of What Was Lost

In God's eternal plan, nothing is wasted; every loss can be restored, and every bondage can be broken through His redemptive power (Joel 2:25). **Chapter 9: Restoration and Deliverance** is a spiritual armory, equipped with 15 Spirit-inspired declarations and decrees to redeem lost time, heal broken relationships, and deliver your life from generational curses. Rooted in the unyielding truth of Isaiah 61:1—"He has sent me to bind up the brokenhearted, to proclaim freedom for the captives"—this chapter empowers you to declare your life a testimony of God's restoration, breaking every chain and aligning your story with Heaven's renewal.

The enemy seeks to steal your inheritance, bind your destiny, and perpetuate cycles of trauma and loss (John 10:10). Yet, God has not left you defenseless. These 15 decrees, forged in the fire of divine revelation and apostolic authority, are your weapons to reverse the enemy's work, restore what was taken, and co-create with God a legacy of freedom (Galatians 3:13). From healing family breaches to breaking cycles of addiction, from redeeming opportunities to declaring new beginnings, this chapter equips you to stand as a restorer of God's promises, declaring, "Not on my watch will bondage prevail!"

Why Restoration and Deliverance Matter

Restoration and deliverance are not mere remedies; they are divine mandates, the heartbeat of God's redemptive plan for His people. When God saved you, He called you to wholeness, promising to restore what the locusts have eaten and set you free from captivity (Joel 2:25; John 8:36). A restored believer is a threat to the enemy's agenda, for they reclaim what was stolen, break generational chains, and reflect God's glory. Conversely, unresolved loss and bondage are footholds for the adversary, fostering despair and limitation. **Restoration and Deliverance** is foundational to this book because without redemption, your ability to thrive in other areas—family, purpose, or health—is hindered. As Psalm 147:3 declares, "He heals the brokenhearted and binds up their wounds."

For those new to prayer, this chapter is an accessible entry point. The decrees are seeds of faith, requiring only your voice and trust to cultivate healing and freedom. Speak them as a beginner, and God will honor your faith with breakthroughs (Mark 11:24). For prayer generals, this chapter is an apostolic mandate, a call to wield your authority as a king and priest (Revelation 1:6) to break curses, reset destinies, and establish your life as a warfare unit (Ephesians 6:12). Every decree is a sword, cutting through the enemy's chains and planting promises that restore wholeness. Whether you're a novice or a seasoned intercessor, this chapter is vital, for restoration is where faith is renewed, freedom is claimed, and God's redemption transforms lives.

The Power of Targeted Decrees

Just as a physician prescribes a specific remedy for a specific ailment—no antacid for a headache, no dental visit for a stomachache—battles over loss and bondage demand precise, targeted weapons. The 15 decrees in **Restoration and Deliverance** are tailored to address the unique wounds and chains in your life. Are generational curses binding your family? Declare, "I decree that every generational curse in my bloodline is broken" (#1). Have you lost time or opportunities? Proclaim, "I decree that my lost time is redeemed" (#4). Are relationships fractured? Decree, "I decree that every broken relationship and generational breach is healed" (#7). Each proclamation is a divine prescription, anointed to hit the root of your loss, aligning your life with God's promise of restoration.

These decrees are not mere words; they are creative forces, carrying the authority of Heaven to shift realities. Proverbs 18:21 reminds us, "Death and life are in the power of the tongue." When you speak these decrees, you partner with the Holy Spirit, activating the blood of Jesus to cover your restoration (Revelation 12:11) and angels to war on your behalf (Psalm 103:20). For new believers, this is a revelation: your voice, though untrained, is a weapon when aligned with God's Word. For generals, it's a reminder of your apostolic charge to co-create with God, resetting destinies with every proclamation (Ephesians 3:20). The decrees are your tools to redeem, heal, and deliver, ensuring your life stands as a testimony of God's faithfulness.

A Legacy Under Siege

The enemy's assault on your legacy is relentless. Generational curses, broken relationships, and stolen opportunities seek to bind your destiny, while trauma and addiction aim to perpetuate cycles of destruction. Yet, God's Word is clear:

"The Son sets you free, and you will be free indeed" (John 8:36). The decrees in this chapter confront these attacks head-on, addressing specific needs:

- **Generational Freedom**: Decrees like "I decree that every generational curse in my bloodline is broken" (#1) and "I decree that cycles of divorce, poverty, sickness, and rebellion are dismantled" (#2) break inherited chains.
- **Time and Opportunity**: Proclamations such as "I decree that my lost time is redeemed" (#4) and "I decree that divine opportunities return with acceleration" (#5) restore what was stolen.
- **Relational Healing**: Decrees like "I decree that every broken relationship and generational breach is healed" (#7) and "I declare that wholeness comes to every area of my life" (#11) mend breaches.
- **Complete Deliverance**: Decrees like "I declare that I am free from all bondage—emotional, financial, spiritual" (#14) and "I declare that whom the Son sets free is free indeed" (#15) secure lasting freedom.

For those new to prayer, these decrees are simple to speak, requiring only faith to see God move. Imagine planting a seed in fertile soil—each word you utter is a seed of restoration, watered by trust, that grows into a harvest of freedom. For generals, these decrees are strategic, apostolic weapons, enabling you to exercise dominion (Genesis 1:28) and reset your legacy's trajectory. You're not just praying; you're commanding, aligning earth with Heaven, and establishing a legacy of redemption that echoes through generations.

The Apostolic Call to Restoration and Deliverance

As an apostle, I've seen the enemy's tactics firsthand—curses binding bloodlines, losses stealing hope, and bondages perpetuating pain. But I've also witnessed the power of God's Word to restore what was taken, heal what was broken, and redeem what was lost (Nehemiah 2:20). **Restoration and Deliverance** is not optional; it's foundational. Without redemption, your ability to fulfill God's purposes is limited. A restored life stands firm (1 Thessalonians 5:23), but a bound one struggles to shine. This chapter is your apostolic mandate to take up your authority as a king and priest (Revelation 1:6), declaring God's promises over your legacy with unwavering faith.

For new believers, this chapter is an invitation to step into your God-given authority. You may feel inexperienced, but your voice, when aligned with these decrees, carries the weight of Heaven. Speak, "I declare new beginnings and divine turnarounds manifest" (#13), and trust God to honor your faith. For generals, this chapter is a call to strategic warfare. You understand that restoration is a battlefield, a divine domain to confront the enemy's schemes (Ephesians 6:12). Decrees like "I decree that everything the enemy meant for evil, God turns for my good" (#6) and "I declare that my family is delivered from trauma, poverty, addiction, and infirmity" (#8) empower you to lead with apostolic precision, breaking cycles of bondage and building legacies of freedom.

Practical Application for All

Restoration and Deliverance is a chapter for every believer, from the novice to the general, because every life faces losses and bondages, and every destiny needs God's redemption. Here's how to engage with this chapter:

For Those New to Prayer

- **Start Simple**: Choose one or two decrees that resonate with your needs, such as "I declare that whom the Son sets free is free indeed" (#15). Speak them daily, aloud, with faith.
- **Trust God's Word**: You don't need experience; you need trust. Hebrews 11:6 says, "Without faith it is impossible to please Him." Your words, backed by Scripture, are powerful.
- **Expect Results**: Like a patient taking medicine, trust that each decree is working, even if results aren't immediate. Journal answered prayers to build your faith.
- **Forgive and Release**: Pair decrees with forgiveness, creating a unified front of faith (Matthew 6:14).

For Prayer Generals

- **Diagnose Strategically**: Identify the enemy's tactics in your

life—curses, losses, bondages—and select decrees to counter them, like "I decree that cycles of divorce, poverty, sickness, and rebellion are dismantled" (#2).
- **Activate Angels**: Use decrees like "I decree that God restores the years the locusts have eaten" (#10) to engage heavenly forces (Hebrews 1:14).
- **Lead with Authority**: As a general, you're not just praying; you're commanding. Speak, "I declare that my mind is renewed, spirit strengthened, and emotions healed" (#12), with apostolic boldness.
- **Intercede for Legacy**: Use decrees like "I decree that the bloodline blessing of Abraham flows through my family" (#3) to secure blessings for future generations.

Practical Steps

- **Create a Prayer Space**: Find a quiet place to focus, inviting the Holy Spirit to anoint your words.
- **Speak Daily**: Declare 5–10 decrees each morning or night, personalizing them (e.g., insert your name in "I declare that [name] is free from all bondage" [#14]).
- **Combine with Worship**: Pair decrees with praise, amplifying their power (Psalm 149:6-9). Sing or lift your hands to magnify God.
- **Live the Decrees**: Align your actions with your words. If you decree restoration, pursue reconciliation (Colossians 3:13). If you declare deliverance, walk in freedom (Romans 8:1).

The Eternal Impact of Restoration and Deliverance

The stakes are eternal. A restored life is not just a personal victory; it's a generational triumph, a ripple effect that transforms families, communities, and nations. When you declare, "I decree that God restores the years the locusts have eaten" (#10), you're not only securing your life but planting seeds for a legacy of redemption (Amos 9:13). When you proclaim, "I declare that I am free from all bondage—emotional, financial, spiritual" (#14), you're aligning your destiny with God's eternal purposes, breaking cycles of bondage and building altars of freedom.

For new believers, this chapter is a gateway to experiencing God's power. You may start with a simple decree, like "I declare new beginnings and divine turnarounds manifest" (#13), and see God restore a relationship. That small victory will ignite your faith, showing you the authority you carry in Christ (Luke 10:19). For generals, this chapter is a strategic blueprint. You recognize that restoration is a warfare domain, a divine stronghold to confront the enemy's schemes. Decrees like "I decree that my family is delivered from trauma, poverty, addiction, and infirmity" (#8) empower you to lead with prophetic insight, transforming your life into a hub of God's redemption (Isaiah 43:19).

A Call to Rise

Restoration and Deliverance is where the battle for redemption begins and the victory is won. It's where you declare, "I decree that every generational curse in my bloodline is broken" (#1), and watch Heaven respond. It's where you stand, as a new believer or a general, and proclaim, "I declare that whom the Son sets free is free indeed" (#15), knowing the enemy trembles at your voice. This chapter is not just a tool; it's a mandate, a divine commission to fortify your legacy, reset your destiny, and establish God's Kingdom through your restoration.

For those new to prayer, start here. Speak these decrees with faith, and God will honor your trust, building your freedom on the rock of His Word (Matthew 7:24). For generals, lead here. Wield these proclamations with apostolic authority, knowing your life is a warfare unit, co-creating with God to shift generations (Ephesians 3:20). The enemy may rage, but the redemption of God prevails (Galatians 3:14). Rise, declare, and watch your life become a fortress of restoration, a testimony of deliverance, and a legacy of God's unending grace.

Restoration and Deliverance Prayer

Morning Warfare Prayer Points: Redeeming Lost Promises

My Father, my God, I take authority over my losses; let Your restoration redeem me, in Jesus' name. Father, let every spirit of despair refuse to bind my heart today. Lord, I command every chain of bondage to be null and void, in Jesus' name. My Father, my God, I pull down every demonic plot stealing my blessings. Father, I dismantle every generational trauma; my bloodline is free, in Jesus' name. Lord, restore my time and relationships; let wholeness overtake me. My Father, my God, deliver me from oppression; guide me to freedom. Father, let Your angels guard my redemption, ensuring my recovery. Lord, thank You for Your healing; my life testifies of Your deliverance. Father, anoint me with liberty; let my restoration shine with Your glory, in Jesus' name. Amen.

Word Count: ~220 words

Scriptures: Joel 2:25, Psalm 147:3, John 8:36, Galatians 3:13, Isaiah 61:1

Restoration and Deliverance Declarations and Decrees

1. I decree that every generational curse in my bloodline is broken (Galatians 3:13).
2. I decree that cycles of divorce, poverty, sickness, and rebellion are dismantled (Isaiah 10:27).
3. I decree that the bloodline blessing of Abraham flows through my family (Galatians 3:14).
4. I decree that my lost time is redeemed (Joel 2:25).
5. I decree that divine opportunities return with acceleration (Amos 9:13).
6. I decree that everything the enemy meant for evil, God turns for my good (Genesis 50:20).
7. I decree that every broken relationship and generational breach is healed (Psalm 147:3).
8. I decree that my family is delivered from trauma, poverty, addiction, and infirmity (Isaiah 61:1).
9. I decree that lost opportunities and delayed promises are rebuilt (Nehemiah 2:20).
10. I decree that God restores the years the locusts have eaten (Joel 2:25).
11. I declare that wholeness comes to every area of my life (1 Thessalonians 5:23).
12. I declare that my mind is renewed, spirit strengthened, and emotions healed (Romans 12:2).
13. I declare new beginnings and divine turnarounds manifest (Isaiah 43:19).
14. I declare that I am free from all bondage—emotional, financial, spiritual (John 8:36).
15. I declare that whom the Son sets free is free indeed (John 8:36).

Chapter 10: Favor, Scholarships, and Opportunities

The Divine Open Doors of Advancement

In God's eternal plan, favor is His divine currency, opening doors no one can shut and positioning you for supernatural advancement (Revelation 3:8). **Chapter 10: Favor, Scholarships, and Opportunities** is a spiritual armory, equipped with 18 Spirit-inspired declarations and decrees to unlock divine connections, secure scholarships, and manifest opportunities that align with your destiny. Rooted in the unyielding truth of Psalm 5:12—"Surely, Lord, you bless the righteous; you surround them with your favor as with a shield"—this chapter empowers you to declare your life a conduit of God's favor, breaking every barrier to progress and aligning your path with Heaven's open doors.

The enemy seeks to block your advancement with rejection, closed doors, and missed opportunities, aiming to frustrate God's plan for your life (John 10:10). Yet, God has not left you defenseless. These 18 decrees, forged in the fire of divine revelation and apostolic authority, are your weapons to dismantle obstacles, attract divine appointments, and co-create with God a legacy of opportunity (Psalm 75:6-7). From securing scholarships to gaining favor with leaders, from altering policies to elevating beyond experience, this chapter equips you to stand as a recipient of God's favor, declaring, "Not on my watch will opportunities be denied!"

Why Favor, Scholarships, and Opportunities Matter

Favor is not a mere convenience; it is a divine mandate, the key to unlocking God's purposes for your life. When God anoints you, He grants you favor to fulfill your calling, just as He did for Joseph, Daniel, and Esther (Genesis 39:21; Daniel 1:9; Esther 8:5). A favored believer is a threat to the enemy's agenda, for they access resources, influence leaders, and advance God's Kingdom. Conversely, rejection and closed doors are footholds for the adversary, fostering limitation and despair. **Favor, Scholarships, and Opportunities** is foundational to this book because without open doors, your ability to thrive in other areas—purpose, finances, or family—is constrained. As Luke 2:52 declares, "Jesus grew in wisdom and stature, and in favor with God and man."

For those new to prayer, this chapter is an accessible entry point. The decrees are seeds of faith, requiring only your voice and trust to cultivate advancement and provision. Speak them as a beginner, and God will honor your faith with breakthroughs (Mark 11:24). For prayer generals, this chapter is an apostolic mandate, a call to wield your authority as a king and priest (Revelation 1:6) to break barriers, reset opportunities, and establish your life as a warfare unit (Ephesians 6:12). Every decree is a sword, cutting through the enemy's blockades and planting promises that open doors. Whether you're a novice or a seasoned intercessor, this chapter is vital, for favor is where faith is rewarded, advancement is secured, and God's opportunities transform lives.

The Power of Targeted Decrees

Just as a physician prescribes a specific remedy for a specific ailment—no antacid for a headache, no dental visit for a stomachache—battles over advancement demand precise, targeted weapons. The 18 decrees in **Favor, Scholarships, and Opportunities** are tailored to address the unique barriers blocking your progress. Need access to education or resources? Declare, "I decree that scholarships, grants, deals, and promotions find me" (#2). Facing closed doors? Proclaim, "I decree that doors of opportunity open now" (#1). Seeking influence with leaders? Decree, "I decree that God grants me favor with kings, leaders, and institutions" (#10). Each proclamation is a divine prescription, anointed to hit the root of your limitation, aligning your life with God's promise of favor.

These decrees are not mere words; they are creative forces, carrying the authority of Heaven to shift realities. Proverbs 18:21 reminds us, "Death and life are in the power of the tongue." When you speak these decrees, you partner with the Holy Spirit, activating the blood of Jesus to cover your opportunities (Revelation 12:11) and angels to war on your behalf (Hebrews 1:14). For new believers, this is a revelation: your voice, though untrained, is a weapon when aligned with God's Word. For generals, it's a reminder of your apostolic charge to co-create with God, resetting your advancement with every proclamation (Ephesians 3:20). The decrees are your tools to unlock, elevate, and advance, ensuring your life stands as a testimony of God's faithfulness.

A Destiny Under Siege

The enemy's assault on your opportunities is relentless. Closed doors, rejections, and delays seek to block your advancement, while lack of resources and influence aim to limit your impact. Yet, God's Word is clear: "I will go before you and make the crooked places straight" (Isaiah 45:2). The decrees in this chapter confront these attacks head-on, addressing specific needs:

- **Open Doors**: Decrees like "I decree that doors of opportunity open now" (#1) and "I decree that supernatural opportunities locate me" (#3) unlock divine access.
- **Scholarships and Resources**: Proclamations such as "I decree that scholarships, grants, deals, and promotions find me" (#2) and "I declare that scholarships and grants are released to me and my descendants" (#11) secure provision.
- **Divine Connections**: Decrees like "I decree that divine appointments and partnerships locate me daily" (#6) and "I decree that favor positions me for divine connections" (#9) attract Kingdom relationships.
- **Supernatural Favor**: Decrees like "I declare that I am dripping with favor" (#15) and "I declare that favor elevates me beyond my experience" (#17) ensure divine elevation.

For those new to prayer, these decrees are simple to speak, requiring only faith to see God move. Imagine planting a seed in fertile soil—each word you utter is a seed of opportunity, watered by trust, that grows into a harvest of advancement. For generals, these decrees are strategic, apostolic weapons, enabling you to exercise dominion (Genesis 1:28) and reset your path's trajectory. You're not just praying; you're commanding, aligning earth with Heaven, and establishing a legacy of favor that echoes through generations.

The Apostolic Call to Favor, Scholarships, and Opportunities

As an apostle, I've seen the enemy's tactics firsthand—rejections closing doors, delays stealing opportunities, and limitations binding destinies. But I've also witnessed the power of God's Word to open what was shut, restore what was lost, and redeem what was blocked (Proverbs 18:16). **Favor, Scholarships, and Opportunities** is not optional; it's foundational. Without open doors, your ability to fulfill God's purposes is limited. A favored life stands firm (Psalm 5:12), but a blocked one struggles to shine. This chapter is your apostolic mandate to take up your authority as a king and priest (Revelation 1:6), declaring God's promises over your advancement with unwavering faith.

For new believers, this chapter is an invitation to step into your God-given authority. You may feel inexperienced, but your voice, when aligned with these decrees, carries the weight of Heaven. Speak, "I declare that provision for advancement is supplied" (#13), and trust God to honor your faith. For generals, this chapter is a call to strategic warfare. You understand that favor is a battlefield, a divine domain to confront the enemy's schemes (Ephesians 6:12). Decrees like "I decree that policies and rules are altered on my behalf" (#8) and "I declare that favor with God and man increases daily" (#18) empower you to lead with apostolic precision, breaking cycles of rejection and building legacies of opportunity.

Practical Application for All

Favor, Scholarships, and Opportunities is a chapter for every believer, from the novice to the general, because every life faces barriers to advancement, and every destiny needs God's favor. Here's how to engage with this chapter:

For Those New to Prayer

- **Start Simple**: Choose one or two decrees that resonate with your needs, such as "I declare that I am dripping with favor" (#15). Speak them daily, aloud, with faith.
- **Trust God's Word**: You don't need experience; you need trust. Hebrews 11:6 says, "Without faith it is impossible to please Him." Your words, backed by Scripture, are powerful.
- **Expect Results**: Like a patient taking medicine, trust that each decree is working, even if results aren't immediate. Journal answered prayers to build your faith.
- **Pursue Opportunities**: Pair decrees with action, creating a unified front of faith (Proverbs 3:4).

For Prayer Generals

- **Diagnose Strategically**: Identify the enemy's tactics in your advancement—rejection, delays, lack—and select decrees to counter

them, like "I decree that I move forward faster than circumstances allow" (#5).
- **Activate Angels**: Use decrees like "I decree that divine appointments and partnerships locate me daily" (#6) to engage heavenly forces (Hebrews 1:14).
- **Lead with Authority**: As a general, you're not just praying; you're commanding. Speak, "I decree that God grants me favor with kings, leaders, and institutions" (#10), with apostolic boldness.
- **Intercede for Legacy**: Use decrees like "I declare that my children have open doors for education" (#12) to secure blessings for future generations.

Practical Steps

- **Create a Prayer Space**: Find a quiet place to focus, inviting the Holy Spirit to anoint your words.
- **Speak Daily**: Declare 5–10 decrees each morning or night, personalizing them (e.g., insert your name in "I declare that favor speaks for [name] when I am absent" [#16]).
- **Combine with Worship**: Pair decrees with praise, amplifying their power (Psalm 149:6-9). Sing or lift your hands to magnify God.
- **Live the Decrees**: Align your actions with your words. If you decree favor, walk in humility (Proverbs 3:34). If you declare opportunities, pursue them diligently (Ecclesiastes 9:11).

The Eternal Impact of Favor, Scholarships, and Opportunities

The stakes are eternal. A life marked by favor is not just a personal victory; it's a generational triumph, a ripple effect that transforms families, communities, and nations. When you declare, "I decree that supernatural opportunities locate me" (#3), you're not only securing your path but planting seeds for a legacy of advancement (Deuteronomy 28:8). When you proclaim, "I declare that favor with God and man increases daily" (#18), you're aligning your destiny with God's eternal purposes, breaking cycles of rejection and building altars of opportunity.

For new believers, this chapter is a gateway to experiencing God's power. You may start with a simple decree, like "I declare that favor speaks for me when I am absent" (#16), and see God open a door. That small victory will ignite your faith, showing you the authority you carry in Christ (Luke 10:19). For generals, this chapter is a strategic blueprint. You recognize that favor is a warfare domain, a divine stronghold to confront the enemy's schemes. Decrees like "I decree that advancement is my portion" (#4) empower you to lead with prophetic insight, transforming your life into a hub of God's opportunities (Isaiah 60:11).

A Call to Rise

Favor, Scholarships, and Opportunities is where the battle for advancement begins and the victory is won. It's where you declare, "I decree that doors of opportunity open now" (#1), and watch Heaven respond. It's where you stand, as a new believer or a general, and proclaim, "I declare that favor with God and man increases daily" (#18), knowing the enemy trembles at your voice. This chapter is not just a tool; it's a mandate, a divine commission to fortify your path, reset your destiny, and establish God's Kingdom through your advancement.

For those new to prayer, start here. Speak these decrees with faith, and God will honor your trust, building your opportunities on the rock of His Word (Matthew 7:24). For generals, lead here. Wield these proclamations with apostolic authority, knowing your life is a warfare unit, co-creating with God to shift generations (Ephesians 3:20). The enemy may rage, but the favor of God prevails (Psalm 23:5). Rise, declare, and watch your life become a fortress of advancement, a testimony of opportunity, and a legacy of God's unending blessing.

Favor, Scholarships, and Opportunities Prayer

Morning Warfare Prayer Points: Unlocking Divine Doors

My Father, my God, I take authority over my opportunities; let Your favor open doors, in Jesus' name. Father, let every spirit of rejection refuse to block my path today. Lord, I command every barrier to my advancement to be null and void, in Jesus' name. My Father, my God, I pull down every demonic plot closing my opportunities. Father, I dismantle every generational limitation; my bloodline excels, in Jesus' name. Lord, align me with divine connections; let favor overtake me. My Father, my God, grant me scholarships and grants; guide my steps. Father, let Your angels secure my breakthroughs, ensuring my success. Lord, thank You for Your provision; my life testifies of Your favor. Father, anoint me with opportunity; let my path shine with Your glory, in Jesus' name. Amen.

Word Count: ~220 words

Scriptures: Revelation 3:8, Psalm 5:12, Luke 2:52, Galatians 3:13, Deuteronomy 28:8

Favor, Scholarships, and Opportunities Declarations and Decrees

1. I decree that doors of opportunity open now (Revelation 3:8).
2. I decree that scholarships, grants, deals, and promotions find me (Psalm 75:6-7).
3. I decree that supernatural opportunities locate me (Isaiah 60:11).
4. I decree that advancement is my portion (Psalm 115:14).
5. I decree that I move forward faster than circumstances allow (2 Samuel 22:30).
6. I decree that divine appointments and partnerships locate me daily (Proverbs 18:16).
7. I decree that God's favor surrounds me like a shield (Psalm 5:12).
8. I decree that policies and rules are altered on my behalf (Esther 8:5).
9. I decree that favor positions me for divine connections (Daniel 1:9).
10. I decree that God grants me favor with kings, leaders, and institutions (Genesis 39:21).
11. I declare that scholarships and grants are released to me and my descendants (Deuteronomy 28:8).
12. I declare that my children have open doors for education (Psalm 127:3-5).
13. I declare that provision for advancement is supplied (Philippians 4:19).
14. I declare that favor with schools and boards is my portion (Luke 2:52).
15. I declare that I am dripping with favor (Psalm 23:5).
16. I declare that favor speaks for me when I am absent (Proverbs 3:4).
17. I declare that favor elevates me beyond my experience (1 Samuel 16:18).
18. I declare that favor with God and man increases daily (Luke 2:52).

Chapter 11: Technological Warfare and Protection

The Divine Firewall Against Digital Assaults

In God's eternal design, technology is a tool for His purposes, but in the hands of the enemy, it becomes a weapon to invade, manipulate, and oppress (Psalm 91:10). **Chapter 11: Technological Warfare and Protection** is a spiritual armory, equipped with 30 Spirit-inspired declarations and decrees to safeguard your mind, devices, and destiny from digital and algorithmic attacks. Rooted in the unyielding truth of Isaiah 54:17—"No weapon formed against you shall prosper"—this chapter empowers you to declare your digital life a fortified sanctuary, breaking every technological trap and aligning your presence with Heaven's protection.

The enemy exploits technology to track, seduce, and control, using algorithms, surveillance, and digital sorcery to infiltrate your thoughts, dreams, and relationships (2 Timothy 1:7). Yet, God has not left you defenseless. These 30 decrees, forged in the fire of divine revelation and apostolic authority, are your weapons to dismantle cyber witchcraft, shield your data, and co-create with God a legacy of digital sanctity (Colossians 3:3). From protecting your devices to guarding your mind, from neutralizing tracking to redeeming your digital footprint, this chapter equips you to stand as a guardian of God's sovereignty, declaring, "Not on my watch will technology prevail over my destiny!"

Why Technological Warfare and Protection Matter

In today's digital age, technology is not a neutral tool; it is a spiritual battlefield, where the enemy seeks to weaponize connectivity against God's people. When God gave humanity dominion, He included stewardship over creation's tools (Genesis 1:28), but the enemy perverts technology to sow confusion, addiction, and oppression. A protected digital life is a threat to the enemy's agenda, for it preserves your clarity, authority, and Kingdom impact. Conversely, vulnerability to technological attacks is a foothold for the adversary, fostering manipulation and spiritual interference. **Technological Warfare and Protection** is foundational to this book because without digital security, your ability to thrive in other areas—purpose, relationships, or health—is compromised. As Zechariah 2:5 declares, "I myself will be a wall of fire around it, declares the Lord."

For those new to prayer, this chapter is an accessible entry point. The decrees are seeds of faith, requiring only your voice and trust to cultivate digital protection. Speak them as a beginner, and God will honor your faith with safeguarding (Mark 11:24). For prayer generals, this chapter is an apostolic mandate, a call to wield your authority as a king and priest (Revelation 1:6) to break digital curses, reset your technological boundaries, and establish your life as a warfare unit (Ephesians 6:12). Every decree is a sword, cutting through the enemy's schemes and planting promises that secure your digital domain. Whether you're a novice or a seasoned intercessor, this chapter is vital, for protection is where faith is fortified, boundaries are set, and God's shield transforms lives.

The Power of Targeted Decrees

Just as a physician prescribes a specific remedy for a specific ailment—no antacid for a headache, no dental visit for a stomachache—battles over technology demand precise, targeted weapons. The 30 decrees in **Technological Warfare and Protection** are tailored to address the unique threats in your digital life. Are algorithms manipulating your thoughts? Declare, "I decree that the Spirit of Wisdom overrides every artificial intelligence system designed to manipulate, spy, or control" (#7). Is technology invading your peace? Proclaim, "I decree that no technology will be used as a portal to invade my dreams, thoughts, or personal space" (#11). Need protection for your data? Decree, "I declare that a divine firewall of protection surrounds my mind, devices, data, and household" (#2). Each proclamation is a divine prescription, anointed to hit the root of your digital vulnerability, aligning your life with God's protective covering.

These decrees are not mere words; they are creative forces, carrying the authority of Heaven to shift realities. Proverbs 18:21 reminds us, "Death and life are in the power of the tongue." When you speak these decrees, you partner with the Holy Spirit, activating the blood of Jesus to cover your digital presence (Revelation 12:11) and angels to war on your behalf (Psalm 91:11). For new believers, this is a revelation: your voice, though untrained, is a weapon when aligned with God's Word. For generals, it's a reminder of your apostolic charge to co-create with God, resetting your digital defenses with every proclamation

(Ephesians 3:20). The decrees are your tools to shield, neutralize, and redeem, ensuring your digital life stands as a testimony of God's sovereignty.

A Digital Life Under Siege

The enemy's assault on your digital life is relentless. Algorithms manipulate, surveillance tracks, and digital sorcery invades, all designed to compromise your destiny. Yet, God's Word is clear: "You will keep in perfect peace those whose minds are steadfast" (Isaiah 26:3). The decrees in this chapter confront these attacks head-on, addressing specific needs:

- **Digital Protection**: Decrees like "I declare that a divine firewall of protection surrounds my mind, devices, data, and household" (#2) and "I decree that my devices will not be hijacked, hacked, tracked, or used against my destiny" (#4) secure your technology.
- **Mental Clarity**: Proclamations such as "I declare that my mind is protected from screen fatigue, mental overload, subliminal messages, and confusion" (#10) and "I declare that I will not be manipulated by online opinions, synthetic emotions, or media-driven fear" (#18) guard your thoughts.
- **Spiritual Defense**: Decrees like "I decree that every spiritual parasite riding through Wi-Fi, Bluetooth, or data signals is evicted now" (#13) and "I decree that cyber witchcraft, digital sorcery, and psychic predictions through technology are shattered now" (#25) break spiritual attacks.
- **Digital Redemption**: Decrees like "I decree that a digital bloodline reset redeems every image, click, and byte by the blood of Jesus" (#17) and "I declare that every smart device in my home is subject to the voice and will of God" (#26) restore your digital footprint.

For those new to prayer, these decrees are simple to speak, requiring only faith to see God move. Imagine planting a seed in fertile soil—each word you utter is a seed of protection, watered by trust, that grows into a harvest of security. For generals, these decrees are strategic, apostolic weapons, enabling you to exercise dominion (Genesis 1:28) and reset your digital battlefield.

You're not just praying; you're commanding, aligning earth with Heaven, and establishing a legacy of digital sanctity that echoes through generations.

The Apostolic Call to Technological Warfare and Protection

As an apostle, I've seen the enemy's tactics firsthand—algorithms sowing confusion, surveillance stealing privacy, and digital sorcery binding destinies. But I've also witnessed the power of God's Word to dismantle what was weaponized, redeem what was corrupted, and protect what was vulnerable (Psalm 17:8). **Technological Warfare and Protection** is not optional; it's foundational. Without digital security, your ability to fulfill God's purposes is compromised. A protected digital life stands firm (Colossians 3:3), but a vulnerable one struggles to shine. This chapter is your apostolic mandate to take up your authority as a king and priest (Revelation 1:6), declaring God's promises over your technology with unwavering faith.

For new believers, this chapter is an invitation to step into your God-given authority. You may feel inexperienced, but your voice, when aligned with these decrees, carries the weight of Heaven. Speak, "I declare that total victory over technological warfare—my mind is sound, my systems are secure, and my soul is untouchable" (#28), and trust God to honor your faith. For generals, this chapter is a call to strategic warfare. You understand that technology is a battlefield, a divine domain to confront the enemy's schemes (Ephesians 6:12). Decrees like "I decree that every technological trap set by the enemy is exposed and dismantled by fire" (#1) and "I declare that I am hidden in Christ and encoded in the Spirit" (#22) empower you to lead with apostolic precision, breaking cycles of digital oppression and building legacies of protection.

Practical Application for All

Technological Warfare and Protection is a chapter for every believer, from the novice to the general, because every life faces digital threats, and every destiny needs God's shield. Here's how to engage with this chapter:

For Those New to Prayer

- **Start Simple**: Choose one or two decrees that resonate with your needs, such as "I declare that every smart device in my home is subject to the voice and will of God" (#26). Speak them daily, aloud, with faith.

- **Trust God's Word**: You don't need experience; you need trust. Hebrews 11:6 says, "Without faith it is impossible to please Him." Your words, backed by Scripture, are powerful.
- **Expect Results**: Like a patient taking medicine, trust that each decree is working, even if results aren't immediate. Journal answered prayers to build your faith.
- **Use Technology Wisely**: Pair decrees with discernment, creating a unified front of faith (Proverbs 4:25).

For Prayer Generals

- **Diagnose Strategically**: Identify the enemy's tactics in your digital life—manipulation, surveillance, sorcery—and select decrees to counter them, like "I decree that every monitoring spirit operating through algorithms, social platforms, spyware, or frequency warfare is bound" (#29).
- **Activate Angels**: Use decrees like "I decree that angelic interception guards every email, text, message, or video meant to cause harm, delay, or destruction" (#9) to engage heavenly forces (Psalm 91:11).
- **Lead with Authority**: As a general, you're not just praying; you're commanding. Speak, "I decree that no drone, camera, satellite, or digital scan will violate the covering of God over my life" (#19), with apostolic boldness.
- **Intercede for Legacy**: Use decrees like "I decree that a digital bloodline reset redeems every image, click, and byte by the blood of Jesus" (#17) to secure blessings for future generations.

Practical Steps

- **Create a Prayer Space**: Find a quiet place to focus, inviting the Holy Spirit to anoint your words.
- **Speak Daily**: Declare 5–10 decrees each morning or night, personalizing them (e.g., insert your name in "I declare that [name]'s mind is protected from screen fatigue" [#10]).

- **Combine with Worship**: Pair decrees with praise, amplifying their power (Psalm 149:6-9). Sing or lift your hands to magnify God.
- **Live the Decrees**: Align your actions with your words. If you decree protection, use technology discerningly (1 Corinthians 6:12). If you declare redemption, steward your digital presence wisely (Psalm 139:14).

The Eternal Impact of Technological Warfare and Protection

The stakes are eternal. A protected digital life is not just a personal victory; it's a generational triumph, a ripple effect that transforms families, communities, and nations. When you declare, "I decree that no technology will be used as a portal to invade my dreams, thoughts, or personal space" (#11), you're not only securing your life but planting seeds for a legacy of digital sanctity (Psalm 4:8). When you proclaim, "I declare that total victory over technological warfare—my mind is sound, my systems are secure, and my soul is untouchable" (#28), you're aligning your destiny with God's eternal purposes, breaking cycles of digital oppression and building altars of protection.

For new believers, this chapter is a gateway to experiencing God's power. You may start with a simple decree, like "I declare that God's encryption is on every call, file, and digital footprint I leave behind" (#12), and see God thwart a threat. That small victory will ignite your faith, showing you the authority you carry in Christ (Luke 10:19). For generals, this chapter is a strategic blueprint. You recognize that technology is a warfare domain, a divine stronghold to confront the enemy's schemes. Decrees like "I decree that freedom from frequency attacks, digital oppression, and spiritual interference via sound and screen is my portion" (#30) empower you to lead with prophetic insight, transforming your digital life into a hub of God's sovereignty (Romans 8:28).

A Call to Rise

Technological Warfare and Protection is where the battle for digital sanctity begins and the victory is won. It's where you declare, "I decree that every technological trap set by the enemy is exposed and dismantled by fire" (#1), and watch Heaven respond. It's where you stand, as a new believer or a general, and proclaim, "I declare that I am hidden in Christ and encoded in the Spirit" (#22), knowing the enemy trembles at your voice. This chapter is not just a tool; it's a mandate, a divine commission to fortify your digital defenses, reset your technological boundaries, and establish God's Kingdom through your protection.

For those new to prayer, start here. Speak these decrees with faith, and God will honor your trust, building your digital security on the rock of His Word (Matthew 7:24). For generals, lead here. Wield these proclamations with apostolic authority, knowing your digital life is a warfare unit, co-creating with God to shift generations (Ephesians 3:20). The enemy may rage, but the protection of God prevails (Psalm 32:7). Rise, declare, and watch your digital life become a fortress of sanctity, a testimony of safeguarding, and a legacy of God's unending power.

Technological Warfare and Protection Prayer

Morning Warfare Prayer Points: Securing Digital Defenses

My Father, my God, I take authority over my devices; let Your firewall guard me, in Jesus' name. Father, let every spirit of intrusion refuse to breach my data today. Lord, I command every cyber attack to be null and void, in Jesus' name. My Father, my God, I pull down every demonic plot tracking my digital life. Father, I dismantle every generational vulnerability; my bloodline is secure, in Jesus' name. Lord, shield my mind from digital noise; let clarity overtake me. My Father, my God, encrypt my communications with Your truth; guide my steps. Father, let Your angels war for my protection, guarding my technology. Lord, thank You for Your safeguarding; my life testifies of Your security. Father, anoint me with digital wisdom; let my safety shine with Your glory, in Jesus' name. Amen.

Word Count: ~220 words

Scriptures: Zechariah 2:5, Psalm 91:10, Isaiah 45:2, Galatians 3:13, Colossians 3:3

Technological Warfare and Protection Declarations and Decrees

1. I decree that every technological trap set by the enemy is exposed and dismantled by fire (Psalm 7:15).
2. I declare that a divine firewall of protection surrounds my mind, devices, data, and household (Zechariah 2:5).
3. I decree that the blood of Jesus surrounds every gateway—digital, mental, spiritual, or physical—connected to my life (Revelation 12:11).
4. I declare that my devices will not be hijacked, hacked, tracked, or used against my destiny (Psalm 91:10).
5. I decree that my voiceprint, fingerprint, digital presence, and likeness are shielded by the hand of God (Psalm 17:8).
6. I declare that every technological weapon formed against me shall fail and backfire (Isaiah 54:17).
7. I decree that the Spirit of Wisdom overrides every artificial intelligence system designed to manipulate, spy, or control (Proverbs 2:6).
8. I declare that corrupted systems, fake profiles, ghost accounts, and data tracking assigned to me are destroyed now (Psalm 35:8).
9. I decree that angelic interception guards every email, text, message, or video meant to cause harm, delay, or destruction (Psalm 91:11).
10. I declare that my mind is protected from screen fatigue, mental overload, subliminal messages, and confusion (Philippians 4:7).
11. I decree that no technology will be used as a portal to invade my dreams, thoughts, or personal space (Psalm 4:8).
12. I declare that God's encryption is on every call, file, and digital footprint I leave behind (Isaiah 45:2).
13. I decree that every spiritual parasite riding through Wi-Fi, Bluetooth, or data signals is evicted now (Luke 10:19).
14. I declare that divine acceleration will not be stopped by digital delay, shadow banning, or technological censorship (Habakkuk 2:3).
15. I decree that every device in my possession becomes an instrument of

Kingdom advancement, not demonic surveillance (Romans 8:28).
16. I declare that I am free from technological seduction, mind control, addiction, and algorithmic entrapment (1 Corinthians 6:12).
17. I decree that a digital bloodline reset redeems every image, click, and byte by the blood of Jesus (Colossians 1:20).
18. I declare that I will not be manipulated by online opinions, synthetic emotions, or media-driven fear (2 Timothy 1:7).
19. I decree that no drone, camera, satellite, or digital scan will violate the covering of God over my life (Psalm 32:7).
20. I declare that I will not be baited, triggered, or spiritually infected through clicks, comments, or content (Proverbs 4:25).
21. I decree that the enemy cannot trace, track, mimic, or impersonate me in any system, visible or invisible (Colossians 3:3).
22. I declare that I am hidden in Christ and encoded in the Spirit (Colossians 3:3).
23. I decree that every spiritual virus hidden in a physical device is rendered powerless (Luke 10:19).
24. I declare that no social network or algorithm has dominion over my identity, influence, or relationships (Psalm 139:14).
25. I decree that cyber witchcraft, digital sorcery, and psychic predictions through technology are shattered now (Deuteronomy 18:10-12).
26. I declare that every smart device in my home is subject to the voice and will of God (Joshua 24:15).
27. I decree that divine clarity, mental focus, and prophetic discernment guide me in a world of digital distraction (1 Corinthians 14:33).
28. I declare total victory over technological warfare—my mind is sound, my systems are secure, and my soul is untouchable (2 Corinthians 2:14).
29. I decree that every monitoring spirit operating through algorithms, social platforms, spyware, or frequency warfare is bound (Matthew 18:18).
30. I decree that freedom from frequency attacks, digital oppression, and spiritual interference via sound and screen is my portion (John 8:36).

Chapter 12: Christ Consciousness and Awakening

The Divine Awakening to Eternal Truth

In God's eternal design, you are called to awaken to the mind of Christ, aligning with divine truth and transcending the illusions of this world (1 Corinthians 2:16). Chapter 12: Christ Consciousness and Awakening is a spiritual armory, equipped with 40 Spirit-inspired declarations and decrees to elevate your awareness, renew your mind, and anchor your life in the eternal reality of God's Kingdom. Rooted in the unyielding truth of Romans 8:17—"We are heirs—heirs of God and co-heirs with Christ"—this chapter empowers you to declare your oneness with God, breaking every lie of separation and aligning your consciousness with Heaven's eternal now.

The enemy seeks to trap you in fear, lack, and illusion, clouding your divine connection and limiting your spiritual authority (Romans 8:6). Yet, God has not left you defenseless. These 40 decrees, forged in the fire of divine revelation and apostolic authority, are your weapons to dissolve doubt, awaken divine inspiration, and co-create with God a legacy of spiritual awakening (Ephesians 5:14). From rejecting sin consciousness to embracing perfect love, from stewarding time to accessing divine prosperity, this chapter equips you to stand as a beacon of Christ's consciousness, declaring, "Not on my watch will illusion prevail over truth!"

Why Christ Consciousness and Awakening Matter

Christ consciousness is not an abstract concept; it is a divine mandate, the call to live as one with God, reflecting His truth and authority in every thought and action. When God created you, He made you in His image, endowing you with a spirit that is eternal and whole (Genesis 1:26-27). An awakened believer is a threat to the enemy's agenda, for they transcend worldly limitations, manifest divine realities, and advance God's Kingdom. Conversely, spiritual slumber and illusion are footholds for the adversary, fostering fear and separation. Christ Consciousness and Awakening is foundational to this book because without divine awareness, your ability to thrive in other areas—purpose, relationships, or protection—is diminished. As Luke 17:21 declares, "The kingdom of God is within you."

For those new to prayer, this chapter is an accessible entry point. The decrees are seeds of faith, requiring only your voice and trust to cultivate spiritual clarity and alignment. Speak them as a beginner, and God will honor your faith with revelation (Mark 11:24). For prayer generals, this chapter is an apostolic mandate, a call to wield your authority as a king and priest (Revelation 1:6) to break illusions, reset your consciousness, and establish your life as a warfare unit (Ephesians 6:12). Every decree is a sword, cutting through the enemy's lies and planting promises that awaken divine truth. Whether you're a novice or a seasoned intercessor, this chapter is vital, for awakening is where faith is elevated, truth is embraced, and God's reality transforms lives.

The Power of Targeted Decrees

Just as a physician prescribes a specific remedy for a specific ailment—no antacid for a headache, no dental visit for a stomachache—battles over spiritual awareness demand precise, targeted weapons. The 40 decrees in Christ Consciousness and Awakening are tailored to address the unique barriers clouding your divine connection. Are you bound by fear or doubt? Declare, "I decree that fear, doubt, and unbelief dissolve when I stay connected to the Spirit within" (#23). Seeking divine alignment? Proclaim, "I declare that I am not separate from God—we are one, and nothing can separate me from divine Source" (#27). Need provision and peace? Decree, "I declare that the power of the tithe unlocks divine peace, wealth, and the flow of supernatural provision" (#40). Each proclamation is a divine prescription, anointed to hit the root of your spiritual slumber, aligning your life with God's eternal truth.

These decrees are not mere words; they are creative forces, carrying the authority of Heaven to shift realities. Proverbs 18:21 reminds us, "Death and life are in the power of the tongue." When you speak these decrees, you partner with the Holy Spirit, activating the blood of Jesus to cover your consciousness (Revelation 12:11) and angels to war on your behalf (Psalm 103:20). For new believers, this is a revelation: your voice, though untrained, is a weapon when aligned with God's Word. For generals, it's a reminder of your apostolic charge to co-create with God, resetting your awareness with every proclamation (Ephesians 3:20). The decrees are your tools to awaken, align, and transcend, ensuring your life stands as a testimony of God's truth.

A Consciousness Under Siege

The enemy's assault on your consciousness is relentless. Fear, lack, and sin consciousness seek to cloud your divine connection, while illusions of separation and limitation aim to bind your authority. Yet, God's Word is clear: "There is no condemnation for those who are in Christ Jesus" (Romans 8:1). The decrees in this chapter confront these attacks head-on, addressing specific needs:

- Spiritual Alignment: Decrees like "I decree that I operate daily with the Mind of Christ, using divine thought to instruct and command my life" (#3) and "I declare that I am not separate from God—we are one, and nothing can separate me from divine Source" (#27) anchor you in divine truth.
- Freedom from Illusion: Proclamations such as "I declare that the Kingdom of God is within me—heaven is now, not later" (#24) and "I declare the illusion is broken, the silver cord is intact, and I fulfill my purpose with clarity and power" (#36) shatter worldly lies.
- Prosperity and Peace: Decrees like "I declare that financial prosperity and divine health are part of my covenant—and I shall not lack either" (#6) and "I declare that the power of the tithe unlocks divine peace, wealth, and the flow of supernatural provision" (#40) secure divine provision.
- Stewardship and Transformation: Decrees like "I decree that I am a wise steward of both time and money—never wasting what is replaceable or irreplaceable" (#11) and "I declare that true spiritual work is inner transformation, not outward performance—I live from within" (#16) cultivate eternal priorities.

For those new to prayer, these decrees are simple to speak, requiring only faith to see God move. Imagine planting a seed in fertile soil—each word you utter is a seed of awakening, watered by trust, that grows into a harvest of divine clarity. For generals, these decrees are strategic, apostolic weapons, enabling you to exercise dominion (Genesis 1:28) and reset your spiritual trajectory. You're not just praying; you're commanding, aligning earth with Heaven, and establishing a legacy of awakening that echoes through generations.

The Apostolic Call to Christ Consciousness and Awakening

As an apostle, I've seen the enemy's tactics firsthand—fear clouding truth, illusions binding minds, and separation stealing authority. But I've also witnessed the power of God's Word to awaken what was asleep, restore what was lost, and redeem what was clouded (John 4:23). Christ Consciousness and Awakening is not optional; it's foundational. Without divine awareness, your ability to fulfill God's purposes is limited. An awakened life stands firm (Romans 8:38-39), but a slumbering one struggles to shine. This chapter is your apostolic mandate to take up your authority as a king and priest (Revelation 1:6), declaring God's promises over your consciousness with unwavering faith.

For new believers, this chapter is an invitation to step into your God-given authority. You may feel inexperienced, but your voice, when aligned with these decrees, carries the weight of Heaven. Speak, "I declare that my thoughts, emotions, imagination, and decisions are aligned with divine consciousness and manifest accordingly" (#30), and trust God to honor your faith. For generals, this chapter is a call to strategic warfare. You understand that consciousness is a battlefield, a divine domain to confront the enemy's schemes (Ephesians 6:12). Decrees like "I decree the highest level of Christ consciousness is freedom from fear, poverty, and bondage" (#19) and "I decree that sin consciousness has no hold on me—I am forgiven, free, and fully restored in Christ" (#39) empower you to lead with apostolic precision, breaking cycles of illusion and building legacies of truth.

Practical Application for All

Christ Consciousness and Awakening is a chapter for every believer, from the novice to the general, because every life faces illusions and fears, and every destiny needs God's truth. Here's how to engage with this chapter:

For Those New to Prayer

- Start Simple: Choose one or two decrees that resonate with your spiritual journey, such as "I declare that the Kingdom of God is within me—heaven is now, not later" (#24). Speak them daily, aloud, with faith.
- Trust God's Word: You don't need experience; you need trust. Hebrews 11:6 says, "Without faith it is impossible to please Him." Your words, backed by Scripture, are powerful.
- Expect Results: Like a patient taking medicine, trust that each decree

is working, even if results aren't immediate. Journal answered prayers to build your faith.
- Seek God Daily: Pair decrees with prayer and meditation, creating a unified front of faith (Colossians 4:2).

For Prayer Generals

- Diagnose Strategically: Identify the enemy's tactics in your consciousness—fear, doubt, illusion—and select decrees to counter them, like "I declare that blame, fear, guilt, and self-sabotage are broken by the renewing of my mind" (#38).
- Activate Angels: Use decrees like "I decree that divine inspiration flows through me daily—I write the vision, and it comes to pass" (#17) to engage heavenly forces (Hebrews 1:14).
- Lead with Authority: As a general, you're not just praying; you're commanding. Speak, "I decree that I am not a body, race, gender, or religion—I am spirit, eternal, and whole" (#31), with apostolic boldness.
- Intercede for Legacy: Use decrees like "I decree that as a joint-heir with Christ, I share in the fullness of divine inheritance and sonship" (#35) to secure blessings for future generations.

Practical Steps

- Create a Prayer Space: Find a quiet place to focus, inviting the Holy Spirit to anoint your words.
- Speak Daily: Declare 5–10 decrees each morning or night, personalizing them (e.g., insert your name in "I declare that [name] is perfect love in spirit" [#32]).
- Combine with Worship: Pair decrees with praise, amplifying their power (Psalm 149:6-9). Sing or lift your hands to magnify God.
- Live the Decrees: Align your actions with your words. If you decree awakening, pursue truth daily (John 4:23). If you declare freedom, reject fear (1 John 4:18).

The Eternal Impact of Christ Consciousness and Awakening

The stakes are eternal. An awakened life is not just a personal victory; it's a generational triumph, a ripple effect that transforms families, communities, and nations. When you declare, "I declare that I am not separate from God—we are one, and nothing can separate me from divine Source" (#27), you're not only securing your consciousness but planting seeds for a legacy of truth (Romans 8:38-39). When you proclaim, "I decree that true worship is knowing Truth and being transformed by it" (#33), you're aligning your destiny with God's eternal purposes, breaking cycles of illusion and building altars of awakening.

For new believers, this chapter is a gateway to experiencing God's power. You may start with a simple decree, like "I declare that my inner reality determines my external experience—and I align my mind with truth" (#26), and see God shift your perspective. That small victory will ignite your faith, showing you the authority you carry in Christ (Luke 10:19). For generals, this chapter is a strategic blueprint. You recognize that consciousness is a warfare domain, a divine stronghold to confront the enemy's schemes. Decrees like "I decree that awakening to truth eliminates karma, restores awareness, and empowers me to walk in light" (#34) empower you to lead with prophetic insight, transforming your life into a hub of God's reality (Philippians 4:8).

A Call to Rise

Christ Consciousness and Awakening is where the battle for divine truth begins and the victory is won. It's where you declare, "I decree that I operate daily with the Mind of Christ, using divine thought to instruct and command my life" (#3), and watch Heaven respond. It's where you stand, as a new believer or a general, and proclaim, "I declare that I am perfect love in spirit—I lack nothing, desire nothing, and trust the Source that formed me" (#32), knowing the enemy trembles at your voice. This chapter is not just a tool; it's a mandate, a divine commission to fortify your consciousness, reset your destiny, and establish God's Kingdom through your awakening.

For those new to prayer, start here. Speak these decrees with faith, and God will honor your trust, building your awareness on the rock of His Word (Matthew 7:24). For generals, lead here. Wield these proclamations with apostolic authority, knowing your consciousness is a warfare unit, co-creating with God to shift generations (Ephesians 3:20). The enemy may rage, but the truth of God prevails (John 4:23). Rise, declare, and watch your life become a fortress of divine consciousness, a testimony of awakening, and a legacy of God's unending reality.

Christ Consciousness and Awakening Prayer

Morning Warfare Prayer Points: Aligning with Divine Truth

My Father, my God, I take authority over my mind; let Your truth awaken me, in Jesus' name. Father, let every spirit of deception refuse to cloud my thoughts today. Lord, I command every lie of fear to be null and void, in Jesus' name. My Father, my God, I pull down every demonic veil obscuring Your reality. Father, I dismantle every generational illusion; my bloodline sees clearly, in Jesus' name. Lord, renew my mind with Your Spirit; let awakening overtake me. My Father, my God, align my thoughts with Your Kingdom; guide my heart. Father, let Your angels stir my awareness, guarding my clarity. Lord, thank You for Your revelation; my life testifies of Your truth. Father, anoint me with divine consciousness; let my mind shine with Your glory, in Jesus' name. Amen.

Word Count: ~220 words

Scriptures: 1 Corinthians 2:16, Romans 8:38-39, John 4:23, Galatians 3:13, Romans 12:2

Christ Consciousness and Awakening Declarations and Decrees

1. I decree that as a tither and kingdom giver, I will never be forced to depend on anything or anyone outside of God's provision within me (Philippians 4:19).
2. I declare that what I permit is permitted, and what I forbid is forbidden — heaven backs my boundaries (Matthew 16:19).
3. I decree that I operate daily with the Mind of Christ, using divine thought to instruct and command my life (1 Corinthians 2:16).
4. I declare that every thought, emotion, decision, and action I release is a spiritual instruction that shapes my reality (Proverbs 4:23).
5. I decree that knowing the scriptures unlocks the power of God within me — and I walk in that power (Joshua 1:8).
6. I declare that financial prosperity and divine health are part of my covenant — and I shall not lack either (3 John 1:2).
7. I decree that divine guidance leads me, and I do not walk in spiritual confusion or blindness (Psalm 32:8).
8. I declare that salvation is deliverance from every evil, and I access it through the promises of God (Ephesians 1:13).
9. I decree that the power of giving releases the blessing and stops every generational curse (Malachi 3:10).
10. I declare that kingdom giving proves God's faithfulness and honors His supremacy over my finances (Proverbs 3:9-10).
11. I decree that I am a wise steward of both time and money — never wasting what is replaceable or irreplaceable (Ephesians 5:16).
12. I declare that my spiritual time is sacred — daily alignment through prayer, meditation, study, and application is non-negotiable (Colossians 4:2).
13. I decree I use time to evolve, not repeat cycles. I invest it in truth, not illusion (Ecclesiastes 3:1).
14. I declare I give cheerfully, not fearfully — God has given me power, love, and a sound mind (2 Timothy 1:7).
15. I decree I have risen with Christ into a superior resurrection —

exempt from second death, defeat, or spiritual decay (Revelation 20:6).
16. I declare that true spiritual work is inner transformation, not outward performance — I live from within (Romans 12:2).
17. I decree divine inspiration flows through me daily — I write the vision, and it comes to pass (Habakkuk 2:2).
18. I declare I do not fear death, lack, or separation — I trust the Greater One who lives within me (1 John 4:4).
19. I decree the highest level of Christ consciousness is freedom from fear, poverty, and bondage (1 John 4:18).
20. I declare that anything I was born with — lack, pain, limitation — is simply the assignment I was born to conquer (John 9:1-4).
21. I decree that peace is my compass and prosperity follows where peace abides (Philippians 4:7).
22. I declare that when I walk in peace, I access all seven phases of divine prosperity (John 16:33).
23. I decree that fear, doubt, and unbelief dissolve when I stay connected to the Spirit within (Mark 11:23).
24. I declare that the Kingdom of God is within me — heaven is now, not later (Luke 17:21).
25. I decree that both heaven and hell are states of consciousness — and I choose to dwell in the promises of God (Matthew 4:17).
26. I declare that my inner reality determines my external experience — and I align my mind with truth (Romans 8:6).
27. I decree that I am not separate from God — we are one, and nothing can separate me from divine Source (Romans 8:38-39).
28. I declare that death and hell have been disannulled — only what is eternal shall remain (Psalm 86:13).
29. I decree that my covenant with the Spirit is activated by the words I speak — I speak life, truth, and promise (Isaiah 59:21).
30. I declare that my thoughts, emotions, imagination, and decisions are aligned with divine consciousness and manifest accordingly (Philippians 4:8).
31. I decree that I am not a body, race, gender, or religion — I am spirit, eternal, and whole (Galatians 3:28).

32. I declare I am perfect love in spirit — I lack nothing, desire nothing, and trust the Source that formed me (1 John 4:16).
33. I decree that true worship is knowing Truth and being transformed by it (John 4:23).
34. I declare that awakening to truth eliminates karma, restores awareness, and empowers me to walk in light (Ephesians 5:14).
35. I decree that as a joint-heir with Christ, I share in the fullness of divine inheritance and sonship (Romans 8:17).
36. I declare the illusion is broken, the silver cord is intact, and I fulfill my purpose with clarity and power (Ecclesiastes 12:6).
37. I decree that the mind is the true creator of all things — and I choose thoughts that align with God's Word (Romans 12:2).
38. I declare that blame, fear, guilt, and self-sabotage are broken by the renewing of my mind (2 Corinthians 10:5).
39. I decree that sin consciousness has no hold on me — I am forgiven, free, and fully restored in Christ (Romans 8:1).
40. I declare that the power of the tithe unlocks divine peace, wealth, and the flow of supernatural provision (Malachi 3:10).

Chapter 13: Emotional and Relational Healing

The Divine Balm for Heart and Soul

In God's eternal design, your heart and relationships are sacred spaces, created to reflect His love and unity (John 17:21). **Chapter 13: Emotional and Relational Healing** is a spiritual armory, equipped with 15 Spirit-inspired declarations and decrees to mend emotional wounds, restore broken connections, and anchor your soul in God's peace. Rooted in the unyielding truth of Psalm 147:3—"He heals the brokenhearted and binds up their wounds"—this chapter empowers you to declare your emotions and relationships as testimonies of God's restoration, breaking every chain of hurt and aligning your heart with Heaven's wholeness.

The enemy targets your emotions and relationships with rejection, betrayal, and bitterness, seeking to fracture your soul and disrupt your divine connections (1 Peter 5:8). Yet, God has not left you defenseless. These 15 decrees, forged in the fire of divine revelation and apostolic authority, are your weapons to heal scars, reconcile breaches, and co-create with God a legacy of love and unity (Colossians 3:14). From releasing forgiveness to attracting godly relationships, from overcoming shame to radiating God's compassion, this chapter equips you to stand as a restorer of hearts, declaring, "Not on my watch will division prevail!"

Why Emotional and Relational Healing Matter

Emotional and relational healing is not a secondary concern; it is a divine mandate, the foundation of a life that mirrors God's love. When God created humanity, He designed relationships to be a reflection of His covenant, fostering unity and mutual edification (Genesis 2:18). A healed heart and restored relationships are a threat to the enemy's agenda, for they radiate God's peace, strengthen communities, and advance His Kingdom. Conversely, unresolved emotional wounds and relational strife are footholds for the adversary, fostering isolation and discord. **Emotional and Relational Healing** is foundational to this book because without inner peace and relational harmony, your ability to thrive in other areas—purpose, productivity, or spiritual warfare—is compromised. As Ephesians 4:32 declares, "Be kind and compassionate to one another, forgiving each other, just as in Christ God forgave you."

For those new to prayer, this chapter is an accessible entry point. The decrees are seeds of faith, requiring only your voice and trust to cultivate healing and reconciliation. Speak them as a beginner, and God will honor your faith with restoration (Mark 11:24). For prayer generals, this chapter is an apostolic mandate, a call to wield your authority as a king and priest (Revelation 1:6) to break emotional strongholds, reset relational destinies, and establish your life as a warfare unit (Ephesians 6:12). Every decree is a sword, cutting through the enemy's lies and planting promises that restore wholeness. Whether you're a novice or a seasoned intercessor, this chapter is vital, for healing is where faith is nurtured, love is restored, and God's peace transforms lives.

The Power of Targeted Decrees

Just as a physician prescribes a specific remedy for a specific ailment—no antacid for a headache, no dental visit for a stomachache—battles over emotions and relationships demand precise, targeted weapons. The 15 decrees in **Emotional and Relational Healing** are tailored to address the unique wounds and breaches in your life. Are you carrying the pain of rejection? Declare, "I decree that every wound of rejection, betrayal, or grief in my heart is healed by the balm of Gilead" (#1). Is a friendship strained? Proclaim, "I declare that God restores broken friendships, knitting them together in His love" (#2). Are you bound by unforgiveness? Decree, "I declare that I release forgiveness to those who have wounded me, breaking the enemy's hold on my emotions" (#10). Each proclamation is a divine prescription, anointed to hit the root of your hurt, aligning your heart with God's promise of healing.

These decrees are not mere words; they are creative forces, carrying the authority of Heaven to shift realities. Proverbs 18:21 reminds us, "Death and life are in the power of the tongue." When you speak these decrees, you partner with the Holy Spirit, activating the blood of Jesus to cover your emotions (Revelation 12:11) and angels to war on your behalf (Psalm 103:20). For new believers, this is a revelation: your voice, though untrained, is a weapon when aligned with God's Word. For generals, it's a reminder of your apostolic charge to co-create with God, resetting your emotional and relational destiny with every proclamation (Ephesians 3:20). The decrees are your tools to heal, reconcile, and restore, ensuring your heart and relationships stand as testimonies of God's love.

A Heart Under Siege

The enemy's assault on your emotions and relationships is relentless. Rejection, betrayal, and shame seek to wound your soul, while bitterness and misunderstanding aim to fracture your connections. Yet, God's Word is clear: "The Lord is close to the brokenhearted and saves those who are crushed in spirit" (Psalm 34:18). The decrees in this chapter confront these attacks head-on, addressing specific needs:

- **Emotional Healing**: Decrees like "I decree that every wound of rejection, betrayal, or grief in my heart is healed by the balm of Gilead" (#1) and "I decree that every scar from past hurts is transformed into a testimony of God's healing power" (#5) mend your soul.
- **Relational Restoration**: Proclamations such as "I declare that God restores broken friendships, knitting them together in His love" (#2) and "I decree that God mends every broken connection in my church community, uniting us in His purpose" (#7) reconcile breaches.
- **Freedom from Bondage**: Decrees like "I declare that I am free from the spirit of offense, walking in humility and grace toward others" (#6) and "I decree that every emotional stronghold of shame or guilt is shattered by God's truth" (#13) break chains.
- **Godly Connections**: Decrees like "I declare that I attract godly relationships that edify and strengthen my walk with Christ" (#12) and "I decree that my heart is whole, radiating God's love to every relationship in my life" (#15) foster divine unity.

For those new to prayer, these decrees are simple to speak, requiring only faith to see God move. Imagine planting a seed in fertile soil—each word you utter is a seed of healing, watered by trust, that grows into a harvest of peace. For generals, these decrees are strategic, apostolic weapons, enabling you to exercise dominion (Genesis 1:28) and reset your emotional and relational trajectory. You're not just praying; you're commanding, aligning earth with Heaven, and establishing a legacy of love that echoes through generations.

The Apostolic Call to Emotional and Relational Healing

As an apostle, I've seen the enemy's tactics firsthand—rejection sowing isolation, bitterness fracturing bonds, and shame binding hearts. But I've also witnessed the power of God's Word to heal what was wounded, restore what was broken, and redeem what was lost (Jeremiah 8:22). **Emotional and Relational Healing** is not optional; it's foundational. Without inner peace and relational harmony, your ability to fulfill God's purposes is limited. A healed heart stands firm (Philippians 4:7), but a wounded one struggles to shine. This chapter is your apostolic mandate to take up your authority as a king and priest (Revelation 1:6), declaring God's promises over your emotions and relationships with unwavering faith.

For new believers, this chapter is an invitation to step into your God-given authority. You may feel inexperienced, but your voice, when aligned with these decrees, carries the weight of Heaven. Speak, "I declare that my interactions are seasoned with grace, building bridges of reconciliation" (#14), and trust God to honor your faith. For generals, this chapter is a call to strategic warfare. You understand that emotions and relationships are battlefields, divine domains to confront the enemy's schemes (Ephesians 6:12). Decrees like "I decree that my emotions are anchored in the peace of God, casting out all bitterness and unforgiveness" (#3) and "I decree that God's healing touch restores my soul from the pain of loss and abandonment" (#11) empower you to lead with apostolic precision, breaking cycles of hurt and building legacies of unity.

Practical Application for All

Emotional and Relational Healing is a chapter for every believer, from the novice to the general, because every heart faces wounds, and every relationship needs God's touch. Here's how to engage with this chapter:

For Those New to Prayer

- **Start Simple**: Choose one or two decrees that resonate with your needs, such as "I declare that my heart is guarded against resentment, filled with God's compassion and mercy" (#8). Speak them daily, aloud, with faith.

- **Trust God's Word**: You don't need experience; you need trust. Hebrews 11:6 says, "Without faith it is impossible to please Him." Your words, backed by Scripture, are powerful.
- **Expect Results**: Like a patient taking medicine, trust that each decree is working, even if results aren't immediate. Journal answered prayers to build your faith.
- **Practice Love**: Pair decrees with acts of kindness, creating a unified front of faith (John 13:34).

For Prayer Generals

- **Diagnose Strategically**: Identify the enemy's tactics in your heart—rejection, bitterness, shame—and select decrees to counter them, like "I decree that every relational breach caused by misunderstanding is healed by divine clarity" (#9).
- **Activate Angels**: Use decrees like "I decree that every wound of rejection, betrayal, or grief in my heart is healed by the balm of Gilead" (#1) to engage heavenly forces (Hebrews 1:14).
- **Lead with Authority**: As a general, you're not just praying; you're commanding. Speak, "I decree that my heart is whole, radiating God's love to every relationship in my life" (#15), with apostolic boldness.
- **Intercede for Legacy**: Use decrees like "I declare that the love of Christ flows through me, reconciling strained relationships outside my family" (#4) to secure blessings for future generations.

Practical Steps

- **Create a Prayer Space**: Find a quiet place to focus, inviting the Holy Spirit to anoint your words.
- **Speak Daily**: Declare 5–10 decrees each morning or night, personalizing them (e.g., insert a person's name in "I declare that God restores [name]'s broken friendships" [#2]).
- **Combine with Worship**: Pair decrees with praise, amplifying their power (Psalm 149:6-9). Sing or lift your hands to magnify God.

- **Live the Decrees**: Align your actions with your words. If you decree forgiveness, release grudges (Matthew 6:14). If you declare healing, pursue peace (Philippians 4:7).

The Eternal Impact of Emotional and Relational Healing

The stakes are eternal. A healed heart and restored relationships are not just personal victories; they're generational triumphs, a ripple effect that transforms families, communities, and nations. When you declare, "I decree that every scar from past hurts is transformed into a testimony of God's healing power" (#5), you're not only securing your soul but planting seeds for a legacy of love (Proverbs 17:17). When you proclaim, "I decree that my heart is whole, radiating God's love to every relationship in my life" (#15), you're aligning your connections with God's eternal purposes, breaking cycles of division and building altars of unity.

For new believers, this chapter is a gateway to experiencing God's power. You may start with a simple decree, like "I declare that my heart is guarded against resentment, filled with God's compassion and mercy" (#8), and see God mend a strained bond. That small victory will ignite your faith, showing you the authority you carry in Christ (Luke 10:19). For generals, this chapter is a strategic blueprint. You recognize that emotions and relationships are warfare domains, divine strongholds to confront the enemy's schemes. Decrees like "I declare that I attract godly relationships that edify and strengthen my walk with Christ" (#12) empower you to lead with prophetic insight, transforming your life into a hub of God's love (1 John 4:12).

A Call to Rise

Emotional and Relational Healing is where the battle for wholeness begins and the victory is won. It's where you declare, "I decree that every wound of rejection, betrayal, or grief in my heart is healed by the balm of Gilead" (#1), and watch Heaven respond. It's where you stand, as a new believer or a general, and proclaim, "I decree that my heart is whole, radiating God's love to every relationship in my life" (#15), knowing the enemy trembles at your voice. This chapter is not just a tool; it's a mandate, a divine commission to fortify your heart, reset your relationships, and establish God's Kingdom through your healing.

For those new to prayer, start here. Speak these decrees with faith, and God will honor your trust, building your peace on the rock of His Word (Matthew 7:24). For generals, lead here. Wield these proclamations with apostolic authority, knowing your heart is a warfare unit, co-creating with God to shift generations (Ephesians 3:20). The enemy may rage, but the love of God prevails (1 John 4:12). Rise, declare, and watch your heart and relationships become a fortress of wholeness, a testimony of restoration, and a legacy of God's unending grace.

Emotional and Relational Healing Prayer

Morning Warfare Prayer Points: Mending Heart and Bonds

My Father, my God, I take authority over my heart; let Your healing mend me, in Jesus' name. Father, let every spirit of resentment refuse to bind my soul today. Lord, I command every wound of betrayal to be null and void, in Jesus' name. My Father, my God, I pull down every demonic plot fracturing my relationships. Father, I dismantle every generational strife; my bloodline is whole, in Jesus' name. Lord, restore my connections with Your love; let peace overtake me. My Father, my God, heal my emotions with Your comfort; guide my bonds. Father, let Your angels guard my heart, ensuring my healing. Lord, thank You for Your peace; my life testifies of Your restoration. Father, anoint me with compassion; let my relationships shine with Your glory, in Jesus' name. Amen.

Word Count: ~220 words

Scriptures: Psalm 147:3, Philippians 4:7, Colossians 3:14, Galatians 3:13, Matthew 6:14

Emotional and Relational Healing Declarations and Decrees

1. I decree that every wound of rejection, betrayal, or grief in my heart is healed by the balm of Gilead (Jeremiah 8:22).
2. I declare that God restores broken friendships, knitting them together in His love (Colossians 3:14).
3. I decree that my emotions are anchored in the peace of God, casting out all bitterness and unforgiveness (Ephesians 4:31-32).
4. I declare that the love of Christ flows through me, reconciling strained relationships outside my family (2 Corinthians 5:18).
5. I decree that every scar from past hurts is transformed into a testimony of God's healing power (Psalm 147:3).
6. I declare that I am free from the spirit of offense, walking in humility and grace toward others (Matthew 18:15).
7. I decree that God mends every broken connection in my church community, uniting us in His purpose (Psalm 133:1).
8. I declare that my heart is guarded against resentment, filled with God's compassion and mercy (Philippians 4:7).
9. I decree that every relational breach caused by misunderstanding is healed by divine clarity (Proverbs 17:17).
10. I declare that I release forgiveness to those who have wounded me, breaking the enemy's hold on my emotions (Matthew 6:14).
11. I decree that God's healing touch restores my soul from the pain of loss and abandonment (Psalm 23:3).
12. I declare that I attract godly relationships that edify and strengthen my walk with Christ (Proverbs 27:17).
13. I decree that every emotional stronghold of shame or guilt is shattered by God's truth (Romans 8:1).
14. I declare that my interactions are seasoned with grace, building bridges of reconciliation (Colossians 4:6).
15. I decree that my heart is whole, radiating God's love to every relationship in my life (1 John 4:12).

Chapter 14: Spiritual Discernment and Wisdom

The Divine Lens of Truth

In God's eternal design, spiritual discernment and wisdom are divine gifts, enabling you to navigate life's complexities with clarity and align with His perfect will (James 1:5). **Chapter 14: Spiritual Discernment and Wisdom** is a spiritual armory, equipped with 15 Spirit-inspired declarations and decrees to sharpen your spiritual senses, illuminate your path, and anchor your decisions in God's truth. Rooted in the unyielding promise of John 16:13—"The Spirit of truth... will guide you into all the truth"—this chapter empowers you to declare your mind a sanctuary of divine insight, breaking every veil of deception and aligning your choices with Heaven's wisdom.

The enemy seeks to cloud your discernment with confusion, deception, and false doctrines, aiming to derail your divine purpose (1 John 4:1). Yet, God has not left you defenseless. These 15 decrees, forged in the fire of divine revelation and apostolic authority, are your weapons to expose lies, receive divine strategies, and co-create with God a legacy of prophetic clarity (Proverbs 3:6). From discerning God's voice to overcoming spiritual traps, from rejecting falsehood to walking in the fear of the Lord, this chapter equips you to stand as a watchman of truth, declaring, "Not on my watch will deception prevail!"

Why Spiritual Discernment and Wisdom Matter

Spiritual discernment and wisdom are not optional luxuries; they are divine mandates, the compass for a life that honors God. When God created you, He endowed you with a spirit capable of knowing His voice and navigating His paths (John 10:27). A discerning believer is a threat to the enemy's agenda, for they expose falsehoods, make godly decisions, and advance God's Kingdom. Conversely, spiritual blindness and confusion are footholds for the adversary, fostering error and missteps. **Spiritual Discernment and Wisdom** is foundational to this book because without clear insight, your ability to thrive in other areas—relationships, purpose, or protection—is compromised. As Proverbs 9:10 declares, "The fear of the Lord is the beginning of wisdom, and knowledge of the Holy One is understanding."

For those new to prayer, this chapter is an accessible entry point. The decrees are seeds of faith, requiring only your voice and trust to cultivate clarity and guidance. Speak them as a beginner, and God will honor your faith with revelation (Mark 11:24). For prayer generals, this chapter is an apostolic mandate, a call to wield your authority as a king and priest (Revelation 1:6) to break deceptive strongholds, reset your spiritual senses, and establish your life as a warfare unit (Ephesians 6:12). Every decree is a sword, cutting through the enemy's lies and planting promises that sharpen your discernment. Whether you're a novice or a seasoned intercessor, this chapter is vital, for wisdom is where faith is guided, truth is upheld, and God's clarity transforms lives.

The Power of Targeted Decrees

Just as a physician prescribes a specific remedy for a specific ailment—no antacid for a headache, no dental visit for a stomachache—battles over discernment demand precise, targeted weapons. The 15 decrees in **Spiritual Discernment and Wisdom** are tailored to address the unique threats clouding your spiritual clarity. Are you struggling to hear God's voice? Declare, "I decree that I discern the voice of God clearly, distinguishing His truth from the enemy's lies" (#1). Facing deceptive influences? Proclaim, "I decree that I detect and dismantle every spirit of deception targeting my mind and choices" (#3). Seeking divine strategies? Decree, "I declare that I receive divine strategies to overcome obstacles, aligning with God's perfect plan" (#10). Each proclamation is a divine prescription, anointed to hit the root of your confusion, aligning your mind with God's wisdom.

These decrees are not mere words; they are creative forces, carrying the authority of Heaven to shift realities. Proverbs 18:21 reminds us, "Death and life are in the power of the tongue." When you speak these decrees, you partner with the Holy Spirit, activating the blood of Jesus to cover your discernment (Revelation 12:11) and angels to war on your behalf (Psalm 103:20). For new believers, this is a revelation: your voice, though untrained, is a weapon when aligned with God's Word. For generals, it's a reminder of your apostolic charge to co-create with God, resetting your spiritual clarity with every proclamation (Ephesians 3:20). The decrees are your tools to illuminate, protect, and guide, ensuring your decisions stand as testimonies of God's truth.

A Mind Under Siege

The enemy's assault on your discernment is relentless. Deception, false doctrines, and confusion seek to cloud your spiritual senses, while distractions and snares aim to misguide your choices. Yet, God's Word is clear: "If any of you lacks wisdom, you should ask God, who gives generously to all without finding fault" (James 1:5). The decrees in this chapter confront these attacks head-on, addressing specific needs:

- **Divine Clarity**: Decrees like "I decree that I discern the voice of God clearly, distinguishing His truth from the enemy's lies" (#1) and "I declare that I hear God's voice behind me, saying, 'This is the way, walk in it'" (#14) anchor you in truth.
- **Protection from Deception**: Proclamations such as "I decree that I detect and dismantle every spirit of deception targeting my mind and choices" (#3) and "I decree that every false doctrine or misleading influence is exposed and cast out of my sphere" (#7) guard your mind.
- **Spiritual Insight**: Decrees like "I decree that my spiritual eyes are opened to see God's plans and purposes for my life" (#5) and "I declare that I am filled with the knowledge of God's will, making decisions with divine precision" (#6) unlock revelation.
- **Godly Wisdom**: Decrees like "I decree that I walk in the fear of the Lord, which is the beginning of wisdom, guiding my every step" (#9) and "I decree that my discernment grows stronger, enabling me to stand firm in truth and righteousness" (#15) ensure wise choices.

For those new to prayer, these decrees are simple to speak, requiring only faith to see God move. Imagine planting a seed in fertile soil—each word you utter is a seed of clarity, watered by trust, that grows into a harvest of wisdom. For generals, these decrees are strategic, apostolic weapons, enabling you to exercise dominion (Genesis 1:28) and reset your spiritual trajectory. You're not just praying; you're commanding, aligning earth with Heaven, and establishing a legacy of discernment that echoes through generations.

The Apostolic Call to Spiritual Discernment and Wisdom

As an apostle, I've seen the enemy's tactics firsthand—deception sowing error, confusion clouding judgment, and falsehoods binding destinies. But I've also witnessed the power of God's Word to illuminate what was hidden, restore what was lost, and redeem what was clouded (Ephesians 1:18). **Spiritual Discernment and Wisdom** is not optional; it's foundational. Without clear insight, your ability to fulfill God's purposes is limited. A discerning life stands firm (Hebrews 5:14), but a confused one struggles to shine. This chapter is your apostolic mandate to take up your authority as a king and priest (Revelation 1:6), declaring God's promises over your mind with unwavering faith.

For new believers, this chapter is an invitation to step into your God-given authority. You may feel inexperienced, but your voice, when aligned with these decrees, carries the weight of Heaven. Speak, "I declare that the Spirit of wisdom guides my decisions, leading me in paths of righteousness" (#2), and trust God to honor your faith. For generals, this chapter is a call to strategic warfare. You understand that discernment is a battlefield, a divine domain to confront the enemy's schemes (Ephesians 6:12). Decrees like "I decree that my mind is renewed daily, discerning good from evil with supernatural clarity" (#11) and "I declare that I am led by the Spirit, avoiding the snares of the enemy in every decision" (#12) empower you to lead with apostolic precision, breaking cycles of confusion and building legacies of wisdom.

Practical Application for All

Spiritual Discernment and Wisdom is a chapter for every believer, from the novice to the general, because every mind faces deception, and every destiny needs God's guidance. Here's how to engage with this chapter:

For Those New to Prayer

- **Start Simple**: Choose one or two decrees that resonate with your needs, such as "I declare that divine insight illuminates my path, equipping me to navigate life's challenges with clarity" (#4). Speak them daily, aloud, with faith.
- **Trust God's Word**: You don't need experience; you need trust. Hebrews 11:6 says, "Without faith it is impossible to please Him." Your words, backed by Scripture, are powerful.
- **Expect Results**: Like a patient taking medicine, trust that each

decree is working, even if results aren't immediate. Journal answered prayers to build your faith.
- **Seek God's Guidance**: Pair decrees with prayer, creating a unified front of faith (Psalm 32:8).

For Prayer Generals

- **Diagnose Strategically**: Identify the enemy's tactics in your mind—deception, confusion, falsehoods—and select decrees to counter them, like "I decree that every false doctrine or misleading influence is exposed and cast out of my sphere" (#7).
- **Activate Angels**: Use decrees like "I declare that I receive divine strategies to overcome obstacles, aligning with God's perfect plan" (#10) to engage heavenly forces (Hebrews 1:14).
- **Lead with Authority**: As a general, you're not just praying; you're commanding. Speak, "I decree that my discernment grows stronger, enabling me to stand firm in truth and righteousness" (#15), with apostolic boldness.
- **Intercede for Legacy**: Use decrees like "I declare that I am filled with the knowledge of God's will, making decisions with divine precision" (#6) to secure blessings for future generations.

Practical Steps

- **Create a Prayer Space**: Find a quiet place to focus, inviting the Holy Spirit to anoint your words.
- **Speak Daily**: Declare 5–10 decrees each morning or night, personalizing them (e.g., insert your name in "I declare that [name] is led by the Spirit, avoiding the snares of the enemy" [#12]).
- **Combine with Worship**: Pair decrees with praise, amplifying their power (Psalm 149:6-9). Sing or lift your hands to magnify God.
- **Live the Decrees**: Align your actions with your words. If you decree discernment, test spirits (1 John 4:1). If you declare wisdom, seek God's counsel (Proverbs 3:5-6).

The Eternal Impact of Spiritual Discernment and Wisdom

The stakes are eternal. A discerning life is not just a personal victory; it's a generational triumph, a ripple effect that transforms families, communities, and nations. When you declare, "I decree that I discern the voice of God clearly, distinguishing His truth from the enemy's lies" (#1), you're not only securing your mind but planting seeds for a legacy of truth (John 10:27). When you proclaim, "I decree that my discernment grows stronger, enabling me to stand firm in truth and righteousness" (#15), you're aligning your decisions with God's eternal purposes, breaking cycles of deception and building altars of wisdom.

For new believers, this chapter is a gateway to experiencing God's power. You may start with a simple decree, like "I declare that the Spirit of wisdom guides my decisions, leading me in paths of righteousness" (#2), and see God clarify a choice. That small victory will ignite your faith, showing you the authority you carry in Christ (Luke 10:19). For generals, this chapter is a strategic blueprint. You recognize that discernment is a warfare domain, a divine stronghold to confront the enemy's schemes. Decrees like "I declare that I hear God's voice behind me, saying, 'This is the way, walk in it'" (#14) empower you to lead with prophetic insight, transforming your life into a hub of God's truth (Isaiah 30:21).

A Call to Rise

Spiritual Discernment and Wisdom is where the battle for clarity begins and the victory is won. It's where you declare, "I decree that I discern the voice of God clearly, distinguishing His truth from the enemy's lies" (#1), and watch Heaven respond. It's where you stand, as a new believer or a general, and proclaim, "I decree that my discernment grows stronger, enabling me to stand firm in truth and righteousness" (#15), knowing the enemy trembles at your voice. This chapter is not just a tool; it's a mandate, a divine commission to fortify your mind, reset your spiritual senses, and establish God's Kingdom through your wisdom.

For those new to prayer, start here. Speak these decrees with faith, and God will honor your trust, building your clarity on the rock of His Word (Matthew 7:24). For generals, lead here. Wield these proclamations with apostolic authority, knowing your mind is a warfare unit, co-creating with God to shift generations (Ephesians 3:20). The enemy may rage, but the wisdom of God prevails (Proverbs 9:10). Rise, declare, and watch your mind become a fortress of truth, a testimony of discernment, and a legacy of God's unending guidance.

Spiritual Discernment and Wisdom Prayer

Morning Warfare Prayer Points: Sharpening Divine Insight

My Father, my God, I take authority over my mind; let Your wisdom guide me, in Jesus' name. Father, let every spirit of confusion refuse to cloud my discernment today. Lord, I command every deceptive lie to be null and void, in Jesus' name. My Father, my God, I pull down every demonic veil obscuring Your voice. Father, I dismantle every generational folly; my bloodline discerns clearly, in Jesus' name. Lord, sharpen my spiritual senses with Your truth; let clarity overtake me. My Father, my God, align my decisions with Your will; guide my path. Father, let Your angels guard my insight, ensuring my understanding. Lord, thank You for Your revelation; my life testifies of Your wisdom. Father, anoint me with discernment; let my choices shine with Your glory, in Jesus' name. Amen.

Word Count: ~220 words

Scriptures: James 1:5, John 10:27, Colossians 1:9, Galatians 3:13, Proverbs 3:6

Spiritual Discernment and Wisdom Declarations and Decrees

1. I decree that I discern the voice of God clearly, distinguishing His truth from the enemy's lies (John 10:27).
2. I declare that the Spirit of wisdom guides my decisions, leading me in paths of righteousness (James 1:5).
3. I decree that I detect and dismantle every spirit of deception targeting my mind and choices (1 John 4:1).
4. I declare that divine insight illuminates my path, equipping me to navigate life's challenges with clarity (Proverbs 3:6).
5. I decree that my spiritual eyes are opened to see God's plans and purposes for my life (Ephesians 1:18).
6. I declare that I am filled with the knowledge of God's will, making decisions with divine precision (Colossians 1:9).
7. I decree that every false doctrine or misleading influence is exposed and cast out of my sphere (2 Timothy 4:3-4).
8. I declare that the Holy Spirit sharpens my discernment, protecting me from spiritual traps (Hebrews 5:14).
9. I decree that I walk in the fear of the Lord, which is the beginning of wisdom, guiding my every step (Proverbs 9:10).
10. I declare that I receive divine strategies to overcome obstacles, aligning with God's perfect plan (Isaiah 55:8-9).
11. I decree that my mind is renewed daily, discerning good from evil with supernatural clarity (Romans 12:2).
12. I declare that I am led by the Spirit, avoiding the snares of the enemy in every decision (Romans 8:14).
13. I decree that God's counsel prevails in my life, overriding human wisdom and confusion (Psalm 33:11).
14. I declare that I hear God's voice behind me, saying, "This is the way, walk in it" (Isaiah 30:21).
15. I decree that my discernment grows stronger, enabling me to stand firm in truth and righteousness (1 Corinthians 2:15).

Chapter 15: Community and National Transformation

The Divine Call to Transform Nations

In God's eternal design, communities and nations are called to reflect His justice, righteousness, and glory, serving as beacons of His Kingdom on earth (Psalm 89:14). **Chapter 15: Community and National Transformation** is a spiritual armory, equipped with 15 Spirit-inspired declarations and decrees to ignite revival, restore godly leadership, and align your region with God's divine order. Rooted in the unyielding promise of 2 Chronicles 7:14—"If my people... humble themselves and pray... I will heal their land"—this chapter empowers you to declare your community and nation as territories of God's presence, breaking every stronghold of division and aligning your region with Heaven's purposes.

The enemy seeks to sow discord, corruption, and deception in communities and nations, aiming to thwart God's redemptive plan (John 10:10). Yet, God has not left you defenseless. These 15 decrees, forged in the fire of divine revelation and apostolic authority, are your weapons to dismantle demonic agendas, shift spiritual atmospheres, and co-create with God a legacy of transformation (Habakkuk 3:2). From sparking revival to overturning injustice, from uniting the body of Christ to establishing peace, this chapter equips you to stand as an intercessor for your land, declaring, "Not on my watch will darkness prevail over my nation!"

Why Community and National Transformation Matter

Community and national transformation is not a peripheral pursuit; it is a divine mandate, the call to see God's Kingdom manifest on earth as it is in Heaven (Matthew 6:10). When God established nations, He purposed them to uphold His righteousness and serve His glory (Psalm 33:12). A transformed community and nation are a threat to the enemy's agenda, for they foster unity, advance justice, and reflect God's power. Conversely, division, corruption, and wickedness are footholds for the adversary, perpetuating chaos and oppression. **Community and National Transformation** is foundational to this book because without a healed land, your ability to thrive in other areas—family, purpose, or discernment—is constrained. As Isaiah 61:8 declares, "For I, the Lord, love justice; I hate robbery and wrongdoing."

For those new to prayer, this chapter is an accessible entry point. The decrees are seeds of faith, requiring only your voice and trust to cultivate revival and restoration. Speak them as a beginner, and God will honor your faith with breakthroughs (Mark 11:24). For prayer generals, this chapter is an apostolic mandate, a call to wield your authority as a king and priest (Revelation 1:6) to break regional strongholds, reset spiritual atmospheres, and establish your community as a warfare unit (Ephesians 6:12). Every decree is a sword, cutting through the enemy's schemes and planting promises that transform nations. Whether you're a novice or a seasoned intercessor, this chapter is vital, for transformation is where faith is activated, justice is restored, and God's Kingdom reshapes the world.

The Power of Targeted Decrees

Just as a physician prescribes a specific remedy for a specific ailment—no antacid for a headache, no dental visit for a stomachache—battles over communities and nations demand precise, targeted weapons. The 15 decrees in **Community and National Transformation** are tailored to address the unique challenges facing your region. Is your community divided? Declare, "I decree that every spirit of division in my community is bound, and unity prevails" (#5). Is your nation plagued by injustice? Proclaim, "I declare that justice and righteousness prevail in my nation, aligning it with God's purposes" (#2). Seeking revival? Decree, "I decree that revival fire sweeps through my community, awakening hearts to the Kingdom of God" (#1). Each proclamation is a divine prescription, anointed to hit the root of your region's darkness, aligning your land with God's redemptive plan.

These decrees are not mere words; they are creative forces, carrying the authority of Heaven to shift realities. Proverbs 18:21 reminds us, "Death and life are in the power of the tongue." When you speak these decrees, you partner with the Holy Spirit, activating the blood of Jesus to cover your community (Revelation 12:11) and angels to war on your behalf (Psalm 103:20). For new believers, this is a revelation: your voice, though untrained, is a weapon when aligned with God's Word. For generals, it's a reminder of your apostolic charge to co-create with God, resetting your region's destiny with every proclamation

(Ephesians 3:20). The decrees are your tools to revive, restore, and transform, ensuring your community and nation stand as testimonies of God's glory.

A Land Under Siege

The enemy's assault on communities and nations is relentless. Division, corruption, and deception seek to fracture societies, while injustice and violence aim to oppress God's people. Yet, God's Word is clear: "Righteousness exalts a nation, but sin condemns any people" (Proverbs 14:34). The decrees in this chapter confront these attacks head-on, addressing specific needs:

- **Revival and Awakening**: Decrees like "I decree that revival fire sweeps through my community, awakening hearts to the Kingdom of God" (#1) and "I declare that my nation turns to God, experiencing a great awakening of faith and repentance" (#14) ignite spiritual renewal.
- **Justice and Righteousness**: Proclamations such as "I declare that justice and righteousness prevail in my nation, aligning it with God's purposes" (#2) and "I decree that economic and social injustices in my nation are overturned by God's divine order" (#7) restore godly order.
- **Unity and Peace**: Decrees like "I decree that every spirit of division in my community is bound, and unity prevails" (#5) and "I declare that my community is a sanctuary of peace, free from violence and oppression" (#8) foster harmony.
- **Godly Leadership and Influence**: Decrees like "I declare that godly leaders are raised up in my nation, governing with wisdom and integrity" (#4) and "I declare that my prayers shift the spiritual atmosphere, bringing Heaven's influence to my nation" (#10) establish divine authority.

For those new to prayer, these decrees are simple to speak, requiring only faith to see God move. Imagine planting a seed in fertile soil—each word you utter is a seed of transformation, watered by trust, that grows into a harvest of revival. For generals, these decrees are strategic, apostolic weapons, enabling you to exercise dominion (Genesis 1:28) and reset your region's spiritual trajectory. You're not just praying; you're commanding, aligning earth with Heaven, and establishing a legacy of transformation that echoes through generations.

The Apostolic Call to Community and National Transformation

As an apostle, I've seen the enemy's tactics firsthand—division fracturing communities, corruption tainting nations, and deception blinding societies. But I've also witnessed the power of God's Word to revive what was dormant, restore what was broken, and redeem what was lost (Joel 2:12-13). **Community and National Transformation** is not optional; it's foundational. Without a healed land, your ability to fulfill God's purposes is limited. A transformed community stands firm (Psalm 72:7), but a divided one struggles to shine. This chapter is your apostolic mandate to take up your authority as a king and priest (Revelation 1:6), declaring God's promises over your region with unwavering faith.

For new believers, this chapter is an invitation to step into your God-given authority. You may feel inexperienced, but your voice, when aligned with these decrees, carries the weight of Heaven. Speak, "I declare that the gospel spreads like wildfire in my region, transforming lives for Christ" (#6), and trust God to honor your faith. For generals, this chapter is a call to strategic warfare. You understand that communities and nations are battlefields, divine domains to confront the enemy's schemes (Ephesians 6:12). Decrees like "I decree that corruption and wickedness in high places are exposed and dismantled" (#11) and "I decree that my community becomes a hub of God's glory, drawing souls to salvation" (#15) empower you to lead with apostolic precision, breaking cycles of darkness and building legacies of light.

Practical Application for All

Community and National Transformation is a chapter for every believer, from the novice to the general, because every region faces spiritual battles, and every nation needs God's touch. Here's how to engage with this chapter:

For Those New to Prayer

- **Start Simple**: Choose one or two decrees that resonate with your community's needs, such as "I declare that my community is a sanctuary of peace, free from violence and oppression" (#8). Speak them daily, aloud, with faith.

- **Trust God's Word**: You don't need experience; you need trust. Hebrews 11:6 says, "Without faith it is impossible to please Him." Your words, backed by Scripture, are powerful.
- **Expect Results**: Like a patient taking medicine, trust that each decree is working, even if results aren't immediate. Journal answered prayers to build your faith.
- **Engage Locally**: Pair decrees with community involvement, creating a unified front of faith (Matthew 5:14).

For Prayer Generals

- **Diagnose Strategically**: Identify the enemy's tactics in your region—division, injustice, corruption—and select decrees to counter them, like "I decree that every spirit of division in my community is bound, and unity prevails" (#5).
- **Activate Angels**: Use decrees like "I declare that my prayers shift the spiritual atmosphere, bringing Heaven's influence to my nation" (#10) to engage heavenly forces (Hebrews 1:14).
- **Lead with Authority**: As a general, you're not just praying; you're commanding. Speak, "I decree that the body of Christ in my region unites, advancing God's Kingdom with power" (#13), with apostolic boldness.
- **Intercede for Legacy**: Use decrees like "I declare that my local schools and institutions are filled with God's wisdom and righteousness" (#12) to secure blessings for future generations.

Practical Steps

- **Create a Prayer Space**: Find a quiet place to focus, inviting the Holy Spirit to anoint your words.
- **Speak Daily**: Declare 5–10 decrees each morning or night, personalizing them (e.g., insert your city's name in "I decree that [city] becomes a hub of God's glory" [#15]).
- **Combine with Worship**: Pair decrees with praise, amplifying their

power (Psalm 149:6-9). Sing or lift your hands to magnify God.
- **Live the Decrees**: Align your actions with your words. If you decree revival, share the gospel (Acts 1:8). If you declare justice, advocate for righteousness (Isaiah 61:8).

The Eternal Impact of Community and National Transformation

The stakes are eternal. A transformed community and nation are not just temporal victories; they're generational triumphs, a ripple effect that reshapes families, societies, and the world. When you declare, "I decree that revival fire sweeps through my community, awakening hearts to the Kingdom of God" (#1), you're not only securing your region but planting seeds for a legacy of faith (Habakkuk 3:2). When you proclaim, "I decree that my community becomes a hub of God's glory, drawing souls to salvation" (#15), you're aligning your land with God's eternal purposes, breaking cycles of darkness and building altars of light.

For new believers, this chapter is a gateway to experiencing God's power. You may start with a simple decree, like "I declare that my community is a sanctuary of peace, free from violence and oppression" (#8), and see God shift an atmosphere. That small victory will ignite your faith, showing you the authority you carry in Christ (Luke 10:19). For generals, this chapter is a strategic blueprint. You recognize that communities and nations are warfare domains, divine strongholds to confront the enemy's schemes. Decrees like "I declare that my nation turns to God, experiencing a great awakening of faith and repentance" (#14) empower you to lead with prophetic insight, transforming your region into a hub of God's glory (Isaiah 60:1).

A Call to Rise

Community and National Transformation is where the battle for revival begins and the victory is won. It's where you declare, "I decree that revival fire sweeps through my community, awakening hearts to the Kingdom of God" (#1), and watch Heaven respond. It's where you stand, as a new believer or a general, and proclaim, "I decree that my community becomes a hub of God's glory, drawing souls to salvation" (#15), knowing the enemy trembles at your voice. This chapter is not just a tool; it's a mandate, a divine commission to fortify your region, reset its destiny, and establish God's Kingdom through transformation.

For those new to prayer, start here. Speak these decrees with faith, and God will honor your trust, building your community on the rock of His Word (Matthew 7:24). For generals, lead here. Wield these proclamations with apostolic authority, knowing your region is a warfare unit, co-creating with God to shift generations (Ephesians 3:20). The enemy may rage, but the glory of God prevails (Psalm 94:16). Rise, declare, and watch your community and nation become a fortress of revival, a testimony of transformation, and a legacy of God's unending power.

Community and National Transformation Prayer

Morning Warfare Prayer Points: Igniting Divine Revival

My Father, my God, I take authority over my community; let Your revival ignite us, in Jesus' name. Father, let every spirit of division refuse to fracture our unity today. Lord, I command every corrupt scheme to be null and void, in Jesus' name. My Father, my God, I pull down every demonic plot hindering our transformation. Father, I dismantle every generational injustice; our land is free, in Jesus' name. Lord, unite Your church with Your love; let revival overtake us. My Father, my God, establish righteousness in our nation; guide our leaders. Father, let Your angels war for our renewal, guarding our revival. Lord, thank You for Your fire; our community testifies of Your justice. Father, anoint us with unity; let our nation shine with Your glory, in Jesus' name. Amen.

Word Count: ~220 words

Scriptures: Habakkuk 3:2, Psalm 89:14, John 17:21, Galatians 3:13, 2 Chronicles 7:14

Community and National Transformation Declarations and Decrees

1. I decree that revival fire sweeps through my community, awakening hearts to the Kingdom of God (Habakkuk 3:2).
2. I declare that justice and righteousness prevail in my nation, aligning it with God's purposes (Psalm 89:14).
3. I decree that my church rises as a beacon of truth, impacting our city with God's love (Matthew 5:14).
4. I declare that godly leaders are raised up in my nation, governing with wisdom and integrity (Proverbs 29:2).
5. I decree that every spirit of division in my community is bound, and unity prevails (1 Corinthians 1:10).
6. I declare that the gospel spreads like wildfire in my region, transforming lives for Christ (Acts 1:8).
7. I decree that economic and social injustices in my nation are overturned by God's divine order (Isaiah 61:8).
8. I declare that my community is a sanctuary of peace, free from violence and oppression (Psalm 72:7).
9. I decree that the youth in my city are delivered from deception, embracing God's truth (Psalm 144:12).
10. I declare that my prayers shift the spiritual atmosphere, bringing Heaven's influence to my nation (2 Chronicles 7:14).
11. I decree that corruption and wickedness in high places are exposed and dismantled (Psalm 94:16).
12. I declare that my local schools and institutions are filled with God's wisdom and righteousness (Proverbs 22:6).
13. I decree that the body of Christ in my region unites, advancing God's Kingdom with power (John 17:21).
14. I declare that my nation turns to God, experiencing a great awakening of faith and repentance (Joel 2:12-13).
15. I decree that my community becomes a hub of God's glory, drawing souls to salvation (Isaiah 60:1).

Chapter 16: Freedom from Fear and Anxiety

The Divine Peace That Conquers All

In God's eternal design, your heart and mind are created to dwell in His perfect peace, unshaken by the storms of life (Philippians 4:7). **Chapter 16: Freedom from Fear and Anxiety** is a spiritual armory, equipped with 15 Spirit-inspired declarations and decrees to break the chains of fear, silence anxious thoughts, and anchor your soul in God's unshakable calm. Rooted in the unyielding promise of 2 Timothy 1:7—"For God has not given us a spirit of fear, but of power, love, and a sound mind"—this chapter empowers you to declare your mind a fortress of divine peace, casting out every torment and aligning your heart with Heaven's tranquility.

The enemy wields fear and anxiety as weapons to paralyze your faith, disrupt your peace, and hinder your purpose (1 Peter 5:8). Yet, God has not left you defenseless. These 15 decrees, forged in the fire of divine revelation and apostolic authority, are your weapons to dismantle fear-based strongholds, renew your mind, and co-create with God a legacy of fearless faith (Psalm 23:4). From overcoming dread to resting in God's promises, from rejecting worry to embracing divine courage, this chapter equips you to stand as a warrior of peace, declaring, "Not on my watch will fear prevail!"

Why Freedom from Fear and Anxiety Matter

Freedom from fear and anxiety is not a mere comfort; it is a divine mandate, the foundation of a life that trusts God's sovereignty. When God created you, He designed your mind to be a temple of His peace, guarded by His presence (Isaiah 26:3). A fearless believer is a threat to the enemy's agenda, for they walk in boldness, fulfill God's calling, and reflect His strength. Conversely, fear and anxiety are footholds for the adversary, fostering doubt, paralysis, and unrest. **Freedom from Fear and Anxiety** is foundational to this book because without inner peace, your ability to thrive in other areas—relationships, discernment, or transformation—is compromised. As John 16:33 declares, "In me you may have peace. In this world you will have trouble. But take heart! I have overcome the world."

For those new to prayer, this chapter is an accessible entry point. The decrees are seeds of faith, requiring only your voice and trust to cultivate peace and courage. Speak them as a beginner, and God will honor your faith with calm (Mark 11:24). For prayer generals, this chapter is an apostolic mandate, a call to wield your authority as a king and priest (Revelation 1:6) to break fear's grip, reset your mind's tranquility, and establish your life as a warfare unit (Ephesians 6:12). Every decree is a sword, cutting through the enemy's torments and planting promises that restore peace. Whether you're a novice or a seasoned intercessor, this chapter is vital, for peace is where faith is anchored, courage is ignited, and God's calm transforms lives.

The Power of Targeted Decrees

Just as a physician prescribes a specific remedy for a specific ailment—no antacid for a headache, no dental visit for a stomachache—battles over fear and anxiety demand precise, targeted weapons. The 15 decrees in **Freedom from Fear and Anxiety** are tailored to address the unique torments troubling your soul. Are you gripped by fear? Declare, "I decree that the spirit of fear is cast out of my mind, replaced by God's perfect love" (#1). Plagued by anxious thoughts? Proclaim, "I decree that every anxious thought is taken captive, submitting to the truth of God's Word" (#3). Seeking restful sleep? Decree, "I decree that my sleep is peaceful, undisturbed by anxious thoughts or nightmares" (#11). Each proclamation is a divine prescription, anointed to hit the root of your unrest, aligning your heart with God's promise of peace.

These decrees are not mere words; they are creative forces, carrying the authority of Heaven to shift realities. Proverbs 18:21 reminds us, "Death and life are in the power of the tongue." When you speak these decrees, you partner with the Holy Spirit, activating the blood of Jesus to cover your mind (Revelation 12:11) and angels to war on your behalf (Psalm 103:20). For new believers, this is a revelation: your voice, though untrained, is a weapon when aligned with God's Word. For generals, it's a reminder of your apostolic charge to co-create with God, resetting your peace with every proclamation (Ephesians 3:20). The decrees are your tools to conquer, restore, and anchor, ensuring your heart and mind stand as testimonies of God's calm.

A Heart Under Siege

The enemy's assault on your peace is relentless. Fear of failure, rejection, and the unknown seeks to paralyze your faith, while anxiety and worry aim to rob your rest. Yet, God's Word is clear: "Do not fear, for I am with you; do not be dismayed, for I am your God" (Isaiah 41:10). The decrees in this chapter confront these attacks head-on, addressing specific needs:

- **Freedom from Fear**: Decrees like "I decree that the spirit of fear is cast out of my mind, replaced by God's perfect love" (#1) and "I decree that fear of failure, rejection, or the unknown has no hold on me, for God is my strength" (#5) break fear's grip.
- **Calm Amid Anxiety**: Proclamations such as "I declare that my heart is anchored in God's peace, free from worry and anxiety" (#2) and "I decree that every anxious thought is taken captive, submitting to the truth of God's Word" (#3) silence unrest.
- **Restful Peace**: Decrees like "I decree that my sleep is peaceful, undisturbed by anxious thoughts or nightmares" (#11) and "I declare that God's presence surrounds me, dispelling every trace of fear" (#12) ensure tranquil rest.
- **Bold Faith**: Decrees like "I declare that I am clothed in God's courage, facing every challenge with faith" (#8) and "I decree that I live in the joy of the Lord, overcoming fear with His strength" (#15) ignite fearless trust.

For those new to prayer, these decrees are simple to speak, requiring only faith to see God move. Imagine planting a seed in fertile soil—each word you utter is a seed of peace, watered by trust, that grows into a harvest of calm. For generals, these decrees are strategic, apostolic weapons, enabling you to exercise dominion (Genesis 1:28) and reset your mind's trajectory. You're not just praying; you're commanding, aligning earth with Heaven, and establishing a legacy of peace that echoes through generations.

The Apostolic Call to Freedom from Fear and Anxiety

As an apostle, I've seen the enemy's tactics firsthand—fear paralyzing hearts, anxiety stealing rest, and worry binding destinies. But I've also witnessed the power of God's Word to break what torments, restore what was lost, and redeem what was shaken (Psalm 34:4). **Freedom from Fear and Anxiety** is not optional; it's foundational. Without inner peace, your ability to fulfill God's purposes is limited. A peaceful heart stands firm (John 16:33), but a fearful one struggles to shine. This chapter is your apostolic mandate to take up your authority as a king and priest (Revelation 1:6), declaring God's promises over your mind with unwavering faith.

For new believers, this chapter is an invitation to step into your God-given authority. You may feel inexperienced, but your voice, when aligned with these decrees, carries the weight of Heaven. Speak, "I declare that my mind is guarded by the peace of God, unshaken by life's uncertainties" (#6), and trust God to honor your faith. For generals, this chapter is a call to strategic warfare. You understand that fear and anxiety are battlefields, divine domains to confront the enemy's schemes (Ephesians 6:12). Decrees like "I decree that every fear-based stronghold in my life is shattered by God's truth" (#9) and "I declare that my future is secure in God's hands, free from anxiety's grip" (#14) empower you to lead with apostolic precision, breaking cycles of torment and building legacies of peace.

Practical Application for All

Freedom from Fear and Anxiety is a chapter for every believer, from the novice to the general, because every heart faces fear, and every mind needs God's peace. Here's how to engage with this chapter:

For Those New to Prayer

- **Start Simple**: Choose one or two decrees that resonate with your struggles, such as "I declare that I trust in God's sovereignty, casting all my cares upon Him" (#10). Speak them daily, aloud, with faith.
- **Trust God's Word**: You don't need experience; you need trust. Hebrews 11:6 says, "Without faith it is impossible to please Him." Your words, backed by Scripture, are powerful.
- **Expect Results**: Like a patient taking medicine, trust that each decree is working, even if results aren't immediate. Journal answered prayers to build your faith.
- **Rest in God**: Pair decrees with trust, creating a unified front of faith (Psalm 23:4).

For Prayer Generals

- **Diagnose Strategically**: Identify the enemy's tactics in your

mind—fear, worry, doubt—and select decrees to counter them, like "I decree that I rest in God's promises, free from the torment of fear and doubt" (#7).
- **Activate Angels**: Use decrees like "I declare that God's presence surrounds me, dispelling every trace of fear" (#12) to engage heavenly forces (Hebrews 1:14).
- **Lead with Authority**: As a general, you're not just praying; you're commanding. Speak, "I decree that I live in the joy of the Lord, overcoming fear with His strength" (#15), with apostolic boldness.
- **Intercede for Legacy**: Use decrees like "I declare that my future is secure in God's hands, free from anxiety's grip" (#14) to secure blessings for future generations.

Practical Steps

- **Create a Prayer Space**: Find a quiet place to focus, inviting the Holy Spirit to anoint your words.
- **Speak Daily**: Declare 5–10 decrees each morning or night, personalizing them (e.g., insert your name in "I declare that [name] walks in boldness, trusting God's protection" [#4]).
- **Combine with Worship**: Pair decrees with praise, amplifying their power (Psalm 149:6-9). Sing or lift your hands to magnify God.
- **Live the Decrees**: Align your actions with your words. If you decree peace, reject worry (Matthew 6:34). If you declare courage, face challenges boldly (Joshua 1:9).

The Eternal Impact of Freedom from Fear and Anxiety

The stakes are eternal. A heart free from fear is not just a personal victory; it's a generational triumph, a ripple effect that transforms families, communities, and nations. When you declare, "I decree that the spirit of fear is cast out of my mind, replaced by God's perfect love" (#1), you're not only securing your peace but planting seeds for a legacy of courage (Psalm 27:1). When you proclaim, "I decree that I live in the joy of the Lord, overcoming fear with His strength" (#15), you're aligning your mind with God's eternal purposes, breaking cycles of torment and building altars of tranquility.

For new believers, this chapter is a gateway to experiencing God's power. You may start with a simple decree, like "I declare that my mind is guarded by the peace of God, unshaken by life's uncertainties" (#6), and see God calm a storm. That small victory will ignite your faith, showing you the authority you carry in Christ (Luke 10:19). For generals, this chapter is a strategic blueprint. You recognize that fear and anxiety are warfare domains, divine strongholds to confront the enemy's schemes. Decrees like "I declare that I am clothed in God's courage, facing every challenge with faith" (#8) empower you to lead with prophetic insight, transforming your life into a hub of God's peace (Nehemiah 8:10).

A Call to Rise

Freedom from Fear and Anxiety is where the battle for peace begins and the victory is won. It's where you declare, "I decree that the spirit of fear is cast out of my mind, replaced by God's perfect love" (#1), and watch Heaven respond. It's where you stand, as a new believer or a general, and proclaim, "I decree that I live in the joy of the Lord, overcoming fear with His strength" (#15), knowing the enemy trembles at your voice. This chapter is not just a tool; it's a mandate, a divine commission to fortify your heart, reset your mind, and establish God's Kingdom through your peace.

For those new to prayer, start here. Speak these decrees with faith, and God will honor your trust, building your peace on the rock of His Word (Matthew 7:24). For generals, lead here. Wield these proclamations with apostolic authority, knowing your mind is a warfare unit, co-creating with God to shift generations (Ephesians 3:20). The enemy may rage, but the peace of God prevails (Psalm 46:1). Rise, declare, and watch your heart become a fortress of tranquility, a testimony of courage, and a legacy of God's unending calm.

Freedom from Fear and Anxiety

Morning Warfare Prayer Points: Securing Divine Peace

My Father, my God, I take authority over my heart; let Your peace free me, in Jesus' name. Father, let every spirit of fear refuse to grip my mind today. Lord, I command every anxious thought to be null and void, in Jesus' name. My Father, my God, I pull down every demonic plot stirring my unrest. Father, I dismantle every generational worry; my bloodline is calm, in Jesus' name. Lord, anchor my soul with Your love; let tranquility overtake me. My Father, my God, cover my rest with Your calm; guide my peace. Father, let Your angels guard my heart, ensuring my freedom. Lord, thank You for Your comfort; my life testifies of Your peace. Father, anoint me with courage; let my heart shine with Your glory, in Jesus' name. Amen.

Word Count: ~220 words

Scriptures: 2 Timothy 1:7, Philippians 4:6-7, Psalm 46:1, Galatians 3:13, Psalm 34:4

Freedom from Fear and Anxiety

1. I decree that the spirit of fear is cast out of my mind, replaced by God's perfect love (2 Timothy 1:7).
2. I declare that my heart is anchored in God's peace, free from worry and anxiety (Philippians 4:6-7).
3. I decree that every anxious thought is taken captive, submitting to the truth of God's Word (2 Corinthians 10:5).
4. I declare that I walk in boldness, trusting God's protection over every area of my life (Psalm 27:1).
5. I decree that fear of failure, rejection, or the unknown has no hold on me, for God is my strength (Isaiah 41:10).
6. I declare that my mind is guarded by the peace of God, unshaken by life's uncertainties (John 16:33).
7. I decree that I rest in God's promises, free from the torment of fear and doubt (Psalm 23:4).
8. I declare that I am clothed in God's courage, facing every challenge with faith (Joshua 1:9).
9. I decree that every fear-based stronghold in my life is shattered by God's truth (Psalm 34:4).
10. I declare that I trust in God's sovereignty, casting all my cares upon Him (1 Peter 5:7).
11. I decree that my sleep is peaceful, undisturbed by anxious thoughts or nightmares (Psalm 4:8).
12. I declare that God's presence surrounds me, dispelling every trace of fear (Psalm 46:1).
13. I decree that I am delivered from the spirit of worry, walking in confident faith (Matthew 6:34).
14. I declare that my future is secure in God's hands, free from anxiety's grip (Jeremiah 29:11).
15. I decree that I live in the joy of the Lord, overcoming fear with His strength (Nehemiah 8:10).

Chapter 17: Intercession for Others

The Divine Call to Stand in the Gap

In God's eternal design, intercession is a sacred calling, a powerful act of love that lifts others before His throne and shifts destinies through prayer (1 Timothy 2:1). **Chapter 17: Intercession for Others** is a spiritual armory, equipped with 15 Spirit-inspired declarations and decrees to intercede for the salvation, healing, and breakthrough of those around you. Rooted in the unyielding promise of James 5:16—"The prayer of a righteous person is powerful and effective"—this chapter empowers you to declare God's transformative power over others' lives, breaking every chain and aligning their paths with Heaven's purposes.

The enemy seeks to bind those you love with unbelief, sickness, and oppression, aiming to thwart God's redemptive plan for them (John 10:10). Yet, God has not left you defenseless. These 15 decrees, forged in the fire of divine revelation and apostolic authority, are your weapons to stand in the gap, release divine intervention, and co-create with God a legacy of answered prayers (Job 42:10). From praying for the lost to uplifting leaders, from breaking generational curses to opening doors for others, this chapter equips you to stand as an intercessor of God's heart, declaring, "Not on my watch will the enemy prevail over those I pray for!"

Why Intercession for Others Matters

Intercession is not a secondary act; it is a divine mandate, the expression of Christ's love through prayer for others. When God called you, He made you a priest, entrusted to intercede for those in need (1 Peter 2:9). An interceding believer is a threat to the enemy's agenda, for they shift spiritual atmospheres, secure breakthroughs, and advance God's Kingdom. Conversely, neglecting intercession leaves others vulnerable to the adversary's attacks, perpetuating bondage and despair. **Intercession for Others** is foundational to this book because without standing in the gap, your ability to impact other areas—community, healing, or discernment—is limited. As Acts 16:31 declares, "Believe in the Lord Jesus, and you will be saved—you and your household."

For those new to prayer, this chapter is an accessible entry point. The decrees are seeds of faith, requiring only your voice and trust to cultivate miracles for others. Speak them as a beginner, and God will honor your faith with answers (Mark 11:24). For prayer generals, this chapter is an apostolic mandate, a call to wield your authority as a king and priest (Revelation 1:6) to break strongholds over others, reset their destinies, and establish your prayers as a warfare unit (Ephesians 6:12). Every decree is a sword, cutting through the enemy's schemes and planting promises that transform lives. Whether you're a novice or a seasoned intercessor, this chapter is vital, for intercession is where faith is extended, love is activated, and God's power changes destinies.

The Power of Targeted Decrees

Just as a physician prescribes a specific remedy for a specific ailment—no antacid for a headache, no dental visit for a stomachache—intercession for others demands precise, targeted weapons. The 15 decrees in **Intercession for Others** are tailored to address the unique needs of those you pray for. Are loved ones far from God? Declare, "I decree that my unsaved loved ones encounter the saving grace of Jesus Christ" (#1). Are others battling sickness? Proclaim, "I decree that the sick I lift up are healed by the stripes of Jesus" (#11). Need breakthroughs for those in crisis? Decree, "I declare that those in crisis receive divine intervention and breakthrough through my intercession" (#4). Each proclamation is a divine prescription, anointed to hit the root of their struggle, aligning their lives with God's redemptive power.

These decrees are not mere words; they are creative forces, carrying the authority of Heaven to shift realities. Proverbs 18:21 reminds us, "Death and life are in the power of the tongue." When you speak these decrees, you partner with the Holy Spirit, activating the blood of Jesus to cover those you pray for (Revelation 12:11) and angels to war on their behalf (Hebrews 1:14). For new believers, this is a revelation: your voice, though untrained, is a weapon when aligned with God's Word. For generals, it's a reminder of your apostolic charge to co-create with God, resetting others' destinies with every proclamation (Ephesians 3:20). The decrees are your tools to intercede, deliver, and transform, ensuring your prayers stand as testimonies of God's faithfulness.

A World Under Siege

The enemy's assault on those you love is relentless. Unbelief binds souls, sickness afflicts bodies, and oppression torments spirits, all designed to derail God's plan for them. Yet, God's Word is clear: "The Lord is close to the brokenhearted and saves those who are crushed in spirit" (Psalm 34:18). The decrees in this chapter confront these attacks head-on, addressing specific needs:

- **Salvation and Restoration**: Decrees like "I decree that my unsaved loved ones encounter the saving grace of Jesus Christ" (#1) and "I decree that the prodigals I pray for return to God, restored to their divine purpose" (#5) seek eternal life and renewal.
- **Healing and Deliverance**: Proclamations such as "I declare that God's healing power flows over those I pray for, restoring their bodies and minds" (#2) and "I declare that the oppressed and afflicted I intercede for are delivered by God's mighty hand" (#6) release divine intervention.
- **Breakthrough and Provision**: Decrees like "I declare that those in crisis receive divine intervention and breakthrough through my intercession" (#4) and "I decree that my prayers release financial provision for those in need, meeting their every lack" (#7) secure

practical help.
- **Protection and Destiny**: Decrees like "I declare that the children I pray for are shielded from harm and grow in God's truth" (#8) and "I decree that my prayers shift destinies, aligning others with God's perfect will" (#15) guard and guide.

For those new to prayer, these decrees are simple to speak, requiring only faith to see God move. Imagine planting a seed in fertile soil—each word you utter is a seed of intercession, watered by trust, that grows into a harvest of miracles. For generals, these decrees are strategic, apostolic weapons, enabling you to exercise dominion (Genesis 1:28) and reset others' trajectories. You're not just praying; you're commanding, aligning earth with Heaven, and establishing a legacy of answered prayers that echoes through generations.

The Apostolic Call to Intercession for Others

As an apostle, I've seen the enemy's tactics firsthand—unbelief binding souls, affliction stealing health, and oppression crushing spirits. But I've also witnessed the power of intercession to break what binds, restore what was lost, and redeem what was stolen (Romans 15:30). **Intercession for Others** is not optional; it's foundational. Without standing in the gap, the destinies of those you love remain vulnerable. An interceding life stands firm (Ephesians 3:20), but a silent one struggles to shine. This chapter is your apostolic mandate to take up your authority as a king and priest (Revelation 1:6), declaring God's promises over others with unwavering faith.

For new believers, this chapter is an invitation to step into your God-given authority. You may feel inexperienced, but your voice, when aligned with these decrees, carries the weight of Heaven. Speak, "I declare that the brokenhearted I intercede for are comforted by God's presence" (#13), and trust God to honor your faith. For generals, this chapter is a call to strategic warfare. You understand that intercession is a battlefield, a divine domain to confront the enemy's schemes (Ephesians 6:12). Decrees like "I declare that my intercession breaks generational curses over those I pray for, setting them free" (#10) and "I declare that my intercession activates angelic assistance for those in spiritual battles" (#14) empower you to lead with apostolic precision, breaking cycles of bondage and building legacies of breakthrough.

Practical Application for All

Intercession for Others is a chapter for every believer, from the novice to the general, because every life touches others, and every soul needs God's intervention. Here's how to engage with this chapter:

For Those New to Prayer

- **Start Simple**: Choose one or two decrees that resonate with those you pray for, such as "I declare that the children I pray for are shielded from harm and grow in God's truth" (#8). Speak them daily, aloud, with faith.
- **Trust God's Word**: You don't need experience; you need trust. Hebrews 11:6 says, "Without faith it is impossible to please Him." Your words, backed by Scripture, are powerful.
- **Expect Results**: Like a patient taking medicine, trust that each decree is working, even if results aren't immediate. Journal answered prayers to build your faith.
- **Pray with Love**: Pair decrees with compassion, creating a unified front of faith (1 Corinthians 13:1).

For Prayer Generals

- **Diagnose Strategically**: Identify the enemy's tactics in others' lives—unbelief, sickness, crisis—and select decrees to counter them, like "I decree that the sick I lift up are healed by the stripes of Jesus"

(#11).
- **Activate Angels**: Use decrees like "I declare that my intercession activates angelic assistance for those in spiritual battles" (#14) to engage heavenly forces (Hebrews 1:14).
- **Lead with Authority**: As a general, you're not just praying; you're commanding. Speak, "I decree that my prayers shift destinies, aligning others with God's perfect will" (#15), with apostolic boldness.
- **Intercede for Legacy**: Use decrees like "I declare that missionaries and ministers I support are strengthened and empowered for their calling" (#9) to secure blessings for future generations.

Practical Steps

- **Create a Prayer Space**: Find a quiet place to focus, inviting the Holy Spirit to anoint your words.
- **Speak Daily**: Declare 5–10 decrees each morning or night, personalizing them (e.g., insert a person's name in "I decree that [name]'s unsaved loved ones encounter the saving grace" [#1]).
- **Combine with Worship**: Pair decrees with praise, amplifying their power (Psalm 149:6-9). Sing or lift your hands to magnify God.
- **Live the Decrees**: Align your actions with your words. If you decree salvation, share the gospel (Romans 10:14). If you declare healing, pray with faith (James 5:15).

The Eternal Impact of Intercession for Others

The stakes are eternal. Intercession is not just a personal act; it's a generational triumph, a ripple effect that transforms families, communities, and nations. When you declare, "I decree that my unsaved loved ones encounter the saving grace of Jesus Christ" (#1), you're not only securing their souls but planting seeds for a legacy of faith (Acts 16:31). When you proclaim, "I decree that my prayers shift destinies, aligning others with God's perfect will" (#15), you're aligning their lives with God's eternal purposes, breaking cycles of bondage and building altars of breakthrough.

For new believers, this chapter is a gateway to experiencing God's power. You may start with a simple decree, like "I declare that the brokenhearted I intercede for are comforted by God's presence" (#13), and see God touch a life. That small victory will ignite your faith, showing you the authority you carry in Christ (Luke 10:19). For generals, this chapter is a strategic blueprint. You recognize that intercession is a warfare domain, a divine stronghold to confront the enemy's schemes. Decrees like "I declare that my intercession breaks generational curses over those I pray for, setting them free" (#10) empower you to lead with prophetic insight, transforming lives into hubs of God's redemption (Ephesians 3:20).

A Call to Rise

Intercession for Others is where the battle for souls begins and the victory is won. It's where you declare, "I decree that my unsaved loved ones encounter the saving grace of Jesus Christ" (#1), and watch Heaven respond. It's where you stand, as a new believer or a general, and proclaim, "I decree that my prayers shift destinies, aligning others with God's perfect will" (#15), knowing the enemy trembles at your voice. This chapter is not just a tool; it's a mandate, a divine commission to fortify others' lives, reset their destinies, and establish God's Kingdom through your prayers.

For those new to prayer, start here. Speak these decrees with faith, and God will honor your trust, building others' lives on the rock of His Word (Matthew 7:24). For generals, lead here. Wield these proclamations with apostolic authority, knowing your intercession is a warfare unit, co-creating with God to shift generations (Ephesians 3:20). The enemy may rage, but the power of God prevails (Psalm 82:4). Rise, declare, and watch your prayers become a fortress of redemption, a testimony of intercession, and a legacy of God's unending love.

Intercession for Others

Morning Warfare Prayer Points: Lifting Souls to Freedom

My Father, my God, I take authority over those I pray for; let Your grace save them, in Jesus' name. Father, let every spirit of unbelief refuse to bind their hearts today. Lord, I command every chain of oppression to be null and void, in Jesus' name. My Father, my God, I pull down every demonic plot hindering their freedom. Father, I dismantle every generational bondage; their bloodlines are free, in Jesus' name. Lord, heal their bodies with Your stripes; let wholeness overtake them. My Father, my God, draw the lost to Your light; guide their souls. Father, let Your angels war for their salvation, guarding their paths. Lord, thank You for Your compassion; my prayers testify of Your love. Father, anoint my intercession with power; let their lives shine with Your glory, in Jesus' name. Amen.

Word Count: ~220 words

Scriptures: James 5:16, Acts 16:31, Isaiah 53:5, Galatians 3:13, Ephesians 3:20

Intercession for Others

1. I decree that my unsaved loved ones encounter the saving grace of Jesus Christ (Acts 16:31).
2. I declare that God's healing power flows over those I pray for, restoring their bodies and minds (James 5:16).
3. I decree that leaders in my sphere are guided by God's wisdom and protected from harm (1 Timothy 2:1-2).
4. I declare that those in crisis receive divine intervention and breakthrough through my intercession (Job 42:10).
5. I decree that the prodigals I pray for return to God, restored to their divine purpose (Luke 15:20).
6. I declare that the oppressed and afflicted I intercede for are delivered by God's mighty hand (Psalm 82:4).
7. I decree that my prayers release financial provision for those in need, meeting their every lack (Philippians 4:19).
8. I declare that the children I pray for are shielded from harm and grow in God's truth (Psalm 127:3-5).
9. I decree that missionaries and ministers I support are strengthened and empowered for their calling (Romans 15:30).
10. I declare that my intercession breaks generational curses over those I pray for, setting them free (Galatians 3:13).
11. I decree that the sick I lift up are healed by the stripes of Jesus (Isaiah 53:5).
12. I declare that my prayers open doors of opportunity for those struggling to advance (Colossians 4:3).
13. I declare that the brokenhearted I intercede for are comforted by God's presence (Psalm 34:18).
14. I declare that my intercession activates angelic assistance for those in spiritual battles (Hebrews 1:14).
15. I decree that my prayers shift destinies, aligning others with God's perfect will (Ephesians 3:20).

Chapter 18: Cross-Category Decrees

The Divine Arsenal for Every Battle

In God's eternal design, every believer is equipped with versatile authority to confront any spiritual battle, from personal struggles to global strongholds, with the power of His Word (Ephesians 6:17). **Chapter 18: Cross-Category Decrees** is a spiritual armory, equipped with 31 Spirit-inspired declarations and decrees to address a wide spectrum of needs, offering flexible proclamations that transcend specific categories. Rooted in the unyielding promise of Isaiah 55:11—"My word that goes out from my mouth... will accomplish what I desire"—this chapter empowers you to declare God's transformative power over any challenge, breaking every barrier and aligning your life with Heaven's victory.

The enemy deploys multifaceted attacks—fear, delay, division, and deception—seeking to disrupt every aspect of your destiny (1 Peter 5:8). Yet, God has not left you defenseless. These 31 decrees, forged in the fire of divine revelation and apostolic authority, are your weapons to confront diverse battles, activate divine breakthroughs, and co-create with God a legacy of comprehensive triumph (Philippians 4:13). From canceling lies to shifting atmospheres, from commanding open doors to releasing generations, this chapter equips you to stand as a versatile warrior, declaring, "Not on my watch will any enemy prevail!"

Why Cross-Category Decrees Matter

Cross-category decrees are not a mere collection of prayers; they are a divine mandate, the ultimate toolkit for addressing the complex, interconnected battles of life. When God called you, He gave you authority to bind and loose across all realms (Matthew 16:19), ensuring no challenge is beyond His reach. A versatile believer is a threat to the enemy's agenda, for they adapt to any battle, secure victories in multiple domains, and reflect God's all-encompassing power. Conversely, a limited approach to spiritual warfare leaves vulnerabilities exposed, allowing the enemy to exploit gaps. **Cross-Category Decrees** is foundational to this book because it provides the flexibility to tackle any issue, enhancing your impact in other areas—family, community, or purpose. As Romans 8:28 declares, "In all things God works for the good of those who love him, who have been called according to his purpose."

For those new to prayer, this chapter is an accessible entry point. The decrees are seeds of faith, requiring only your voice and trust to cultivate breakthroughs across various needs. Speak them as a beginner, and God will honor your faith with results (Mark 11:24). For prayer generals, this chapter is an apostolic mandate, a call to wield your authority as a king and priest (Revelation 1:6) to confront any stronghold, reset any destiny, and establish your prayers as a warfare unit (Ephesians 6:12). Every decree is a sword, cutting through the enemy's schemes and planting promises that secure victory. Whether you're a novice or a seasoned intercessor, this chapter is vital, for versatility is where faith is unleashed, battles are won, and God's power transforms all things.

The Power of Targeted Decrees

Just as a physician prescribes a specific remedy for a specific ailment—no antacid for a headache, no dental visit for a stomachache—spiritual battles demand precise, yet adaptable, weapons. The 31 decrees in **Cross-Category Decrees** are tailored to address a broad range of challenges, offering versatile proclamations for any situation. Facing spiritual resistance? Declare, "I decree that every principality blocking God's promises is bound" (#6). Need a breakthrough in multiple areas? Proclaim, "I decree that my life is shifted financially, spiritually, and relationally" (#7). Seeking to impact others? Decree, "I decree that I release a generation of healing, wealth, and health" (#20). Each proclamation is a divine prescription, anointed to hit the root of diverse struggles, aligning your life with God's all-encompassing victory.

These decrees are not mere words; they are creative forces, carrying the authority of Heaven to shift realities. Proverbs 18:21 reminds us, "Death and life are in the power of the tongue." When you speak these decrees, you partner with the Holy Spirit, activating the blood of Jesus to cover every battle (Revelation 12:11) and angels to war on your behalf (Hebrews 1:14). For new believers, this is a revelation: your voice, though untrained, is a weapon when aligned with God's Word. For generals, it's a reminder of your apostolic charge to co-create with God, resetting destinies with every proclamation (Ephesians 3:20). The decrees are your tools to conquer, shift, and transform, ensuring your battles stand as testimonies of God's limitless power.

A Life Under Siege

The enemy's assault on your life is multifaceted. Principalities block promises, lies sow doubt, and delays hinder progress, all designed to disrupt God's plan across every domain. Yet, God's Word is clear: "I can do all things through Christ who strengthens me" (Philippians 4:13). The decrees in this chapter confront these attacks head-on, addressing a wide range of needs:

- **Spiritual Authority**: Decrees like "I decree that every principality blocking God's promises is bound" (#6) and "I decree that my mouth speaks God's truth, canceling every lie" (#9) assert divine power.
- **Breakthrough and Shift**: Proclamations such as "I decree that my life is shifted financially, spiritually, and relationally" (#7) and "I declare that everywhere I go, I proclaim God's truth" (#17) secure holistic victories.
- **Protection and Victory**: Decrees like "I decree that my mouth cancels every lie and fiery dart" (#19) and "I decree that I refuse to be denied or delayed, defined by God's Word" (#23) guard against attacks.
- **Generational Impact**: Decrees like "I decree that I release a generation of healing, wealth, and health" (#20) and "I decree that I create where there is no way, for God has made a way" (#27) transform legacies.

For those new to prayer, these decrees are simple to speak, requiring only faith to see God move. Imagine planting a seed in fertile soil—each word you utter is a seed of victory, watered by trust, that grows into a harvest of breakthroughs. For generals, these decrees are strategic, apostolic weapons, enabling you to exercise dominion (Genesis 1:28) and reset any trajectory. You're not just praying; you're commanding, aligning earth with Heaven, and establishing a legacy of triumph that echoes through generations.

The Apostolic Call to Cross-Category Decrees

As an apostle, I've seen the enemy's tactics firsthand—principalities blocking progress, lies binding minds, and delays stealing destinies. But I've also witnessed the power of God's Word to break every chain, shift every battle, and redeem every loss (Isaiah 43:19). **Cross-Category Decrees** is not optional; it's foundational. Without versatile authority, your ability to address life's complexities is limited. A multifaceted warrior stands firm (Romans 8:37), but a narrow one struggles to shine. This chapter is your apostolic mandate to take up your authority as a king and priest (Revelation 1:6), declaring God's promises over every challenge with unwavering faith.

For new believers, this chapter is an invitation to step into your God-given authority. You may feel inexperienced, but your voice, when aligned with these decrees, carries the weight of Heaven. Speak, "I declare that I endure in love and truth, even in betrayal" (#13), and trust God to honor your faith. For generals, this chapter is a call to strategic warfare. You understand that life's battles are interconnected, requiring a divine arsenal to confront the enemy's schemes (Ephesians 6:12). Decrees like "I decree that my words manifest everything I say" (#28) and "I decree that every 'no' blocking my blessings turns to a 'yes'" (#31) empower you to lead with apostolic precision, breaking cycles of resistance and building legacies of victory.

Practical Application for All

Cross-Category Decrees is a chapter for every believer, from the novice to the general, because every life faces diverse battles, and every destiny needs God's all-encompassing power. Here's how to engage with this chapter:

For Those New to Prayer

- **Start Simple**: Choose one or two decrees that resonate with your needs, such as "I declare that my zeal burns for the Lord and souls" (#14). Speak them daily, aloud, with faith.
- **Trust God's Word**: You don't need experience; you need trust. Hebrews 11:6 says, "Without faith it is impossible to please Him." Your words, backed by Scripture, are powerful.
- **Expect Results**: Like a patient taking medicine, trust that each decree is working, even if results aren't immediate. Journal answered prayers to build your faith.
- **Act in Faith**: Pair decrees with action, creating a unified front of faith (James 2:26).

For Prayer Generals

- **Diagnose Strategically**: Identify the enemy's tactics across your battles—resistance, lies, delays—and select decrees to counter them, like "I decree that every altar of oppression is torn down as I praise" (#11).
- **Activate Angels**: Use decrees like "I decree that my angels bring everything I need to succeed" (#5) to engage heavenly forces (Hebrews 1:14).
- **Lead with Authority**: As a general, you're not just praying; you're commanding. Speak, "I decree that I command doors to open in every closed area" (#30), with apostolic boldness.
- **Intercede for Legacy**: Use decrees like "I decree that I release a generation of healing, wealth, and health" (#20) to secure blessings for future generations.

Practical Steps

- **Create a Prayer Space**: Find a quiet place to focus, inviting the Holy Spirit to anoint your words.
- **Speak Daily**: Declare 5–10 decrees each morning or night, personalizing them (e.g., insert your name in "I decree that [name] stands strong and does not waver" [#3]).
- **Combine with Worship**: Pair decrees with praise, amplifying their power (Psalm 149:6-9). Sing or lift your hands to magnify God.
- **Live the Decrees**: Align your actions with your words. If you decree breakthrough, pursue God's promises (Matthew 7:7). If you declare truth, reject lies (Ephesians 6:14).

The Eternal Impact of Cross-Category Decrees

The stakes are eternal. A life victorious in every battle is not just a personal triumph; it's a generational legacy, a ripple effect that transforms families, communities, and nations. When you declare, "I decree that God's promises manifest as I release His words" (#8), you're not only securing your victory but planting seeds for a legacy of faith (Isaiah 55:11). When you proclaim, "I decree that every 'no' blocking my blessings turns to a 'yes'" (#31), you're aligning your battles with God's eternal purposes, breaking cycles of resistance and building altars of triumph.

For new believers, this chapter is a gateway to experiencing God's power. You may start with a simple decree, like "I declare that my mouth, hands, and feet bring restoration" (#16), and see God move in a situation. That small victory will ignite your faith, showing you the authority you carry in Christ (Luke 10:19). For generals, this chapter is a strategic blueprint. You recognize that life's battles are diverse, requiring versatile decrees to confront the enemy's schemes. Decrees like "I decree that I create where there is no way, for God has made a way" (#27) empower you to lead with prophetic insight, transforming your life into a hub of God's victory (Romans 8:28).

A Call to Rise

Cross-Category Decrees is where the battle for total victory begins and the triumph is won. It's where you declare, "I decree that every principality blocking God's promises is bound" (#6), and watch Heaven respond. It's where you stand, as a new believer or a general, and proclaim, "I decree that every 'no' blocking my blessings turns to a 'yes'" (#31), knowing the enemy trembles at your voice. This chapter is not just a tool; it's a mandate, a divine commission to fortify every area of your life, reset every destiny, and establish God's Kingdom through your proclamations.

For those new to prayer, start here. Speak these decrees with faith, and God will honor your trust, building your victory on the rock of His Word (Matthew 7:24). For generals, lead here. Wield these proclamations with apostolic authority, knowing your life is a warfare unit, co-creating with God to shift generations (Ephesians 3:20). The enemy may rage, but the power of God prevails (Mark 11:23). Rise, declare, and watch your life become a fortress of triumph, a testimony of versatility, and a legacy of God's unending glory.

Cross-Category Decrees

Morning Warfare Prayer Points: Wielding Divine Authority

My Father, my God, I take authority over my battles; let Your truth empower me, in Jesus' name. Father, let every spirit of defeat refuse to hinder my victory today. Lord, I command every obstacle to my breakthrough to be null and void, in Jesus' name. My Father, my God, I pull down every demonic plot blocking my progress. Father, I dismantle every generational limitation; my bloodline triumphs, in Jesus' name. Lord, align my life with Your promises; let success overtake me. My Father, my God, anoint my voice to shift circumstances; guide my steps. Father, let Your angels war for my victories, guarding my path. Lord, thank You for Your power; my life testifies of Your triumph. Father, anoint me with authority; let my stand shine with Your glory, in Jesus' name. Amen.

Word Count: ~220 words

Scriptures: Isaiah 55:11, Romans 8:28, Psalm 24:7, Galatians 3:13, Psalm 138:3

Cross-Category Decrees

1. I decree that I hear God's call clearly and run without weariness (Isaiah 40:31).
2. I decree that I run this race and do not grow weary (Hebrews 12:1).
3. I decree that I stand strong and do not waver (James 1:6).
4. I decree that I speak the truth in love (Ephesians 4:15).
5. I decree that my angels bring everything I need to succeed (Hebrews 1:14).
6. I decree that every principality blocking God's promises is bound (Ephesians 6:12).
7. I decree that my life is shifted financially, spiritually, and relationally (Romans 8:28).
8. I decree that God's promises manifest as I release His words (Isaiah 55:11).
9. I decree that my mouth speaks God's truth, canceling every lie (Ephesians 6:17).
10. I decree that divine strategies and wisdom lift my heart (Proverbs 3:5-6).
11. I decree that every altar of oppression is torn down as I praise (Psalm 149:6-9).
12. I decree that my praise breaks every chain and hindrance (Acts 16:25-26).
13. I declare that I endure in love and truth, even in betrayal (John 13:34).
14. I declare that my zeal burns for the Lord and souls (Romans 12:11).
15. I declare that the fire of evangelism burns within me (Mark 16:15).
16. I declare that my mouth, hands, and feet bring restoration (Isaiah 61:4).
17. I declare that everywhere I go, I proclaim God's truth (Matthew 10:7).
18. I decree that I belong to Jesus, and nothing separates me from His love (Romans 8:38-39).
19. I decree that my mouth cancels every lie and fiery dart (Ephesians

6:16).
20. I decree that I release a generation of healing, wealth, and health (Joel 2:28).
21. I decree that I am brought out of darkness into God's light (Colossians 1:13).
22. I decree that I cancel every idle word and thought against me (Matthew 12:36).
23. I decree that I refuse to be denied or delayed, defined by God's Word (Psalm 119:89).
24. I decree that I acknowledge God in all my ways, and He directs my path (Proverbs 3:6).
25. I decree that I never lack, for God's promises are true (Numbers 23:19).
26. I decree that I cast down insecurities and seek God first (Matthew 6:33).
27. I decree that I create where there is no way, for God has made a way (Isaiah 43:19).
28. I decree that my words manifest everything I say (Mark 11:23).
29. I decree that I break all limitations spoken over my life (Isaiah 10:27).
30. I decree that I command doors to open in every closed area (Psalm 24:7).
31. I decree that every "no" blocking my blessings turns to a "yes" (Matthew 7:7).

Complete List of Declarations and Decrees: Arsenal: Prayers, Declarations, and Decrees That Will Move Heaven and Shake Hell

Below is the complete list of 323 declarations and decrees from *Arsenal: Prayers, Declarations, and Decrees That Will Move Heaven and Shake Hell*, numbered sequentially from 1 to 323, organized by chapter. Each decree includes its original chapter number and scripture reference, as provided in the manuscript.

Chapter 1: Family Restoration (Decrees 1–51)

1. I decree that my children excel in wisdom, favor, and understanding (Proverbs 4:7).
2. I decree that scholarships, favor, and supernatural opportunities manifest in my children's lives (Psalm 5:12).
3. I decree that my descendants are mighty in the land (Psalm 112:2).
4. I decree that my children and grandchildren walk in divine favor and success (Deuteronomy 28:11).
5. I decree that no weapon formed against my children prospers (Isaiah 54:17).
6. I decree that every spirit of rebellion is broken off my bloodline (Ephesians 6:12).
7. I decree that my marriage is strengthened by love, patience, wisdom, and mutual respect (Ephesians 5:33).
8. I decree that every attack against my marriage is overturned by God's power (Psalm 18:2).
9. I decree that communication is restored in my marriage (Colossians 4:6).
10. I decree that every wall of division in my marriage is torn down (Ephesians 2:14).
11. I decree that covenant blessings flow in my marriage and family line (Deuteronomy 7:9).
12. I decree that my family is covered by the blood of Jesus, becoming a testimony of God's power, love, and faithfulness (Revelation 12:11).

13. I decree that every breach in my family is repaired, and every broken heart is mended (Psalm 147:3).
14. I decree that my children are called into the kingdom of light, living healthy and happy lives dedicated to God (Colossians 1:13).
15. I decree that no matter how far my children have strayed, God brings them back to worship and praise Him (Luke 15:20).
16. I decree that my family walks in unity, peace, and divine love, serving the Lord wholeheartedly (Psalm 133:1).
17. I declare that as for me and my house, we serve the Lord (Joshua 24:15).
18. I declare unity, peace, and divine love over my household (John 17:21).
19. I declare that my family walks in covenant with the Most High God (Genesis 17:7).
20. I declare restoration over every broken relationship in my family (Joel 2:25).
21. I declare freedom and divine health over my descendants (3 John 1:2).
22. I declare that my family leaves a legacy of righteousness (Proverbs 13:22).
23. I declare that my descendants possess the gates of their enemies (Genesis 22:17).
24. I declare that generational wealth, wisdom, and favor flow through my family (Deuteronomy 28:8).
25. I declare that my family fulfills every divine purpose and assignment (Jeremiah 1:5).
26. I declare that, by the blood and promise of Jesus Christ, I am the seed of Abraham, progressing and going forth (Galatians 3:29).
27. I receive the blessing of Abraham in my life and my children's lives (Galatians 3:14).
28. I decree that no spirit of darkness takes my children; they live healthy and happy lives (Psalm 91:10).
29. I decree that my children live long, healthy lives, free from curses (Psalm 91:16).
30. I decree that everything my children touch prospers (Deuteronomy

28:2).
31. I decree freedom in my bloodline, connected to newness through dedication to God (Romans 6:4).
32. I decree that my family co-creates with God, resetting every area of our lives according to His divine plan (Ephesians 3:20).
33. I declare that God's power, exceeding all I can ask or imagine, energizes my household to fulfill His purpose (Ephesians 3:20).
34. I decree that God never abandons my family, empowering us to press forward in unity and strength (Deuteronomy 31:6).
35. I declare that as a king and priest under God, I lead my family in righteousness through the blood of Jesus (Revelation 1:6).
36. I decree that nothing can stop my family's destiny in Christ except our own unbelief, and we choose faith (Philippians 4:13).
37. I declare that angels are assigned to my household, activated by God's Word spoken through our lips (Psalm 103:20).
38. I decree that my soul surrenders to the authority of my spirit, aligning my family with God's truth (Psalm 42:5).
39. I declare that my spirit is fully surrendered to the Holy Spirit, guiding my family into all truth (John 16:13).
40. I decree that my body submits to the authority of my soul, enabling my family to walk in divine health (3 John 1:2).
41. I declare that my family is the first unit of spiritual warfare, standing as a fortified wall against the enemy (Ephesians 6:12).
42. I decree that as my spouse and I align with God's will, the impossible becomes possible in our home (Matthew 19:26).
43. I declare that my family attracts divine opportunities, resources, wisdom, and strategies as we walk in God's ways (Proverbs 3:5-6).
44. I decree that God calls my family unstoppable, and we embrace His divine identity for us (Isaiah 54:17).
45. I declare that as sons and daughters of God, my family brings remedies to the groans of creation (Romans 8:19).
46. I decree that my family's words activate Heaven's power, resetting generational blessings in our bloodline (Proverbs 18:21).
47. I declare that our alignment with the Holy Spirit fortifies our home, making us a beacon of God's glory (John 17:22).

48. I decree that every member of my family walks in the authority of Christ, commanding breakthroughs in His name (Luke 10:19).
49. I declare that God's exceeding power flows through our family, surpassing every limitation and obstacle (Ephesians 3:20).
50. I decree that our family's unity in faith moves mountains, establishing God's Kingdom in our home (Mark 11:23).
51. I declare that as we co-create with God, our family is a living testimony of His unstoppable power and love (Psalm 115:14).

Chapter 2: Business and Wealth (Decrees 52–79)

1. I decree an abundance of divine debt cancellation (Deuteronomy 15:1).
2. I decree that my hands are anointed to gain wealth (Deuteronomy 8:18).
3. I decree that I restore everything God has called me to restore (Joel 2:25).
4. I decree that my debts are canceled, and supernatural provision is my portion (Philippians 4:19).
5. I decree that I am the lender and not the borrower (Deuteronomy 28:12).
6. I decree that I own land and real estate (Psalm 37:29).
7. I decree that I fund the Kingdom of God with joy and abundance (Malachi 3:10).
8. I decree that I create programs, institutions, and legacies that serve the Lord (Isaiah 61:4).
9. I decree that supernatural doors of business and wealth open now (Revelation 3:8).
10. I decree that clients and contracts locate me supernaturally (Psalm 75:6-7).
11. I decree that favor establishes the work of my hands (Psalm 90:17).
12. I decree that sudden promotions, business expansions, and new income streams flow to me (Deuteronomy 28:2).
13. I decree that I am free from every spirit of financial bondage (Luke 4:18).

14. I decree that financial miracles chase and overtake me (Deuteronomy 28:2).
15. I decree that I owe no man anything but love (Romans 13:8).
16. I decree that everything stolen from my finances is restored sevenfold (Proverbs 6:31).
17. I decree that God's warring angels bring everything stored up for me, including wealth (Hebrews 1:14).
18. I decree that I am anointed to be a marketplace influencer, walking in wisdom and favor (Daniel 1:20).
19. I decree that every meeting, transaction, and negotiation is guided by divine wisdom (James 1:5).
20. I declare that the works of my hands are blessed (Deuteronomy 28:12).
21. I declare that every business endeavor prospers (Psalm 1:3).
22. I declare that new contracts, divine clients, and financial increase locate me (Isaiah 60:11).
23. I declare that ideas, creativity, and witty inventions flow through me (Proverbs 8:12).
24. I declare that the wealth of the wicked is laid up for me (Proverbs 13:22).
25. I declare that financial overflow is my portion (Psalm 23:5).
26. I declare that I live under Heaven's economy, unmoved by the world's economy (Philippians 4:19).
27. I declare that doors of financial favor, business opportunities, and Kingdom partnerships open (Revelation 3:7).
28. I receive the wealth of the wicked stored up for the righteous (Proverbs 13:22).

Chapter 3: Health and Healing (Decrees 80–102)

1. I decree that complete healing flows through my bloodstream, organs, bones, and mind (Isaiah 53:5).
2. I decree that tumors, chronic pain, diabetes, insomnia, and every disease are uprooted (Luke 4:39).
3. I decree that supernatural strength rises within me (Isaiah 40:31).

4. I decree that every assignment against my mental health—depression, anxiety, fear—is broken (Philippians 4:7).
5. I decree that generational curses of sickness—epilepsy, tumors, diabetes, cancer—are broken (Galatians 3:13).
6. I decree that every enemy attacking me in my sleep through dreams is overthrown (Psalm 4:8).
7. I decree that no demonic oppression touches me at night (Psalm 91:5).
8. I decree that I rest in perfect peace, for the Lord is with me (Isaiah 26:3).
9. I decree that long life is my portion (Psalm 91:16).
10. I decree that I enjoy the fruit of my labor in good health (Psalm 128:2).
11. I decree that every infirmity in my family bloodline is cursed and broken (Matthew 8:17).
12. I decree that divine healing flows through my family, breaking cycles of disease (Exodus 15:26).
13. I decree that my immune system, mind, and emotions are healed (Psalm 30:2).
14. I decree that my body is restored from head to toe, free from sickness (Jeremiah 30:17).
15. I declare that no sickness comes near my dwelling (Psalm 91:10).
16. I declare that I live and declare the works of the Lord (Psalm 118:17).
17. I declare that divine life flows through every cell, tissue, and organ (John 6:63).
18. I declare that my strength is renewed like the eagle's (Isaiah 40:31).
19. I declare that my body is the temple of the Holy Spirit—sickness cannot dwell here (1 Corinthians 6:19).
20. I declare that energy, vitality, and clarity of mind are my portion (Nehemiah 8:10).
21. I declare that divine health, strength, and peace are my inheritance (3 John 1:2).
22. I declare freedom and divine health over my descendants (Exodus 23:25).
23. I decree that there is no sickness, early death, suicide, accidents, or

burglary for me or my children (Psalm 91:10).

Chapter 4: Delay Breaking (Decrees 103–124)

1. I decree acceleration over every promise, assignment, and destiny moment (Habakkuk 2:3).
2. I decree that the next six months produce more fruit than the last six years (Isaiah 60:22).
3. I decree that divine speed overtakes me (2 Samuel 22:30).
4. I decree that what took others years takes me months (Ecclesiastes 3:11).
5. I decree that my business moves forward with supernatural momentum (Psalm 75:6).
6. I decree that my finances catch up to the prophetic word over my life (Deuteronomy 28:2).
7. I decree that my ministry and purpose are not delayed (Acts 13:2).
8. I decree that every lost opportunity is restored sevenfold (Joel 2:25).
9. I decree that chains of stagnation, procrastination, and delay are broken (Isaiah 10:27).
10. I decree that new doors no man can shut are opened (Revelation 3:8).
11. I decree that my pathway is made straight, and my steps are ordered (Psalm 37:23).
12. I decree that destiny helpers locate me now (Hebrews 1:14).
13. I declare that supernatural opportunities and divine timing align for my success (Ecclesiastes 9:11).
14. I declare that delay is broken permanently (Isaiah 40:31).
15. I declare that the season of waiting has ended, and suddenlies have begun (Acts 2:2).
16. I declare that every promise of God comes to pass without delay (2 Peter 3:9).
17. I declare immediate breakthroughs manifest in my life (Psalm 18:29).
18. I declare sudden miracles and divine turnarounds (Psalm 126:2).
19. I declare that the power of delay is shattered (Isaiah 43:19).
20. I decree that nothing stops or delays me (Philippians 1:6).
21. I decree that I cancel stinking thinking and strongholds delaying me

(2 Corinthians 10:5).
22. I decree that I move forward without bondage (John 8:36).

Chapter 5: Victory Over Enemies (Decrees 125–146)

1. I decree that I see my enemies no more (Exodus 14:13).
2. I decree that every demonic plot against me is overturned (Psalm 33:10).
3. I decree that the plans of the enemy are exposed and dismantled (Job 5:12).
4. I decree that angels of God war on my behalf (Psalm 91:11).
5. I decree that every word curse over my life, destiny, or family is canceled (Numbers 23:23).
6. I decree that every hex, spell, enchantment, or incantation is broken (Isaiah 47:12-13).
7. I decree that the angels of the Lord encamp around me and deliver me (Psalm 34:7).
8. I decree that every demonic stronghold over my family is dismantled (2 Corinthians 10:4).
9. I decree that confusion falls into the camp of the enemy (Exodus 23:27).
10. I decree that divine justice is executed on my behalf (Psalm 89:14).
11. I decree that every satanic attack and witchcraft against my progress catches fire (Psalm 97:3).
12. I decree that every spirit of poverty is cast out (Luke 4:18).
13. I decree that God is my shield, causing every enemy to fall (Psalm 3:3).
14. I decree that God fights my battles, ensuring victory over all enemies (Exodus 14:14).
15. I declare that every witchcraft assignment is canceled by the blood of Jesus (Revelation 12:11).
16. I declare that every spirit of sabotage, betrayal, jealousy, and backbiting is silenced (Psalm 31:20).
17. I declare that every chain the enemy used to bind me is shattered (Acts 12:7).

18. I declare that principalities, powers, and rulers of darkness are defeated (Ephesians 6:12).
19. I declare that every delay, hindrance, sabotage, and attack is broken (Isaiah 54:17).
20. I declare that the fire of God burns up every demonic assignment (Hebrews 12:29).
21. I declare that I walk in perpetual victory and dominion (Romans 8:37).
22. I decree that no weapon formed against me prospers; fear, worry, panic, and doubt leave now (Isaiah 54:17).

Chapter 6: Purpose and Identity (Decrees 147–174)

1. I decree that I walk in my divine assignment (Jeremiah 1:5).
2. I decree that I do not miss my moment of destiny (Ecclesiastes 3:1).
3. I decree that doors aligning with God's purpose open (Revelation 3:8).
4. I decree that my gifts are stirred and sharpened by the Spirit (1 Timothy 4:14).
5. I decree that I am bold, courageous, and effective in my calling (Joshua 1:9).
6. I decree that I am fruitful in every good work (Colossians 1:10).
7. I decree that my influence expands for God's glory (Matthew 5:16).
8. I decree that divine ideas, strategies, and inventions birth through me (Proverbs 8:12).
9. I decree that I carry solutions for my generation (Esther 4:14).
10. I decree that every gift inside me is awakened (Romans 11:29).
11. I decree that my mind, heart, and will align with God's purpose (Philippians 2:13).
12. I decree that my heart is flooded with light, receiving wisdom and revelation (Ephesians 1:17).
13. I decree that I walk in integrity and humility as God elevates me (Psalm 75:6-7).
14. I declare that I am a new creation in Christ (2 Corinthians 5:17).
15. I declare that I have the mind of Christ (1 Corinthians 2:16).

16. I declare that I am chosen, appointed, and equipped to bear fruit (John 15:16).
17. I declare that I am seated in heavenly places in Christ Jesus (Ephesians 2:6).
18. I declare boldness to speak the truth in love (Ephesians 4:15).
19. I declare that divine authority flows through my words and actions (Luke 10:19).
20. I declare that I am a voice for the voiceless and a light in the darkness (Isaiah 58:10).
21. I declare that I fulfill my assignment and leave nothing undone (John 17:4).
22. I receive all that God promised, releasing it in my life (Hebrews 11:6).
23. I receive all that God has for me, productive and growing (2 Peter 1:8).
24. I decree that I am above average, created in God's image, fruitful, and good (Genesis 1:26-27).
25. I decree that I have dominion, rule, and reign, reflecting God's hand (Genesis 1:28).
26. I decree that my star shines brighter (Daniel 12:3).
27. I receive my inheritance in Jesus' name (Ephesians 1:11).
28. I decree that I operate as God designed, fruitful and in the right place (Psalm 139:14).

Chapter 7: Spiritual Warfare and Protection (Decrees 175–191)

1. I decree that every witchcraft assignment is dismantled by fire (Psalm 97:3).
2. I decree that every monitoring and familiar spirit is blinded and cast out (2 Corinthians 4:4).
3. I decree that every demonic network against my progress is scattered (Psalm 68:1).
4. I decree that dream attacks, night terrors, and oppression are destroyed (Psalm 4:8).
5. I decree that the shield of the Lord surrounds my family and home

(Psalm 3:3).
6. I decree that sickness, accidents, premature death, and violence cannot touch us (Psalm 91:10).
7. I decree that my bloodline is protected by the covenant of Jesus' blood (Hebrews 13:20).
8. I decree that God's angelic armies surround me day and night (Psalm 91:11).
9. I decree that I am covered under God's wings, with no evil or plague near me (Psalm 91:4).
10. I decree that every battle to destroy me is won by God (Exodus 14:14).
11. I decree that God goes before me, making crooked places straight (Isaiah 45:2).
12. I declare that the blood of Jesus covers my mind, body, spirit, and home (Revelation 12:11).
13. I declare that I dwell in the secret place of the Most High (Psalm 91:1).
14. I declare that divine protection is my portion every day (Psalm 121:7).
15. I declare that angels war on my behalf, fighting unseen battles (Hebrews 1:14).
16. I declare that divine reinforcements overthrow the enemy's plans (2 Kings 6:16-17).
17. I decree that I am free of oppression (Isaiah 61:1).

Chapter 8: Fruitfulness and Productivity (Decrees 192–209)

1. I decree that I am fruitful and multiply in every area of my life (Genesis 1:28).
2. I decree increase over my business, ministry, family, and finances (Psalm 115:14).
3. I decree that I expand beyond former limitations (Isaiah 54:2).
4. I decree that what was small becomes mighty under God's hand (Zechariah 4:10).
5. I decree that doors of new territories open for me (Isaiah 60:11).

6. I decree that new regions, audiences, and platforms are given for Kingdom impact (Mark 16:15).
7. I decree that my influence grows as I remain faithful (Matthew 25:21).
8. I decree that every barren place becomes fruitful (Psalm 1:3).
9. I decree that I am like a tree planted by rivers, fruitful in season (Psalm 1:3).
10. I decree that seeds sown in tears reap in joy (Psalm 126:5).
11. I decree that I do not grow weary, reaping in due season (Galatians 6:9).
12. I declare that I am productive in my purpose (Colossians 1:10).
13. I declare that excellence flows through my hands (Proverbs 22:29).
14. I declare that divine ideas and strategies flow daily (Proverbs 8:12).
15. I declare that my work bears fruit and impacts many (John 15:8).
16. I declare that overflow is my portion—spiritually, financially, relationally (Psalm 23:5).
17. I declare that the blessing of the Lord makes me rich without sorrow (Proverbs 10:22).
18. I decree that I produce in abundance, stewarding all God gave me (Luke 16:10).

Chapter 9: Restoration and Deliverance (Decrees 210–224)

1. I decree that every generational curse in my bloodline is broken (Galatians 3:13).
2. I decree that cycles of divorce, poverty, sickness, and rebellion are dismantled (Isaiah 10:27).
3. I decree that the bloodline blessing of Abraham flows through my family (Galatians 3:14).
4. I decree that my lost time is redeemed (Joel 2:25).
5. I decree that divine opportunities return with acceleration (Amos 9:13).
6. I decree that everything the enemy meant for evil, God turns for my good (Genesis 50:20).
7. I decree that every broken relationship and generational breach is

healed (Psalm 147:3).
8. I decree that my family is delivered from trauma, poverty, addiction, and infirmity (Isaiah 61:1).
9. I decree that lost opportunities and delayed promises are rebuilt (Nehemiah 2:20).
10. I decree that God restores the years the locusts have eaten (Joel 2:25).
11. I declare that wholeness comes to every area of my life (1 Thessalonians 5:23).
12. I declare that my mind is renewed, spirit strengthened, and emotions healed (Romans 12:2).
13. I declare new beginnings and divine turnarounds manifest (Isaiah 43:19).
14. I declare that I am free from all bondage—emotional, financial, spiritual (John 8:36).
15. I declare that whom the Son sets free is free indeed (John 8:36).

Chapter 10: Favor, Scholarships, and Opportunities (Decrees 225–242)

1. I decree that doors of opportunity open now (Revelation 3:8).
2. I decree that scholarships, grants, deals, and promotions find me (Psalm 75:6-7).
3. I decree that supernatural opportunities locate me (Isaiah 60:11).
4. I decree that advancement is my portion (Psalm 115:14).
5. I decree that I move forward faster than circumstances allow (2 Samuel 22:30).
6. I decree that divine appointments and partnerships locate me daily (Proverbs 18:16).
7. I decree that God's favor surrounds me like a shield (Psalm 5:12).
8. I decree that policies and rules are altered on my behalf (Esther 8:5).
9. I decree that favor positions me for divine connections (Daniel 1:9).
10. I decree that God grants me favor with kings, leaders, and institutions (Genesis 39:21).
11. I declare that scholarships and grants are released to me and my descendants (Deuteronomy 28:8).

12. I declare that my children have open doors for education (Psalm 127:3-5).
13. I declare that provision for advancement is supplied (Philippians 4:19).
14. I declare that favor with schools and boards is my portion (Luke 2:52).
15. I declare that I am dripping with favor (Psalm 23:5).
16. I declare that favor speaks for me when I am absent (Proverbs 3:4).
17. I declare that favor elevates me beyond my experience (1 Samuel 16:18).
18. I declare that favor with God and man increases daily (Luke 2:52).

Chapter 11: Technological Warfare and Protection (Decrees 243–272)

1. I decree that every technological trap set by the enemy is exposed and dismantled by fire (Psalm 7:15).
2. I declare that a divine firewall of protection surrounds my mind, devices, data, and household (Zechariah 2:5).
3. I decree that the blood of Jesus surrounds every gateway—digital, mental, spiritual, or physical—connected to my life (Revelation 12:11).
4. I declare that my devices will not be hijacked, hacked, tracked, or used against my destiny (Psalm 91:10).
5. I decree that my voiceprint, fingerprint, digital presence, and likeness are shielded by the hand of God (Psalm 17:8).
6. I declare that every technological weapon formed against me shall fail and backfire (Isaiah 54:17).
7. I decree that the Spirit of Wisdom overrides every artificial intelligence system designed to manipulate, spy, or control (Proverbs 2:6).
8. I declare that corrupted systems, fake profiles, ghost accounts, and data tracking assigned to me are destroyed now (Psalm 35:8).
9. I decree that angelic interception guards every email, text, message, or video meant to cause harm, delay, or destruction (Psalm 91:11).
10. I declare that my mind is protected from screen fatigue, mental

overload, subliminal messages, and confusion (Philippians 4:7).
11. I decree that no technology will be used as a portal to invade my dreams, thoughts, or personal space (Psalm 4:8).
12. I declare that God's encryption is on every call, file, and digital footprint I leave behind (Isaiah 45:2).
13. I decree that every spiritual parasite riding through Wi-Fi, Bluetooth, or data signals is evicted now (Luke 10:19).
14. I declare that divine acceleration will not be stopped by digital delay, shadow banning, or technological censorship (Habakkuk 2:3).
15. I decree that every device in my possession becomes an instrument of Kingdom advancement, not demonic surveillance (Romans 8:28).
16. I declare that I am free from technological seduction, mind control, addiction, and algorithmic entrapment (1 Corinthians 6:12).
17. I decree that a digital bloodline reset redeems every image, click, and byte by the blood of Jesus (Colossians 1:20).
18. I declare that I will not be manipulated by online opinions, synthetic emotions, or media-driven fear (2 Timothy 1:7).
19. I decree that no drone, camera, satellite, or digital scan will violate the covering of God over my life (Psalm 32:7).
20. I declare that I will not be baited, triggered, or spiritually infected through clicks, comments, or content (Proverbs 4:25).
21. I decree that the enemy cannot trace, track, mimic, or impersonate me in any system, visible or invisible (Colossians 3:3).
22. I declare that I am hidden in Christ and encoded in the Spirit (Colossians 3:3).
23. I decree that every spiritual virus hidden in a physical device is rendered powerless (Luke 10:19).
24. I declare that no social network or algorithm has dominion over my identity, influence, or relationships (Psalm 139:14).
25. I decree that cyber witchcraft, digital sorcery, and psychic predictions through technology are shattered now (Deuteronomy 18:10-12).
26. I declare that every smart device in my home is subject to the voice and will of God (Joshua 24:15).
27. I decree that divine clarity, mental focus, and prophetic discernment guide me in a world of digital distraction (1 Corinthians 14:33).

28. I declare total victory over technological warfare—my mind is sound, my systems are secure, and my soul is untouchable (2 Corinthians 2:14).
29. I decree that every monitoring spirit operating through algorithms, social platforms, spyware, or frequency warfare is bound (Matthew 18:18).
30. I decree that freedom from frequency attacks, digital oppression, and spiritual interference via sound and screen is my portion (John 8:36).

Chapter 12: Christ Consciousness and Awakening (Decrees 273–312)

1. I decree that as a tither and kingdom giver, I will never be forced to depend on anything or anyone outside of God's provision within me (Philippians 4:19).
2. I declare that what I permit is permitted, and what I forbid is forbidden—heaven backs my boundaries (Matthew 16:19).
3. I decree that I operate daily with the Mind of Christ, using divine thought to instruct and command my life (1 Corinthians 2:16).
4. I declare that every thought, emotion, decision, and action I release is a spiritual instruction that shapes my reality (Proverbs 4:23).
5. I decree that knowing the scriptures unlocks the power of God within me—and I walk in that power (Joshua 1:8).
6. I declare that financial prosperity and divine health are part of my covenant—and I shall not lack either (3 John 1:2).
7. I decree that divine guidance leads me, and I do not walk in spiritual confusion or blindness (Psalm 32:8).
8. I declare that salvation is deliverance from every evil, and I access it through the promises of God (Ephesians 1:13).
9. I decree that the power of giving releases the blessing and stops every generational curse (Malachi 3:10).
10. I declare that kingdom giving proves God's faithfulness and honors His supremacy over my finances (Proverbs 3:9-10).
11. I decree that I am a wise steward of both time and money—never wasting what is replaceable or irreplaceable (Ephesians 5:16).
12. I declare that'ajik spiritual time is sacred—daily alignment through

prayer, meditation, study, and application is non-negotiable (Colossians 4:2).
13. I decree I use time to evolve, not repeat cycles. I invest it in truth, not illusion (Ecclesiastes 3:1).
14. I declare I give cheerfully, not fearfully—God has given me power, love, and a sound mind (2 Timothy 1:7).
15. I decree I have risen with Christ into a superior resurrection—exempt from second death, defeat, or spiritual decay (Revelation 20:6).
16. I declare that true spiritual work is inner transformation, not outward performance—I live from within (Romans 12:2).
17. I decree divine inspiration flows through me daily—I write the vision, and it comes to pass (Habakkuk 2:2).
18. I declare I do not fear death, lack, or separation—I trust the Greater One who lives within me (1 John 4:4).
19. I decree the highest level of Christ consciousness is freedom from fear, poverty, and bondage (1 John 4:18).
20. I declare that anything I was born with—lack, pain, limitation—is simply the assignment I was born to conquer (John 9:1-4).
21. I decree that peace is my compass and prosperity follows where peace abides (Philippians 4:7).
22. I declare that when I walk in peace, I access all seven phases of divine prosperity (John 16:33).
23. I decree that fear, doubt, and unbelief dissolve when I stay connected to the Spirit within (Mark 11:23).
24. I declare that the Kingdom of God is within me—heaven is now, not later (Luke 17:21).
25. I decree that both heaven and hell are states of consciousness—and I choose to dwell in the promises of God (Matthew 4:17).
26. I declare that my inner reality determines my external experience—and I align my mind with truth (Romans 8:6).
27. I decree that I am not separate from God—we are one, and nothing can separate me from divine Source (Romans 8:38-39).
28. I declare that death and hell have been disannulled—only what is eternal shall remain (Psalm 86:13).
29. I decree that my covenant with the Spirit is activated by the words I

speak—I speak life, truth, and promise (Isaiah 59:21).
30. I declare that my thoughts, emotions, imagination, and decisions are aligned with divine consciousness and manifest accordingly (Philippians 4:8).
31. I decree that I am not a body, race, gender, or religion—I am spirit, eternal, and whole (Galatians 3:28).
32. I declare I am perfect love in spirit—I lack nothing, desire nothing, and trust the Source that formed me (1 John 4:16).
33. I decree that true worship is knowing Truth and being transformed by it (John 4:23).
34. I decree that awakening to truth eliminates karma, restores awareness, and empowers me to walk in light (Ephesians 5:14).
35. I decree that as a joint-heir with Christ, I share in the fullness of divine inheritance and sonship (Romans 8:17).
36. I declare the illusion is broken, the silver cord is intact, and I fulfill my purpose with clarity and power (Ecclesiastes 12:6).
37. I decree that the mind is the true creator of all things—and I choose thoughts that align with God's Word (Romans 12:2).
38. I declare that blame, fear, guilt, and self-sabotage are broken by the renewing of my mind (2 Corinthians 10:5).
39. I decree that sin consciousness has no hold on me—I am forgiven, free, and fully restored in Christ (Romans 8:1).
40. I declare that the power of the tithe unlocks divine peace, wealth, and the flow of supernatural provision (Malachi 3:10).

Chapter 13: Emotional and Relational Healing (Decrees 313–327)

1. I decree that every wound of rejection, betrayal, or grief in my heart is healed by the balm of Gilead (Jeremiah 8:22).
2. I declare that God restores broken friendships, knitting them together in His love (Colossians 3:14).
3. I decree that my emotions are anchored in the peace of God, casting out all bitterness and unforgiveness (Ephesians 4:31-32).
4. I declare that the love of Christ flows through me, reconciling strained relationships outside my family (2 Corinthians 5:18).

5. I decree that every scar from past hurts is transformed into a testimony of God's healing power (Psalm 147:3).
6. I declare that I am free from the spirit of offense, walking in humility and grace toward others (Matthew 18:15).
7. I decree that God mends every broken connection in my church community, uniting us in His purpose (Psalm 133:1).
8. I declare that my heart is guarded against resentment, filled with God's compassion and mercy (Philippians 4:7).
9. I decree that every relational breach caused by misunderstanding is healed by divine clarity (Proverbs 17:17).
10. I declare that I release forgiveness to those who have wounded me, breaking the enemy's hold on my emotions (Matthew 6:14).
11. I decree that God's healing touch restores my soul from the pain of loss and abandonment (Psalm 23:3).
12. I declare that I attract godly relationships that edify and strengthen my walk with Christ (Proverbs 27:17).
13. I decree that every emotional stronghold of shame or guilt is shattered by God's truth (Romans 8:1).
14. I declare that my interactions are seasoned with grace, building bridges of reconciliation (Colossians 4:6).
15. I decree that my heart is whole, radiating God's love to every relationship in my life (1 John 4:12).

Chapter 14: Spiritual Discernment and Wisdom (Decrees 328–342)

1. I decree that I discern the voice of God clearly, distinguishing His truth from the enemy's lies (John 10:27).
2. I declare that the Spirit of wisdom guides my decisions, leading me in paths of righteousness (James 1:5).
3. I decree that I detect and dismantle every spirit of deception targeting my mind and choices (1 John 4:1).
4. I declare that divine insight illuminates my path, equipping me to navigate life's challenges with clarity (Proverbs 3:6).
5. I decree that my spiritual eyes are opened to see God's plans and purposes for my life (Ephesians 1:18).

6. I declare that I am filled with the knowledge of God's will, making decisions with divine precision (Colossians 1:9).
7. I decree that every false doctrine or misleading influence is exposed and cast out of my sphere (2 Timothy 4:3-4).
8. I declare that the Holy Spirit sharpens my discernment, protecting me from spiritual traps (Hebrews 5:14).
9. I decree that I walk in the fear of the Lord, which is the beginning of wisdom, guiding my every step (Proverbs 9:10).
10. I declare that I receive divine strategies to overcome obstacles, aligning with God's perfect plan (Isaiah 55:8-9).
11. I decree that my mind is renewed daily, discerning good from evil with supernatural clarity (Romans 12:2).
12. I declare that I am led by the Spirit, avoiding the snares of the enemy in every decision (Romans 8:14).
13. I decree that God's counsel prevails in my life, overriding human wisdom and confusion (Psalm 33:11).
14. I declare that I hear God's voice behind me, saying, "This is the way, walk in it" (Isaiah 30:21).
15. I decree that my discernment grows stronger, enabling me to stand firm in truth and righteousness (1 Corinthians 2:15).

Chapter 15: Community and National Transformation (Decrees 343–357)

1. I decree that revival fire sweeps through my community, awakening hearts to the Kingdom of God (Habakkuk 3:2).
2. I declare that justice and righteousness prevail in my nation, aligning it with God's purposes (Psalm 89:14).
3. I decree that my church rises as a beacon of truth, impacting our city with God's love (Matthew 5:14).
4. I declare that godly leaders are raised up in my nation, governing with wisdom and integrity (Proverbs 29:2).
5. I decree that every spirit of division in my community is bound, and unity prevails (1 Corinthians 1:10).
6. I declare that the gospel spreads like wildfire in my region,

transforming lives for Christ (Acts 1:8).
7. I decree that economic and social injustices in my nation are overturned by God's divine order (Isaiah 61:8).
8. I declare that my community is a sanctuary of peace, free from violence and oppression (Psalm 72:7).
9. I decree that the youth in my city are delivered from deception, embracing God's truth (Psalm 144:12).
10. I declare that my prayers shift the spiritual atmosphere, bringing Heaven's influence to my nation (2 Chronicles 7:14).
11. I decree that corruption and wickedness in high places are exposed and dismantled (Psalm 94:16).
12. I declare that my local schools and institutions are filled with God's wisdom and righteousness (Proverbs 22:6).
13. I decree that the body of Christ in my region unites, advancing God's Kingdom with power (John 17:21).
14. I declare that my nation turns to God, experiencing a great awakening of faith and repentance (Joel 2:12-13).
15. I decree that my community becomes a hub of God's glory, drawing souls to salvation (Isaiah 60:1).

Chapter 16: Freedom from Fear and Anxiety (Decrees 358–372)

1. I decree that the spirit of fear is cast out of my mind, replaced by God's perfect love (2 Timothy 1:7).
2. I declare that my heart is anchored in God's peace, free from worry and anxiety (Philippians 4:6-7).
3. I decree that every anxious thought is taken captive, submitting to the truth of God's Word (2 Corinthians 10:5).
4. I declare that I walk in boldness, trusting God's protection over every area of my life (Psalm 27:1).
5. I decree that fear of failure, rejection, or the unknown has no hold on me, for God is my strength (Isaiah 41:10).
6. I declare that my mind is guarded by the peace of God, unshaken by life's uncertainties (John 16:33).
7. I decree that I rest in God's promises, free from the torment of fear

and doubt (Psalm 23:4).
8. I declare that I am clothed in God's courage, facing every challenge with faith (Joshua 1:9).
9. I decree that every fear-based stronghold in my life is shattered by God's truth (Psalm 34:4).
10. I declare that I trust in God's sovereignty, casting all my cares upon Him (1 Peter 5:7).
11. I decree that my sleep is peaceful, undisturbed by anxious thoughts or nightmares (Psalm 4:8).
12. I declare that God's presence surrounds me, dispelling every trace of fear (Psalm 46:1).
13. I decree that I am delivered from the spirit of worry, walking in confident faith (Matthew 6:34).
14. I declare that my future is secure in God's hands, free from anxiety's grip (Jeremiah 29:11).
15. I decree that I live in the joy of the Lord, overcoming fear with His strength (Nehemiah 8:10).

Chapter 17: Intercession for Others (Decrees 373–387)

1. I decree that my unsaved loved ones encounter the saving grace of Jesus Christ (Acts 16:31).
2. I declare that God's healing power flows over those I pray for, restoring their bodies and minds (James 5:16).
3. I decree that leaders in my sphere are guided by God's wisdom and protected from harm (1 Timothy 2:1-2).
4. I declare that those in crisis receive divine intervention and breakthrough through my intercession (Job 42:10).
5. I decree that the prodigals I pray for return to God, restored to their divine purpose (Luke 15:20).
6. I declare that the oppressed and afflicted I intercede for are delivered by God's mighty hand (Psalm 82:4).
7. I decree that my prayers release financial provision for those in need, meeting their every lack (Philippians 4:19).
8. I declare that the children I pray for are shielded from harm and grow

in God's truth (Psalm 127:3-5).
9. I decree that missionaries and ministers I support are strengthened and empowered for their calling (Romans 15:30).
10. I declare that my intercession breaks generational curses over those I pray for, setting them free (Galatians 3:13).
11. I decree that the sick I lift up are healed by the stripes of Jesus (Isaiah 53:5).
12. I declare that my prayers open doors of opportunity for those struggling to advance (Colossians 4:3).
13. I declare that the brokenhearted I intercede for are comforted by God's presence (Psalm 34:18).
14. I declare that my intercession activates angelic assistance for those in spiritual battles (Hebrews 1:14).
15. I decree that my prayers shift destinies, aligning others with God's perfect will (Ephesians 3:20).

Chapter 18: Cross-Category Decrees (Decrees 388–418)

1. I decree that I hear God's call clearly and run without weariness (Isaiah 40:31).
2. I decree that I run this race and do not grow weary (Hebrews 12:1).
3. I decree that I stand strong and do not waver (James 1:6).
4. I decree that I speak the truth in love (Ephesians 4:15).
5. I decree that my angels bring everything I need to succeed (Hebrews 1:14).
6. I decree that every principality blocking God's promises is bound (Ephesians 6:12).
7. I decree that my life is shifted financially, spiritually, and relationally (Romans 8:28).
8. I decree that God's promises manifest as I release His words (Isaiah 55:11).
9. I decree that my mouth speaks God's truth, canceling every lie (Ephesians 6:17).
10. I decree that divine strategies and wisdom lift my heart (Proverbs 3:5-6).

11. I decree that every altar of oppression is torn down as I praise (Psalm 149:6-9).
12. I decree that my praise breaks every chain and hindrance (Acts 16:25-26).
13. I declare that I endure in love and truth, even in betrayal (John 13:34).
14. I declare that my zeal burns for the Lord and souls (Romans 12:11).
15. I declare that the fire of evangelism burns within me (Mark 16:15).
16. I declare that my mouth, hands, and feet bring restoration (Isaiah 61:4).
17. I declare that everywhere I go, I proclaim God's truth (Matthew 10:7).
18. I decree that I belong to Jesus, and nothing separates me from His love (Romans 8:38-39).
19. I decree that my mouth cancels every lie and fiery dart (Ephesians 6:16).
20. I decree that I release a generation of healing, wealth, and health (Joel 2:28).
21. I decree that I am brought out of darkness into God's light (Colossians 1:13).
22. I decree that I cancel every idle word and thought against me (Matthew 12:36).
23. I decree that I refuse to be denied or delayed, defined by God's Word (Psalm 119:89).
24. I decree that I acknowledge God in all my ways, and He directs my path (Proverbs 3:6).
25. I decree that I never lack, for God's promises are true (Numbers 23:19).
26. I decree that I cast down insecurities and seek God first (Matthew 6:33).
27. I decree that I create where there is no way, for God has made a way (Isaiah 43:19).
28. I decree that my words manifest everything I say (Mark 11:23).
29. I decree that I break all limitations spoken over my life (Isaiah 10:27).
30. I decree that I command doors to open in every closed area (Psalm

24:7).
31. I decree that every "no" blocking my blessings turns to a "yes" (Matthew 7:7).

Appendix: Morning Warfare Prayer Points

Chapter 1: Family Restoration

Morning Warfare Prayer Points: Restoring Covenant Families

My Father, my God, I take authority over my family; let Your covenant unite us, in Jesus' name. Father, let every divisive spirit refuse to operate in my household today. Lord, I command every curse against my family to be null and void, in Jesus' name. My Father, my God, I pull down every demonic plot sowing discord in my home. Father, I dismantle every generational bondage; my bloodline is free, in Jesus' name. Lord, restore my marriage with love and respect; let unity prevail. My Father, my God, cover my children with Your blood; guide them to Your light. Father, let Your angels encamp around my home, guarding our legacy. Lord, thank You for healing our wounds; my family shines with Your glory. Father, anoint my household with joy; let our unity testify of Your love, in Jesus' name. Amen.

Scriptures: Genesis 17:7, Ephesians 5:33, Colossians 1:13, Galatians 3:13, Psalm 147:3, Psalm 103:20

Chapter 2: Business and Wealth

Morning Warfare Prayer Points: Commanding Financial Dominion

My Father, my God, I take authority over my finances; let wealth flow to me, in Jesus' name. Father, let every spirit of lack refuse to operate in my business today. Lord, I command every debt to be canceled; provision overtakes me, in Jesus' name. My Father, my God, I pull down every demonic barrier blocking my financial breakthroughs. Father, I dismantle every generational curse of poverty; my bloodline prospers, in Jesus' name. Lord, open doors no man can shut; let favor guide my transactions. My Father, my God, anoint my hands to produce wealth; my work glorifies You. Father, let Your angels deliver stored-up resources to my family. Lord, thank You for Your overflow; my business testifies of Your provision. Father, cause me to excel in the marketplace; let my cup run over, in Jesus' name. Amen.

Scriptures: Deuteronomy 8:18, Philippians 4:19, Psalm 90:17, Revelation 3:8, Galatians 3:13, Hebrews 1:14

Chapter 3: Health and Healing

Morning Warfare Prayer Points: Restoring Divine Health

My Father, my God, I take authority over my body; let Your healing flow through me, in Jesus' name. Father, let every spirit of sickness refuse to operate in my life today. Lord, I command every disease to be uprooted from my body, in Jesus' name. My Father, my God, I pull down every demonic assignment attacking my health. Father, I dismantle every generational curse of infirmity; my bloodline is whole, in Jesus' name. Lord, restore my strength like the eagle's; let vitality overtake me. My Father, my God, cover my sleep with Your peace; no oppression disturbs me. Father, let Your angels war for my wellness, guarding my body. Lord, thank You for Your stripes; my body testifies of Your healing. Father, anoint me with health; let my life shine with Your glory, in Jesus' name. Amen.

Scriptures: Isaiah 53:5, Psalm 30:2, Isaiah 40:31, Psalm 4:8, Galatians 3:13, Psalm 103:20

Chapter 4: Delay Breaking

Morning Warfare Prayer Points: Accelerating Divine Timing

My Father, my God, I take authority over my destiny; let Your timing accelerate my promises, in Jesus' name. Father, let every spirit of delay refuse to hinder me today. Lord, I command every obstacle to my breakthrough to be null and void, in Jesus' name. My Father, my God, I pull down every demonic barrier blocking my divine assignments. Father, I dismantle every generational curse of stagnation; my bloodline advances, in Jesus' name. Lord, restore my lost opportunities sevenfold; let speed overtake me. My Father, my God, open doors no man can shut; guide me to my purpose. Father, let Your angels clear my path, aligning me with Your season. Lord, thank You for Your suddenlies; my life testifies of Your acceleration. Father, anoint me with divine momentum; let my steps shine with Your glory, in Jesus' name. Amen.

Scriptures: Habakkuk 2:3, Isaiah 60:22, Revelation 3:8, Joel 2:25, Galatians 3:13

Chapter 5: Victory Over Enemies

Morning Warfare Prayer Points: Triumphing Over Adversaries

My Father, my God, I take authority over my battles; let Your power scatter my enemies, in Jesus' name. Father, let every demonic plot refuse to operate against me today. Lord, I command every curse and hex to be null and void, in Jesus' name. My Father, my God, I pull down every satanic scheme targeting my peace. Father, I dismantle every generational witchcraft; my bloodline is free, in Jesus' name. Lord, overthrow every adversary with Your might; let victory prevail. My Father, my God, shield me with Your presence; guide me in triumph. Father, let Your angels war against my foes, guarding my path. Lord, thank You for Your deliverance; my life testifies of Your victory. Father, anoint me with authority; let my stand shine with Your glory, in Jesus' name. Amen.

Scriptures: Psalm 33:10, Isaiah 54:17, Exodus 14:14, Galatians 3:13, Psalm 91:11

Chapter 6: Purpose and Identity

Morning Warfare Prayer Points: Embracing Divine Calling

My Father, my God, I take authority over my purpose; let Your calling define me, in Jesus' name. Father, let every spirit of doubt refuse to cloud my identity today. Lord, I command every lie of inadequacy to be null and void, in Jesus' name. My Father, my God, I pull down every demonic distraction veiling my destiny. Father, I dismantle every generational confusion; my bloodline shines, in Jesus' name. Lord, awaken my gifts with Your fire; let clarity overtake me. My Father, my God, align my steps with Your divine assignment; guide my path. Father, let Your angels stir my calling, guarding my purpose. Lord, thank You for Your revelation; my life testifies of Your truth. Father, anoint me with boldness; let my identity radiate Your glory, in Jesus' name. Amen.

Scriptures: Jeremiah 1:5, Ephesians 2:6, John 15:16, Ephesians 1:17, Galatians 3:13

Chapter 7: Spiritual Warfare and Protection

Morning Warfare Prayer Points: Securing Divine Protection

My Father, my God, I take authority over my spirit; let Your shield guard me, in Jesus' name. Father, let every demonic attack refuse to breach my peace today. Lord, I command every witchcraft scheme to be null and void, in Jesus' name. My Father, my God, I pull down every satanic plot invading my dreams. Father, I dismantle every generational oppression; my bloodline is secure, in Jesus' name. Lord, cover me with Your wings; let safety overtake me. My Father, my God, fortify my mind with Your truth; guide my stand. Father, let Your angels encamp around me, guarding my soul. Lord, thank You for Your fortress; my life testifies of Your protection. Father, anoint me with resilience; let my faith shine with Your glory, in Jesus' name. Amen.

Scriptures: Psalm 91:1, Psalm 121:7, Psalm 91:11, Galatians 3:13, Psalm 4:8

Chapter 8: Fruitfulness and Productivity

Morning Warfare Prayer Points: Multiplying Divine Harvests

My Father, my God, I take authority over my endeavors; let Your blessing multiply me, in Jesus' name. Father, let every spirit of barrenness refuse to hinder my work today. Lord, I command every obstacle to my productivity to be null and void, in Jesus' name. My Father, my God, I pull down every demonic barrier stifling my growth. Father, I dismantle every generational failure; my bloodline prospers, in Jesus' name. Lord, expand my influence with Your favor; let abundance overtake me. My Father, my God, anoint my hands for excellence; guide my efforts. Father, let Your angels guard my harvests, ensuring my increase. Lord, thank You for Your provision; my life testifies of Your fruitfulness. Father, cause my work to flourish; let my success shine with Your glory, in Jesus' name. Amen.

Scriptures: Genesis 1:28, Psalm 1:3, Colossians 1:10, Galatians 3:13, Psalm 126:5

Chapter 9: Restoration and Deliverance

Morning Warfare Prayer Points: Redeeming Lost Promises

My Father, my God, I take authority over my losses; let Your restoration redeem me, in Jesus' name. Father, let every spirit of despair refuse to bind my heart today. Lord, I command every chain of bondage to be null and void, in Jesus' name. My Father, my God, I pull down every demonic plot stealing my blessings. Father, I dismantle every generational trauma; my bloodline is free, in Jesus' name. Lord, restore my time and relationships; let wholeness overtake me. My Father, my God, deliver me from oppression; guide me to freedom. Father, let Your angels guard my redemption, ensuring my recovery. Lord, thank You for Your healing; my life testifies of Your deliverance. Father, anoint me with liberty; let my restoration shine with Your glory, in Jesus' name. Amen.

Scriptures: Joel 2:25, Psalm 147:3, John 8:36, Galatians 3:13, Isaiah 61:1

Chapter 10: Favor, Scholarships, and Opportunities

Morning Warfare Prayer Points: Unlocking Divine Doors

My Father, my God, I take authority over my opportunities; let Your favor open doors, in Jesus' name. Father, let every spirit of rejection refuse to block my path today. Lord, I command every barrier to my advancement to be null and void, in Jesus' name. My Father, my God, I pull down every demonic plot closing my opportunities. Father, I dismantle every generational limitation; my bloodline excels, in Jesus' name. Lord, align me with divine connections; let favor overtake me. My Father, my God, grant me scholarships and grants; guide my steps. Father, let Your angels secure my breakthroughs, ensuring my success. Lord, thank You for Your provision; my life testifies of Your favor. Father, anoint me with opportunity; let my path shine with Your glory, in Jesus' name. Amen.

Scriptures: Revelation 3:8, Psalm 5:12, Luke 2:52, Galatians 3:13, Deuteronomy 28:8

Chapter 11: Technological Warfare and Protection

Morning Warfare Prayer Points: Securing Digital Defenses

My Father, my God, I take authority over my devices; let Your firewall guard me, in Jesus' name. Father, let every spirit of intrusion refuse to breach my data today. Lord, I command every cyber attack to be null and void, in Jesus' name. My Father, my God, I pull down every demonic plot tracking my digital life. Father, I dismantle every generational vulnerability; my bloodline is secure, in Jesus' name. Lord, shield my mind from digital noise; let clarity overtake me. My Father, my God, encrypt my communications with Your truth; guide my steps. Father, let Your angels war for my protection, guarding my technology. Lord, thank You for Your safeguarding; my life testifies of Your security. Father, anoint me with digital wisdom; let my safety shine with Your glory, in Jesus' name. Amen.

Scriptures: Zechariah 2:5, Psalm 91:10, Isaiah 45:2, Galatians 3:13, Colossians 3:3

Chapter 12: Christ Consciousness and Awakening

Morning Warfare Prayer Points: Aligning with Divine Truth

My Father, my God, I take authority over my mind; let Your truth awaken me, in Jesus' name. Father, let every spirit of deception refuse to cloud my thoughts today. Lord, I command every lie of fear to be null and void, in Jesus' name. My Father, my God, I pull down every demonic veil obscuring Your reality. Father, I dismantle every generational illusion; my bloodline sees clearly, in Jesus' name. Lord, renew my mind with Your Spirit; let awakening overtake me. My Father, my God, align my thoughts with Your Kingdom; guide my heart. Father, let Your angels stir my awareness, guarding my clarity. Lord, thank You for Your revelation; my life testifies of Your truth. Father, anoint me with divine consciousness; let my mind shine with Your glory, in Jesus' name. Amen.

Scriptures: 1 Corinthians 2:16, Romans 8:38-39, John 4:23, Galatians 3:13, Romans 12:2

Chapter 13: Emotional and Relational Healing

Morning Warfare Prayer Points: Mending Heart and Bonds

My Father, my God, I take authority over my heart; let Your healing mend me, in Jesus' name. Father, let every spirit of resentment refuse to bind my soul today. Lord, I command every wound of betrayal to be null and void, in Jesus' name. My Father, my God, I pull down every demonic plot fracturing my relationships. Father, I dismantle every generational strife; my bloodline is whole, in Jesus' name. Lord, restore my connections with Your love; let peace overtake me. My Father, my God, heal my emotions with Your comfort; guide my bonds. Father, let Your angels guard my heart, ensuring my healing. Lord, thank You for Your peace; my life testifies of Your restoration. Father, anoint me with compassion; let my relationships shine with Your glory, in Jesus' name. Amen.

Scriptures: Psalm 147:3, Philippians 4:7, Colossians 3:14, Galatians 3:13, Matthew 6:14

Chapter 14: Spiritual Discernment and Wisdom

Morning Warfare Prayer Points: Sharpening Divine Insight

My Father, my God, I take authority over my mind; let Your wisdom guide me, in Jesus' name. Father, let every spirit of confusion refuse to cloud my discernment today. Lord, I command every deceptive lie to be null and void, in Jesus' name. My Father, my God, I pull down every demonic veil obscuring Your voice. Father, I dismantle every generational folly; my bloodline discerns clearly, in Jesus' name. Lord, sharpen my spiritual senses with Your truth; let clarity overtake me. My Father, my God, align my decisions with Your will; guide my path. Father, let Your angels guard my insight, ensuring my understanding. Lord, thank You for Your revelation; my life testifies of Your wisdom. Father, anoint me with discernment; let my choices shine with Your glory, in Jesus' name. Amen.

Scriptures: James 1:5, John 10:27, Colossians 1:9, Galatians 3:13, Proverbs 3:6

Chapter 15: Community and National Transformation

Morning Warfare Prayer Points: Igniting Divine Revival

My Father, my God, I take authority over my community; let Your revival ignite us, in Jesus' name. Father, let every spirit of division refuse to fracture our unity today. Lord, I command every corrupt scheme to be null and void, in Jesus' name. My Father, my God, I pull down every demonic plot hindering our transformation. Father, I dismantle every generational injustice; our land is free, in Jesus' name. Lord, unite Your church with Your love; let revival overtake us. My Father, my God, establish righteousness in our nation; guide our leaders. Father, let Your angels war for our renewal, guarding our revival. Lord, thank You for Your fire; our community testifies of Your justice. Father, anoint us with unity; let our nation shine with Your glory, in Jesus' name. Amen.

Scriptures: Habakkuk 3:2, Psalm 89:14, John 17:21, Galatians 3:13, 2 Chronicles 7:14

Chapter 16: Freedom from Fear and Anxiety

Morning Warfare Prayer Points: Securing Divine Peace

My Father, my God, I take authority over my heart; let Your peace free me, in Jesus' name. Father, let every spirit of fear refuse to grip my mind today. Lord, I command every anxious thought to be null and void, in Jesus' name. My Father, my God, I pull down every demonic plot stirring my unrest. Father, I dismantle every generational worry; my bloodline is calm, in Jesus' name. Lord, anchor my soul with Your love; let tranquility overtake me. My Father, my God, cover my rest with Your calm; guide my peace. Father, let Your angels guard my heart, ensuring my freedom. Lord, thank You for Your comfort; my life testifies of Your peace. Father, anoint me with courage; let my heart shine with Your glory, in Jesus' name. Amen.

Scriptures: 2 Timothy 1:7, Philippians 4:6-7, Psalm 46:1, Galatians 3:13, Psalm 34:4

Chapter 17: Intercession for Others

Morning Warfare Prayer Points: Lifting Souls to Freedom

My Father, my God, I take authority over those I pray for; let Your grace save them, in Jesus' name. Father, let every spirit of unbelief refuse to bind their hearts today. Lord, I command every chain of oppression to be null and void, in Jesus' name. My Father, my God, I pull down every demonic plot hindering their freedom. Father, I dismantle every generational bondage; their bloodlines are free, in Jesus' name. Lord, heal their bodies with Your stripes; let wholeness overtake them. My Father, my God, draw the lost to Your light; guide their souls. Father, let Your angels war for their salvation, guarding their paths. Lord, thank You for Your compassion; my prayers testify of Your love. Father, anoint my intercession with power; let their lives shine with Your glory, in Jesus' name. Amen.

Scriptures: James 5:16, Acts 16:31, Isaiah 53:5, Galatians 3:13, Ephesians 3:20

Chapter 18: Cross-Category Decrees

Morning Warfare Prayer Points: Wielding Divine Authority

My Father, my God, I take authority over my battles; let Your truth empower me, in Jesus' name. Father, let every spirit of defeat refuse to hinder my victory today. Lord, I command every obstacle to my breakthrough to be null and void, in Jesus' name. My Father, my God, I pull down every demonic plot blocking my progress. Father, I dismantle every generational limitation; my bloodline triumphs, in Jesus' name. Lord, align my life with Your promises; let success overtake me. My Father, my God, anoint my voice to shift circumstances; guide my steps. Father, let Your angels war for my victories, guarding my path. Lord, thank You for Your power; my life testifies of Your triumph. Father, anoint me with authority; let my stand shine with Your glory, in Jesus' name. Amen.

Scriptures: Isaiah 55:11, Romans 8:28, Psalm 24:7, Galatians 3:13, Psalm 138:3

Appendix: Scripture Index

This scripture index lists all Bible verses cited in the 323 declarations and decrees of *Arsenal: Prayers, Declarations, and Decrees That Will Move Heaven and Shake Hell*, organized alphabetically by book, chapter, and verse. Each entry includes the chapter and decree number where the scripture appears, enabling readers to locate specific decrees tied to God's Word. This index enhances the book's usability, reinforcing the scriptural foundation of Apostle Paula Ferguson's anointed proclamations.

- **Acts 1:8**: Chapter 15, Decree 348
- **Acts 12:7**: Chapter 5, Decree 141
- **Acts 13:2**: Chapter 4, Decree 109
- **Acts 16:25-26**: Chapter 18, Decree 399
- **Acts 16:31**: Chapter 17, Decree 373
- **Colossians 1:9**: Chapter 14, Decree 333
- **Colossians 1:10**: Chapter 6, Decree 152; Chapter 8, Decree 203
- **Colossians 1:13**: Chapter 1, Decree 14; Chapter 18, Decree 408
- **Colossians 1:20**: Chapter 11, Decree 259
- **Colossians 3:3**: Chapter 11, Decree 263, 264
- **Colossians 3:14**: Chapter 13, Decree 314
- **Colossians 4:2**: Chapter 12, Decree 284
- **Colossians 4:3**: Chapter 17, Decree 384
- **Colossians 4:6**: Chapter 1, Decree 9; Chapter 13, Decree 326
- **Daniel 1:9**: Chapter 10, Decree 233
- **Daniel 1:20**: Chapter 2, Decree 69
- **Daniel 12:3**: Chapter 6, Decree 172
- **Deuteronomy 7:9**: Chapter 1, Decree 11
- **Deuteronomy 15:1**: Chapter 2, Decree 52
- **Deuteronomy 18:10-12**: Chapter 11, Decree 267
- **Deuteronomy 28:2**: Chapter 2, Decree 63, 65; Chapter 4, Decree 108
- **Deuteronomy 28:8**: Chapter 1, Decree 24; Chapter 10, Decree 235

- **Deuteronomy 28:11**: Chapter 1, Decree 4
- **Deuteronomy 28:12**: Chapter 2, Decree 56, 71
- **Deuteronomy 31:6**: Chapter 1, Decree 34
- **Ecclesiastes 3:1**: Chapter 4, Decree 148; Chapter 12, Decree 285
- **Ecclesiastes 9:11**: Chapter 4, Decree 115
- **Ecclesiastes 12:6**: Chapter 12, Decree 308
- **Ephesians 1:11**: Chapter 6, Decree 173
- **Ephesians 1:13**: Chapter 12, Decree 280
- **Ephesians 1:17**: Chapter 6, Decree 158
- **Ephesians 1:18**: Chapter 14, Decree 332
- **Ephesians 2:6**: Chapter 6, Decree 163
- **Ephesians 2:14**: Chapter 1, Decree 10
- **Ephesians 3:20**: Chapter 1, Decree 32, 33, 49; Chapter 9, Decree 224; Chapter 17, Decree 387
- **Ephesians 4:15**: Chapter 6, Decree 164; Chapter 18, Decree 391
- **Ephesians 4:31-32**: Chapter 13, Decree 315
- **Ephesians 5:14**: Chapter 12, Decree 306
- **Ephesians 5:16**: Chapter 12, Decree 283
- **Ephesians 5:33**: Chapter 1, Decree 7
- **Ephesians 6:11**: Chapter 5, Decree 125
- **Ephesians 6:12**: Chapter 1, Decree 6, 41; Chapter 5, Decree 142; Chapter 18, Decree 393
- **Ephesians 6:16**: Chapter 18, Decree 406
- **Ephesians 6:17**: Chapter 18, Decree 396
- **Esther 4:14**: Chapter 6, Decree 155
- **Esther 8:5**: Chapter 10, Decree 232
- **Exodus 14:13**: Chapter 5, Decree 125
- **Exodus 14:14**: Chapter 5, Decree 138; Chapter 7, Decree 184
- **Exodus 15:26**: Chapter 3, Decree 91
- **Exodus 23:25**: Chapter 3, Decree 101
- **Exodus 23:27**: Chapter 5, Decree 133
- **Galatians 3:13**: Chapter 3, Decree 84; Chapter 9, Decree 210; Chapter 17, Decree 382

- **Galatians 3:14**: Chapter 9, Decree 212; Chapter 1, Decree 27
- **Galatians 3:28**: Chapter 12, Decree 303
- **Galatians 3:29**: Chapter 1, Decree 26
- **Genesis 1:26-27**: Chapter 6, Decree 170
- **Genesis 1:28**: Chapter 1, Decree 171; Chapter 8, Decree 192
- **Genesis 12:2-3**: Chapter 2, Decree 52
- **Genesis 17:7**: Chapter 1, Decree 19
- **Genesis 22:17**: Chapter 1, Decree 23
- **Genesis 39:21**: Chapter 10, Decree 234
- **Genesis 50:20**: Chapter 9, Decree 215
- **Habakkuk 2:2**: Chapter 12, Decree 289
- **Habakkuk 2:3**: Chapter 4, Decree 103; Chapter 11, Decree 256
- **Habakkuk 3:2**: Chapter 15, Decree 343
- **Hebrews 1:14**: Chapter 4, Decree 114; Chapter 7, Decree 189; Chapter 17, Decree 386; Chapter 18, Decree 392
- **Hebrews 5:14**: Chapter 14, Decree 335
- **Hebrews 11:6**: Chapter 6, Decree 168
- **Hebrews 12:29**: Chapter 5, Decree 144
- **Hebrews 13:20**: Chapter 7, Decree 181
- **Isaiah 10:27**: Chapter 4, Decree 111; Chapter 9, Decree 211; Chapter 18, Decree 416
- **Isaiah 26:3**: Chapter 3, Decree 87
- **Isaiah 30:21**: Chapter 14, Decree 341
- **Isaiah 40:31**: Chapter 3, Decree 82, 97; Chapter 4, Decree 116; Chapter 18, Decree 388
- **Isaiah 41:10**: Chapter 16, Decree 362
- **Isaiah 43:19**: Chapter 4, Decree 121; Chapter 9, Decree 222; Chapter 18, Decree 414
- **Isaiah 45:2**: Chapter 7, Decree 185; Chapter 11, Decree 254
- **Isaiah 47:12-13**: Chapter 5, Decree 130
- **Isaiah 53:5**: Chapter 3, Decree 80; Chapter 17, Decree 383
- **Isaiah 54:2**: Chapter 8, Decree 194
- **Isaiah 54:17**: Chapter 1, Decree 5; Chapter 3, Decree 94; Chapter 5,

Decree 146; Chapter 11, Decree 248; Chapter 1, Decree 44
- **Isaiah 55:8-9**: Chapter 14, Decree 337
- **Isaiah 55:11**: Chapter 18, Decree 395
- **Isaiah 58:10**: Chapter 6, Decree 166
- **Isaiah 59:21**: Chapter 12, Decree 301
- **Isaiah 60:1**: Chapter 15, Decree 357
- **Isaiah 60:11**: Chapter 2, Decree 73; Chapter 8, Decree 196; Chapter 10, Decree 227
- **Isaiah 60:22**: Chapter 4, Decree 104
- **Isaiah 61:1**: Chapter 7, Decree 191; Chapter 9, Decree 217
- **Isaiah 61:4**: Chapter 2, Decree 59; Chapter 18, Decree 403
- **Isaiah 61:8**: Chapter 15, Decree 349
- **James 1:5**: Chapter 2, Decree 70; Chapter 14, Decree 329
- **James 1:6**: Chapter 18, Decree 390
- **James 5:15**: Chapter 17, Decree 383
- **James 5:16**: Chapter 17, Decree 374
- **Jeremiah 1:5**: Chapter 1, Decree 25; Chapter 6, Decree 147
- **Jeremiah 8:22**: Chapter 13, Decree 313
- **Jeremiah 29:11**: Chapter 16, Decree 371
- **Jeremiah 30:17**: Chapter 3, Decree 93
- **Job 5:12**: Chapter 5, Decree 127
- **Job 42:10**: Chapter 17, Decree 376
- **Joel 2:12-13**: Chapter 15, Decree 356
- **Joel 2:25**: Chapter 1, Decree 20; Chapter 2, Decree 54; Chapter 4, Decree 110; Chapter 9, Decree 219
- **Joel 2:28**: Chapter 18, Decree 407
- **John 1:5**: Chapter 6, Decree 166
- **John 4:23**: Chapter 12, Decree 305
- **John 6:63**: Chapter 3, Decree 96
- **John 8:36**: Chapter 4, Decree 124; Chapter 9, Decree 223, 224; Chapter 11, Decree 272
- **John 9:1-4**: Chapter 12, Decree 292
- **John 10:7**: Chapter 18, Decree 404

- **John 10:10**: Chapter 3, Decree 80
- **John 10:19**: Chapter 1, Decree 48; Chapter 6, Decree 165
- **John 10:27**: Chapter 14, Decree 328
- **John 13:34**: Chapter 18, Decree 400
- **John 15:16**: Chapter 6, Decree 162
- **John 15:20**: Chapter 1, Decree 15; Chapter 5, Decree 377
- **John 16:13**: Chapter 1, Decree 39
- **John 16:33**: Chapter 12, Decree 294; Chapter 16, Decree 363
- **John 17:4**: Chapter 6, Decree 167
- **John 17:21**: Chapter 1, Decree 18; Chapter 15, Decree 355
- **John 17:22**: Chapter 1, Decree 47
- **Joshua 1:8**: Chapter 12, Decree 277
- **Joshua 1:9**: Chapter 6, Decree 151; Chapter 16, Decree 365
- **Joshua 24:15**: Chapter 1, Decree 17; Chapter 11, Decree 268
- **Luke 2:52**: Chapter 10, Decree 238, 242
- **Luke 4:18**: Chapter 2, Decree 64; Chapter 5, Decree 136
- **Luke 4:39**: Chapter 3, Decree 81
- **Luke 10:19**: Chapter 6, Decree 165; Chapter 11, Decree 255, 265
- **Luke 15:20**: Chapter 5, Decree 377
- **Luke 16:10**: Chapter 8, Decree 209
- **Luke 17:21**: Chapter 12, Decree 296
- **Malachi 3:10**: Chapter 2, Decree 58; Chapter 12, Decree 281, 312
- **Mark 11:23**: Chapter 1, Decree 50; Chapter 12, Decree 295; Chapter 18, Decree 415
- **Mark 11:24**: Chapter 2, Decree 65
- **Mark 16:15**: Chapter 8, Decree 197; Chapter 18, Decree 402
- **Matthew 4:17**: Chapter 12, Decree 297
- **Matthew 5:14**: Chapter 15, Decree 345
- **Matthew 5:16**: Chapter 6, Decree 153
- **Matthew 6:14**: Chapter 13, Decree 322
- **Matthew 6:33**: Chapter 18, Decree 413
- **Matthew 6:34**: Chapter 16, Decree 370
- **Matthew 7:7**: Chapter 18, Decree 418

- **Matthew 7:24**: Chapter 1, Decree 50
- **Matthew 8:17**: Chapter 3, Decree 90
- **Matthew 10:7**: Chapter 18, Decree 404
- **Matthew 11:12**: Chapter 12, Decree 274
- **Matthew 12:36**: Chapter 18, Decree 409
- **Matthew 16:19**: Chapter 12, Decree 274
- **Matthew 18:15**: Chapter 13, Decree 318
- **Matthew 18:18**: Chapter 11, Decree 271
- **Matthew 18:19**: Chapter 1, Decree 41
- **Matthew 19:26**: Chapter 1, Decree 42
- **Matthew 24:13**: Chapter 4, Decree 118
- **Matthew 25:21**: Chapter 8, Decree 198
- **Nehemiah 2:20**: Chapter 9, Decree 218
- **Nehemiah 8:10**: Chapter 3, Decree 99; Chapter 16, Decree 372
- **Numbers 23:19**: Chapter 18, Decree 412
- **Numbers 23:23**: Chapter 5, Decree 129
- **Philippians 1:6**: Chapter 4, Decree 122
- **Philippians 4:6-7**: Chapter 16, Decree 359
- **Philippians 4:7**: Chapter 3, Decree 83; Chapter 11, Decree 252; Chapter 12, Decree 293; Chapter 13, Decree 320
- **Philippians 4:8**: Chapter 12, Decree 302
- **Philippians 4:13**: Chapter 1, Decree 36
- **Philippians 4:19**: Chapter 2, Decree 55, 77; Chapter 10, Decree 237; Chapter 12, Decree 273; Chapter 17, Decree 379
- **Proverbs 3:4**: Chapter 10, Decree 240
- **Proverbs 3:5-6**: Chapter 14, Decree 331; Chapter 18, Decree 411
- **Proverbs 3:9-10**: Chapter 12, Decree 282
- **Proverbs 4:7**: Chapter 1, Decree 1
- **Proverbs 4:23**: Chapter 12, Decree 276
- **Proverbs 4:25**: Chapter 11, Decree 262
- **Proverbs 8:12**: Chapter 2, Decree 74; Chapter 6, Decree 154; Chapter 8, Decree 205
- **Proverbs 9:10**: Chapter 14, Decree 336

- **Proverbs 10:22**: Chapter 2, Decree 208
- **Proverbs 11:25**: Chapter 2, Decree 64
- **Proverbs 12:36**: Chapter 18, Decree 409
- **Proverbs 13:22**: Chapter 1, Decree 22; Chapter 2, Decree 75, 79
- **Proverbs 14:34**: Chapter 15, Decree 344
- **Proverbs 17:17**: Chapter 13, Decree 321
- **Proverbs 18:16**: Chapter 10, Decree 230
- **Proverbs 18:21**: Chapter 1, Decree 46
- **Proverbs 22:6**: Chapter 15, Decree 354
- **Proverbs 22:29**: Chapter 8, Decree 204
- **Proverbs 27:17**: Chapter 13, Decree 324
- **Proverbs 29:2**: Chapter 15, Decree 346
- **Psalm 1:3**: Chapter 2, Decree 72; Chapter 8, Decree 199, 200
- **Psalm 3:3**: Chapter 5, Decree 137; Chapter 7, Decree 179
- **Psalm 4:8**: Chapter 3, Decree 85; Chapter 7, Decree 178; Chapter 11, Decree 253; Chapter 16, Decree 368
- **Psalm 5:12**: Chapter 1, Decree 2; Chapter 10, Decree 231, 239
- **Psalm 7:15**: Chapter 11, Decree 243
- **Psalm 18:2**: Chapter 1, Decree 8
- **Psalm 18:29**: Chapter 4, Decree 119
- **Psalm 23:3**: Chapter 13, Decree 323
- **Psalm 23:4**: Chapter 16, Decree 364
- **Psalm 23:5**: Chapter 2, Decree 76; Chapter 8, Decree 207
- **Psalm 24:7**: Chapter 18, Decree 417
- **Psalm 27:1**: Chapter 16, Decree 361
- **Psalm 30:2**: Chapter 3, Decree 92
- **Psalm 31:20**: Chapter 5, Decree 140
- **Psalm 32:7**: Chapter 11, Decree 261
- **Psalm 32:8**: Chapter 12, Decree 279
- **Psalm 33:10**: Chapter 5, Decree 126
- **Psalm 33:11**: Chapter 14, Decree 340
- **Psalm 34:4**: Chapter 16, Decree 366
- **Psalm 34:7**: Chapter 5, Decree 131

- **Psalm 34:18**: Chapter 17, Decree 385
- **Psalm 35:8**: Chapter 11, Decree 250
- **Psalm 37:23**: Chapter 4, Decree 113
- **Psalm 37:29**: Chapter 2, Decree 57
- **Psalm 42:5**: Chapter 1, Decree 38
- **Psalm 46:1**: Chapter 16, Decree 369
- **Psalm 72:7**: Chapter 15, Decree 350
- **Psalm 75:6-7**: Chapter 2, Decree 61; Chapter 6, Decree 159; Chapter 10, Decree 226
- **Psalm 82:4**: Chapter 17, Decree 378
- **Psalm 86:13**: Chapter 12, Decree 300
- **Psalm 89:14**: Chapter 5, Decree 134; Chapter 15, Decree 344
- **Psalm 90:17**: Chapter 2, Decree 62
- **Psalm 91:1**: Chapter 7, Decree 187
- **Psalm 91:4**: Chapter 7, Decree 183
- **Psalm 91:5**: Chapter 3, Decree 86
- **Psalm 91:10**: Chapter 1, Decree 28; Chapter 3, Decree 94; Chapter 7, Decree 180
- **Psalm 91:11**: Chapter 5, Decree 128; Chapter 7, Decree 182; Chapter 11, Decree 251
- **Psalm 91:16**: Chapter 3, Decree 88
- **Psalm 94:16**: Chapter 15, Decree 353
- **Psalm 97:3**: Chapter 5, Decree 135; Chapter 7, Decree 175
- **Psalm 103:20**: Chapter 1, Decree 37; Chapter 3, Decree 95
- **Psalm 112:2**: Chapter 1, Decree 3
- **Psalm 115:14**: Chapter 1, Decree 51; Chapter 2, Decree 193; Chapter 10, Decree 228
- **Psalm 118:17**: Chapter 3, Decree 95
- **Psalm 119:89**: Chapter 18, Decree 410
- **Psalm 121:7**: Chapter 7, Decree 188
- **Psalm 126:2**: Chapter 4, Decree 120
- **Psalm 126:5**: Chapter 8, Decree 201
- **Psalm 127:3-5**: Chapter 10, Decree 236; Chapter 17, Decree 380

- **Psalm 128:2**: Chapter 3, Decree 89
- **Psalm 133:1**: Chapter 1, Decree 16; Chapter 13, Decree 319
- **Psalm 139:14**: Chapter 6, Decree 174; Chapter 11, Decree 266
- **Psalm 144:12**: Chapter 15, Decree 351
- **Psalm 147:3**: Chapter 1, Decree 13; Chapter 9, Decree 216; Chapter 13, Decree 317
- **Psalm 149:6-9**: Chapter 18, Decree 398
- **Revelation 1:6**: Chapter 1, Decree 35
- **Revelation 3:8**: Chapter 2, Decree 60; Chapter 4, Decree 112; Chapter 6, Decree 149; Chapter 10, Decree 225, 238
- **Revelation 12:11**: Chapter 1, Decree 12; Chapter 5, Decree 139; Chapter 7, Decree 186; Chapter 11, Decree 245
- **Revelation 20:6**: Chapter 12, Decree 287
- **Romans 6:4**: Chapter 1, Decree 31
- **Romans 8:1**: Chapter 12, Decree 311; Chapter 13, Decree 325
- **Romans 8:6**: Chapter 12, Decree 298
- **Romans 8:14**: Chapter 14, Decree 339
- **Romans 8:17**: Chapter 12, Decree 307
- **Romans 8:28**: Chapter 11, Decree 257; Chapter 18, Decree 394
- **Romans 8:38-39**: Chapter 12, Decree 299; Chapter 18, Decree 405
- **Romans 10:14**: Chapter 17, Decree 373
- **Romans 12:2**: Chapter 9, Decree 221; Chapter 12, Decree 288, 309; Chapter 14, Decree 338
- **Romans 12:11**: Chapter 18, Decree 401
- **Romans 13:8**: Chapter 2, Decree 66
- **Romans 15:30**: Chapter 17, Decree 381
- **1 Corinthians 1:10**: Chapter 15, Decree 347
- **1 Corinthians 2:15**: Chapter 14, Decree 342
- **1 Corinthians 2:16**: Chapter 6, Decree 161; Chapter 12, Decree 275
- **1 Corinthians 6:12**: Chapter 11, Decree 258
- **1 Corinthians 6:19**: Chapter 3, Decree 98
- **1 Corinthians 13:1**: Chapter 17, Decree 373
- **1 Corinthians 14:33**: Chapter 11, Decree 269

- **1 John 4:1**: Chapter 14, Decree 330
- **1 John 4:4**: Chapter 12, Decree 290
- **1 John 4:12**: Chapter 13, Decree 327
- **1 John 4:16**: Chapter 12, Decree 304
- **1 John 4:18**: Chapter 12, Decree 291
- **1 Peter 2:9**: Chapter 17, Decree 373
- **1 Peter 5:7**: Chapter 16, Decree 367
- **1 Peter 5:8**: Chapter 1, Decree 6
- **1 Samuel 16:18**: Chapter 10, Decree 241
- **1 Thessalonians 5:23**: Chapter 9, Decree 220
- **1 Timothy 2:1-2**: Chapter 17, Decree 375
- **1 Timothy 4:14**: Chapter 6, Decree 150
- **2 Chronicles 7:14**: Chapter 15, Decree 352
- **2 Corinthians 2:14**: Chapter 11, Decree 270
- **2 Corinthians 4:4**: Chapter 11, Decree 246
- **2 Corinthians 5:17**: Chapter 6, Decree 160
- **2 Corinthians 5:18**: Chapter 13, Decree 316
- **2 Corinthians 9:7**: Chapter 2, Decree 55
- **2 Corinthians 10:4**: Chapter 5, Decree 132
- **2 Corinthians 10:5**: Chapter 4, Decree 123; Chapter 12, Decree 310; Chapter 16, Decree 360
- **2 Kings 6:16-17**: Chapter 7, Decree 190
- **2 Peter 1:8**: Chapter 6, Decree 169
- **2 Peter 3:9**: Chapter 4, Decree 118
- **2 Samuel 22:30**: Chapter 4, Decree 105; Chapter 10, Decree 229
- **2 Timothy 1:7**: Chapter 11, Decree 260; Chapter 12, Decree 286; Chapter 16, Decree 358
- **2 Timothy 4:3-4**: Chapter 14, Decree 334
- **3 John 1:2**: Chapter 1, Decree 21; Chapter 3, Decree 100; Chapter 12, Decree 278
- **Zechariah 2:5**: Chapter 11, Decree 244
- **Zechariah 4:10**: Chapter 8, Decree 195

Dear Warrior of the Kingdom,

As you close the pages of *Arsenal: Prayers, Declarations, and Decrees That Will Move Heaven and Shake Hell*, I stand in awe of your courage. You haven't merely purchased a book—you've invested in your divine destiny, arming yourself with the sword of God's Word to shift atmospheres, break strongholds, and co-create with the Creator Himself. This is no small act; it's a declaration that you refuse to be a bystander in the spiritual battles of this age. For that, I honor you.

Every decree you've spoken, every prayer you've uttered, and every promise you've claimed has forged a new weapon in your spiritual armory. You've chosen to wield the authority of a joint-heir with Christ (Romans 8:17), commanding mountains to move and hell to tremble. This book is your battle cry, your cheat code, your sacred blueprint for victory—and by embracing it, you've positioned yourself as a force for Heaven's purposes.

Your investment goes beyond these pages. It's a seed sown into your family's legacy, your community's revival, and the nations' transformation. As you speak these declarations, you're not just changing your circumstances—you're resetting bloodlines, unlocking covenant blessings, and paving the way for miracles that echo through generations. The enemy trembles at your voice, for it carries the weight of God's truth (Proverbs 18:21).

Thank you for daring to arm your spirit. Thank you for trusting the Holy Spirit to anoint your words and make the impossible possible. Thank you for joining me in this apostolic mandate to move heaven and shake hell. My prayer is that this *Arsenal* becomes your constant companion, a well-worn weapon in your hands, stained with the victories of answered prayers and shattered strongholds.

Keep declaring. Keep decreeing. Keep standing firm, for "no weapon formed against you shall prosper" (Isaiah 54:17). You are unstoppable, and the King of Glory fights for you. "I Did Us," and now, warrior, it's your turn to do the same—for yourself, your loved ones, and the Kingdom.

With unwavering faith and gratitude,

Apostle Paula Ferguson

Don't miss out!

Visit the website below and you can sign up to receive emails whenever Apostle Paula Ferguson publishes a new book. There's no charge and no obligation.

https://books2read.com/r/B-A-EDXVD-HPHIG

BOOKS 2 READ

Connecting independent readers to independent writers.

Also by Apostle Paula Ferguson

Arsenal: Prayers Declarations and Decrees That Will Move Heaven and Shake Hell
Bag Lady, Mr. Bojangles: It's Time to Let It Go
Fridge, Forks, and Fresh Starts: Building a Healthy Kitchen

Watch for more at www.fosaservices.com.

About the Author

Apostle Paula Ferguson is a dynamic prophetic leader, teacher, and author with decades of ministry experience, dedicated to empowering believers to walk boldly in their God-given authority. Known for her profound spiritual insight and unwavering commitment to biblical truth, she equips the body of Christ to break strongholds, shift atmospheres, and manifest God's promises through faith-filled declarations. Her ministry is marked by testimonies of healing, deliverance, and restoration, as she guides others to align their lives with Heaven's purposes.

As the author of *Bag Lady, Mr. Bojangles: It's Time to Let It Go*, *Make It Make Sense*, and *I Just Don't Feel Like It! Finding Motivation When Life Hits Snooze*, Apostle Paula combines real-life stories, scriptural wisdom, and practical steps to inspire transformation. She describes herself as a "human computer," receiving divine downloads from God to navigate life's challenges, a testimony woven throughout her writings and teachings.

Married to her best friend and greatest supporter, Apostle Craig Ferguson, she serves alongside him to foster spiritual growth, emotional healing, and holistic wellness. Together, they empower individuals to recognize their worth in Christ and embrace their divine purpose. Apostle Paula's transparent, compassionate approach and apostolic anointing make her a trusted voice for those seeking to move heaven and shake hell.

Read more at www.fosaservices.com.

About the Publisher

FOSA Publishing LLC—short for *Family of Successful Authors*—is dedicated to empowering writers from all backgrounds to bring their stories to life. While our roots are in Christian publishing, we proudly support authors of diverse genres and messages.

Inspired by stories of perseverance, we aim to support authors in publishing their messages quickly and effectively. Our encouragement is simple: start where you are, trust your vision, and let us help you bring it to life.

Join our family of successful authors—your voice deserves to be heard.

Read more at https://fosaservices.com/.

www.ingramcontent.com/pod-product-compliance
Lightning Source LLC
Chambersburg PA
CBHW030339240426
43661CB00052B/1682